Alessandro Vianello

STAFF BUILDING
all together at the same time

NOVEL

© 2013 Alessandro Vianello

Alessandro Vianello
via Giampiccoli, 74
32100 – Belluno
Italia

Original title:
STAFF BUILDING tutti insieme nello stesso momento

Translated by Licia Scandola

ISBN 978-88-907774-1-7

IT Consultant Corrado Polentes

Cover by Alberto Bogo

SUMMARY

Dedication 5

Acknowledgements 7

Preface 9
    Gianni Caprara 11
    Piero Monestier 15
    Federico Bisazza 17
    Roberto Oliva 21
    Giuliano Vantaggi 23
    Renato Padoan 25

Introduction 29

SECTION I 31
My staff

1. A staff for me 33
2. What is your challenge? 39
3. Winning together: Gianni Caprara 45
4. Who do you want with tou? 63
5. The righteous men: Piero Monestier 73
6. What are you looking for? 85
7. Specific skills: Federico Bisazza 97
8. What matters? 109
9. The result: Roberto Oliva 121
10. What do you really need? 139
11. Enthusiasm: Giuliano Vantaggi 161
12. Who are you? 177
13. A leader: Renato Padoan 187

SECTION II 201
Selection criteria

14. Selection 203

SECTION III 223
My way

15. Believe 225
16. State 231
17. Goal 235
18. Momentum 243
19. Pre-bonus 247
20. Equipment 251
21. Anchors 257
22. The alarm clock 263
23. Scheme's interruptions 267
24. Questions 277

SECTION IV 283
3 experiences in staff

25. Company: Certottica 285
26. Sport: Sirio Pallavolo Perugia 307
27. Volunteering: Ridere per Vivere 339

SECTION V 355
Tam-Tam

28. All together at the same time 357
29. Transparency 359
30. Ninja pajamas 361
31. Contacts 363
32. Mat-Mat 365

Dedicated to life and love.

ACKNOWLEDGEMENTS

My first thank is for you!

As you may know, I am a Coach and a Volunteer of Smile, I live and work with people. And I'm also the father of a marvellous creature named Riccardo.

For these reasons my desire in Staff Building is triple:

Writing a simple, useful and funny book;

Bringing a message of *hope* and *solidarity*, because all together at the same time is a way of living;

Creating an out break of *gratitude and giggles*. Ha ha ha, the giggles!

Have fun! I wish you all the best!

Alessandro Vianello

PREFACE

Staff Building's preface begins with this e-mail I sent simultaneously to Gianni Caprara, Piero Monestier, Federico Bisazza, Roberto Oliva, Giuliano Vantaggi, Renato Padoan.

OBJECT: Staff Building: a story that will entertain, excite and inspire.

Dear Friends,

I write to You, *all together at the same time*, to get you involved in Staff Building. In my novel, I explain how to build a successful staff right through my personal account of the experiences I lived with You. Staff Building is my way to say thank you and to be *all together at the same time*.

Many of You have never met in person, you know each other through my stories. You have different ages, do different things, live in different places, but all have an extraordinary spirit, high skills and a friend in common: me. You're making me grow, so I admire you and I love you. You are my great fortune, a fortune to donate.

To do this at best I ask you something special: a great little story, born from your experiences in living and working constantly *with* people in a team. This letter and all of your little big stories will be my Staff Building's preface. A special preface, because it isn't about the writer, but the reader.

In this sense, Staff Building is also our opportunity to be together again. This is my greatest wish, this is my commitment, this is my promise: a big party *all together at the same time.*

For Staff Building I aspect from you what you want, what you feel. The reader is only interested in something that is yours, something free, without knowing what I've written about You. Have fun!

Thank you very much,
all the best,
Ale

GIANNI CAPRARA

Professional Italian volleyball coach among the biggest international names.

Hi Ale,

I've been thinking a lot about which story to tell you and I've come to the conclusion that it would be worth it to start from the beginning, from how we came about to win the world championship. Hopefully I'll manage to be concise and I'll remember all the important facts. Of course, feel free to change anything you reckon necessary, you know, my Italian isn't that great!

Here we go!!!

In 2006 the Russian National women volleyball team starts to work on winning the world championship in Japan, held in November.

We have two positive factors:
1- all our best players are extremely motivated and ready for anything;
2- we have enough time (from May to November) and a very important date to play, like the Gran Prix.

These are very important starting points. Now we should figure out how we want our team to play and how to beat the strongest team: Brazil.

We play with the best idea in mind right from the start. After 6 matches we realize that our game level is not enough to reach the top. Our first move is that to change our setter and make the older players think they prefer their oldest team mate. All the staff urges to make this change accepted. We play other 7 matches with the new setter (fortunately, 2 matches against Brazil). In the first race we lose 3 to 0 and improve during the match. In the second competition (which will be the final of the Grand Prix) we lose 3 to 1 and play as equals to 3 sets, but in the fourth set we don't hold the rhythm anymore.

After a week of vacation we resume our workouts. There are still two months to the world championship. Very well: we still have a lot of time to convince the players to work on some technical aspects if we want to beat the best in the world. From that moment our work is based only on the video images testifying the differences between Brazil and Russia and on the gym work to eliminate that gap. The faces of the athletes in the video room and the determination they bring in the gym make us realize that we are on the right track: the problem is not only ours but it also became theirs. At the same time we understand that to achieve our aim we need another exchange within the regular team. We must be consistent with what we are asking the players and then enter an athlete who best performs the technical tasks the team needs.

During the week before leaving to Japan, we tactically worked only on the key-game we would have played in the leg: China, which has a very unique game.
We are more than ready: we're off to Japan one week before the first race, for acclimatization.
We have a very difficult leg and we know that losing a game can mean being out of the semi-finals.
We win the first 5 games, even surpassing China for 3 to 1. We play more and more better in every game.

In the next leg we have 4 other matches and the last one against Brazil. If we win all the matches that against Brazil might be ineffective (only to assign 1st or 2nd place in the leg). It happens just what I hoped. We lose 3 to 1 against Brazil, but we play every set at the same pace... with our strongest player on the bench for muscle problems. We reach the semi-finals, as second in our leg, and we meet Italy winning 3 to 0. During the Grand Prix we had only won 3 to 2 in the semi-final against Italy. It is undeniable that the team has improved.

In the final we play against Brazil that had won the three previous meetings. But this time we are ready and we play to their level capping a dream that involved all the players, the coaching staff and the managers who followed us.

I hope that this story may be useful and that will meet your approval.

An affectionate hug
Gianni

STAFF BUILDING

PIERO MONESTIER

Coach, Trainer, Mentor among the highest Italian names.

Ale, You are mad as a March hare.

If you believe that this is good for your book, I will share it also with the others. If you want, you can make all the modifications which can be congenial for your aim.

"Alessandro Vianello, what kind of person!
We meet up to delight someone else, and immediately there is a tune which allows us to create "Alta Formazione" right from the beginning.
A lot of stuff, this expression has still rung out in my head, after a year we met, how much stuff, how much sharing and how many reflections.
Desire to bring up, desire to be responsible, desire to look for values.
The capacity to help people, to follow them also after the training meeting. How much stuff.
What is our value? Helping others, being able to listen to them and then helping people to take their internal resources and to use them in their lives.
Well, this is what I found in my collaboration with Alessandro."

A hug.
Piero

FEDERICO BISAZZA

*Former European Tour professional golfer
and Golf Coach of the Italian National Team.*

I received a mad e-mail from my big associate Alessandro some time ago. The traditional e-mail which a person writes after having smoked a field of dope. I had not understood a fucking thing of it, so I told him: Ale, come here! I cook you "meat balls with sauce" for dinner, so you can explain me. I had not understood a fucking thing of it again, so I told him: "make me some questions".
And here we are…

What is a staff, Fede?

For me, a staff is a group of people who work together to reach a single objective. In my experience as a Coach for the Italian National Golf Team, the staff is led by a captain and by experts in different fields.
The management decisions and the primary and secondary objectives are shared and all work in the same direction.
In my sport, golf, reaching a goal can take a long time, years.
It can all depend on the level of the players with which we work. We have 14-years old boys and more mature ones of 20 or more years, so you can imagine the diversity of managing these groups.
At the beginning of my career, I was considered the "bad cop" of the coaches. So they gave me always the more mature ones to manage as they feared that I would terrorize the little ones. The truth is that the competitive determination and meanness, with which I have always approached my career as a player, have made me also a tough teacher.
I expected a lot, but I also gave a lot.

Our captain was able, through patient work and with excellent results, to guide me and transform me in order to improve my attitude with the boys. In fact, to my considerable surprise, I was in this year much in demanded by the same boys, who had asked me to follow them a bit during all transfers.

Like all crazy people (in fact I considered myself absolutely as such), I am two-faced. The extreme seriousness, with which I face certain situations, alternates with an overall enjoyment, shared and adored by Alessandro.

In fact, my toughness is almost always ironic and playful; these two characteristics are according to me the foundation of the joint work of any team that deals with sport. If you are not happy, ironic or you don't smile, you will have a difficult time being Coach and playing.

Thank you mate, can you tell me now about a time as a coach when you were the protagonist?

I'm two-faced, so I'll tell you two episodes: a negative one and a positive one.

Two years ago I went as assistant coach to European Team Championship. Spin, turn, fight, play, we win the title, quarters and we are in the semi-final against England.

The crux of the match: I find myself at 17 hole with my player ahead of a hole (to explain to those who don't know, the golf holes are 18, then winning the 17 we won). My radio seethed with Cape game orders and I, as assistant coach, couldn't theoretically talk with the player. However, as Italians, we devised a system of communicating all signals and gestures.

At that crucial moment I had to warn the player about the changes in the wind and the iron to play, so I tried in every way to attract his attention. But he didn't pay attention to me.

Arrogant and unsympathetic as all lone wolves, (not for nothing his nickname was Ezekiel Wolf) he didn't smear shitted days. He performed his "stupendous and stupidest" shot straight at the flag, but alas short into the water.

Then he turned towards me with an amazed face and looked at me inquiringly about why I had given no advice.
I wanted "to castrate him and rape him" but I said nothing.
The gentleman then, to protect himself, has also reported the incident to the Head Coach who has used my ass like discharge of all his anger and before everyone has filled me with expletives. And I always shut up.
At night I hear a knock at the door of my room and, even with pain in the butt, I stand in front of the boss, who apologizes and wants to know the truth. He explains to me that the day after we played for the bronze medal and that boys should have been prepared. It was necessary de-empower them of the blame for the defeat.
In the following years the thing has never popped out and I am convinced that the player is still sure that I did not wanted to help him with suggestions. A deaf would have heard my pssssst, but in sport arrogance sometimes makes ugly jokes. In this case, the lack of communication between Coach and player, due to too much safety, cost us a lot. My ability to stay in a team however has secured the bronze medal. If I had answered that evening and defended myself, I don't know how it would end.

A positive episode happened to me earlier this year (2012).
For the first time the Italian Golf Federation has decided to send a group of boys in South Africa in January for some competitions in the local circuit. For those who do not know, for them it's summer in January and then the South African players are in full form. For us, January means skiing or frozen ass, but no golf.
Clearly, for the "short and easy" trip they choose me. It must have been that wonderful country, the African warmth or a bit of luck, but in three competitions we rocked. In a race I even managed to place five of my six players in the top ten. At that point, South Africa hated us...

Seriously, I think I managed to create a competitive, joyful and eager climate, ideal for my boys. This thing has surprised everyone, me at first. No one could have expected such results from a group of six youths who took turns in splendid performances.

The ideal climate of flow for a team is when you all have fun and you feel good all the time, on and off the field.

Working, sweating, try again, swearing, it doesn't cost any effort and you do not even know it. Time flies and everything runs smoothly.

I think it was a classic example of perfect Coaching: I had to give it and the boys wanted to receive.

Of one thing I am sure: my partnership with Alessandro in recent years has helped a lot to enhance the level of my coaching and I hope this will continue.

Up and Joy,
Federico

ROBERTO OLIVA

Entrepreneur and General Agent Ina Assitalia Vignola.

Dear Friends,

I wondered what was the best way to begin this new emotion, and then, thinking about Ale's way to involve us, I decided not to think and not to do things straight off. So here below, with great humility, I write my preface.

What matters: the Result.

Be "all together at the same time."

A very beautiful phrase, born from the intimate, hidden, subtle thought of a tireless dreamer. I share with him, not an experience, not a job but a piece of heart, illuminating the path of our future.

What matters?

What matters is what we are, what we can shape on others. As former athlete, as former teacher of Physical Education, the cult of work = performance = result is the basis of my culture. But over the years this philosophy, although full of experiences, patterns, planning, organization and provisional plans, has changed more and more, letting space to colors, sounds and emotions.

Everyone, who is an essential part of every result is the most beautiful expression of an art: "the ability to enjoy his life."

Each goal is reached and acquired only if the inner passion overwhelms the action. Every "sterile" action is unfinished and therefore inexperienced. Only by shaping a group toward an "Olympic" goal you can create an enterprise system.

The daily struggle consists only in sharing themselves with the others without hesitations and fears.

Alessandro has taught me to listen, not with the words through the mind, but themselves through the silence.

Thanks Ale... kiss

GIULIANO VANTAGGI

Consultant for Communication, Marketing and Tourism Training in Italy.

Hi Crazy man,

what can I write?

If you ask me, if you want to build a team the first thing to do is get everyone sitting down at a round table (preferably with food on it) and make them share an idea.

Well, not so much share it as think they've had the idea themselves. This takes a good deal of preparation by the "puppet-master" so that the idea gets straight on the right tracks from the word go.

Now it's time for brainstorming. Everyone chips in (you can usually count on using 2 or 3 ideas out of every 100, but keep the others in a drawer as they can always be re-hashed and used again).

You need to think of ideas like dresses, and the project is the model. Ideas become great the minute they dress the project (model) perfectly for the occasion. If they don't do this they're just good ideas "on paper".

It's like the Rubik's cube. Only one idea solves all the sides. The others let you solve one side, or two, three at most.

After all this you have your team but you still have to manage it carefully to keep everyone on course. With good supervision you'll get outstanding results.

This is my experience with the best projects. Sometimes you're one of the team, sometimes the puppet-master, other times you might arrive halfway through the project. The important thing is to understand straight away where you stand.

Bye, Giuli

RENATO PADOAN

*Teacher of life, Actor, Director, Production Designer,
Art Director, University Professor.*

The experience of directing includes necessarily that of obeying. To directors like me, the comprehension of obeying is that of an actor. As an actor I have been so obedient, as a director I was always authoritarian. The director is at the service of the work to be successful and nothing is more importunate of an actor who does not understand that who directs answers of what it does to the group only. He has in mind not the benefit of the individual but the statement of the group. He is the first to sacrifice all, and not only his personal ambition to the group. Such sweeping statements are reliable if uttered by someone like me who loves loneliness ultimately. Loneliness concentrated in one person's obedience and domination! It's also true, therefore, that towards common tolerance the man who leads the team to its most innocent eyes stained with some guilt.

I don't think I've told the dear Alessandro this anecdote of my experience as Artistic Director and director of the University of Venice's Teatro Ca' Foscari. I am going for the first time to render it "public"! This is an example of how we should conduct in such circumstances.

The theatrical season was bloody due to a contest that seen me opposed to all the Associations and Weapon Fighters in Italy because of the fact that I had set the Parliament of Ruzante in the frame of the defeat of Caporetto!

My interpretation had aroused curiosity and a journalist of Toulon had contacted the Theatre for a tour in Toulon. The tour was very important for the theater because the ministerial contribution (that was the only real subsidy and financial support of the Theatre) depended on it. Except that this journalist, after coming to Venice to agree on the time and manner of the tour, had disappeared leaving a harmless letter in which she said that the tour was not to be done. Impossible! This was essential for the survival of the theater. I decided that I would go with the company in Toulon anyway. I did not say anything to anyone, not even to my right arm (my dear Zambonini), who disappeared prematurely in Atlanta, Georgia, where he became Dean of the Faculty of Architecture, after he graduated in Venice. As mark of the tour I got printed some playbills in French, in Venice, by the imaginary Jacquard typography that I made up. I booked a bus from Venice Brusutti company and I put in there the whole company for Toulon. *At the end the agreement was cancelled but in a way the show had already been announced.* Just before to get to Toulon I told my loyal Zambonini the truth. And astonished he said «And now what do we do?» And I answered «I don't know, we'll do something». When we arrived in Toulon I called the consul to tell him we had been deceived, that we were on the street and that we did not know what to do. The consul provided the company for the accommodation in a modest but passable hotel. Zambonini and I went to the journalist and we imperatively explained her we did not care about her theatre festival but that we had to do a show abroad and, most of all, we had to have the confirmation of the journalistic criticism and of the French playbill "printed in Venice", we needed all this to confirm the costs and have access to the ministerial contribution. More scared of our determination than else, she set to it and, unlike other times – when everything took place properly but there was any journalistic review – it was a big critical success even with a little audience. The funny thing about the show was that the sound of crickets and cicadas seemed to be a good sound comment for the show to me. We struggled a lot to get that sound recorded. Well, the show was offered outdoors, in a sort of

Roman theatre where, for the duration of it, a natural sound of crickets and cicadas raged. There were endowment and satisfaction. With such brazenness Paolo Grassi built the Piccolo Theatre of Milan. Debts and sudden attacks. In this theatrical expedition in the role of the leading man there was an excellent lawyer from Venice, a top-level criminal lawyer… I don't mention his name! According to Sun Tzu – who was the first author I have translated from Italian into Chinese – in war this has to do with the combat ground and with sending the troops to certain defeat because *men are like stones, they roll only if you put them on the top of a cliff!* Cortés' ships are another version of such strategy, the ships that he burned so they will have never thought about going back to Spain… and in this way they won Mexico! For us of the Theatre it was more simply to win the subvention that, in the late 60s, wasn't little because it amounted to about 10 millions of lire.

Renato, the master

INTRODUCTION

None of us is as smart as all of us.
ANCIENT JAPANESE PROVERB

Hello, it is a pleasure and an honor to welcome you.

In my life I had the luck to work as a Coach in the sports and business world for great Italian coaches and businessmen who taught me a lot about leadership and building a successful staff.

When you want your team or your business to have great results, first you have to invest your time and energies in the Staff Building process because you need a united, loyal, qualified, creative and strong staff to succeed.

Among my "duties" I have always given greater importance to aligning the staff human resources toward one direction to achieve the expected goals the faster, more secure and enjoyable way.

In my mind, the members of a successful staff must always be able to amplify the leader's voice and at the same time they must be a continuous stimulus to take good decisions.

Besides, the leader must be able *to involve everyone and create the proper environment* for a continuous feedback exchange among all the staff members, regardless of everyone's roles and responsibilities.

Staff Building collects some of my experiences in this wonderful trip to the world of people and their interaction for achieving success, so they can be useful to your trip, whatever this is.

This is the story of human beings who are committed with other human beings to win their challenges together, or to do all they can to succeed *all together at the same time.*

To you and to them I extend my thanks.

Have fun!

SECTION I

MY STAFF

With you I want to fill my days...

TOSCA E FIORELLO, My start is you (Il mio inizio sei tu)

1. A STAFF FOR ME

> *I'm a lucky guy because they gave me the world.*
> JOVANOTTI

In my opinion, the definition of staff is based on the evolution of the sociological concept of *the peer group*, i.e. a group of people with similar characteristics who share common tasks.

On Wikipedia we read that "*Peer group* may be defined as a group of people who share similarities such as age, background, and social status. A form of spontaneous social gathering typical of adolescence. The *peer group* is of great importance in the process of formation and growth of individuals, but in some cases may be a potential risk factor for health. It can be considered as an *agency of socialization* able to form opinions and guide the behavior of individuals."

I like the term agency of socialization!
Hello, you what do you do?
"I have an *agency of socialization*..."
That's nice! I thought there were only dating agencies and social networks...

In fact, the *peer group* is much more. As Ligabue would say, to me is "the center of the world," *the first Bengal light shot in the sky when I get lost*. Gianni, Piero, Federico, Roberto, Giuliano, Renato, are part of my peer group. Indeed, they are my personal Bod, the board of directors of the 1coach Alessandro Vianello SpA and I take advantage of Staff Building to tell them officially. They are my points of reference, they are people I've chosen. I respect them deeply and I keep them close to me because they stimulate me, make me grow and laugh. We have fun together and we become one. That's why I want them *all together at the same time* in my personal life staff.

To explain myself even better, I ask you to forgive my French, "but if you keep close to you assholes you'll get a fucking life." The law of attraction, of which so much is written and spoken, is infallible. Everyone draws in their own lives what thoughts and emotions focus on. If you give off vibrations such as anger, fear, cynicism therefore you'll attract corresponding experiences. But when you give off vibrations of joy, love, passion, you'll attract events and experiences in tune with them.

Sharon Stone, unforgettable icon of "Basic Instinct", when she turned 50 she did some clearing eliminating people she considered false friends, as if they were panties in her closet. Better naked than in bad company. I fully agree. A choice of great intelligence and wisdom, because *life is a thrill flying away, it's all a balance above the craziness,* as Vasco sings.

Well, I'm not telling you to go around without your underwear or to murder certain "snakes relatives " or truncate definitely those friendships with the lowercase a, I'm telling you to put your energy where you feel something good for you. I'm telling you to choose. Choose means deciding that derives from excise, i.e. cut out.

"The choice of happiness begins choosing who you want next to you in your life, from your personal staff of life. Surrounded by smiling people who exude positive energy, who you have fun with, with who time flies and as a consequence even your life soars. Elementary my dear Watson!" Sherlock Holmes would say. This way, I feel that I have evolved over time, because I have learnt to choose who I want next to me and start from scratch my *peer group*, my personal Bod, my staff.

The evolution is the choice.

A technical, electoral, corporate or voluntary staff can't be, indeed, "a spontaneous social aggregation of people with similar characteristics", maybe "typical of adolescence", as in origin is the *peer group*.

In a staff that takes the responsibility of being born to achieve results together, the components are selected on the basis of values they express and the skills that are required.

In a staff we enter as adults, unless embarrassing regressions into the childhood age I have witnessed. We also enter with at least a definite identity and started established skills. Afterwards, we can and should acquire others, working together with the idea of becoming a team.

In a well-trained, aligned and close-knit staff, "the risks associated with health", mentioned in the Wikipedia definition, disappear completely or almost, because it's nice to be part of something bigger than us, that we have consciously chosen. In the staff system we are fine and we want to be fine because there are many things to do to get any illness or those prolonged moments of unproductive discomfort that may be formed instead in a *peer group*, due to the constraints and psychological pressures of others.

In a staff we grow up, "opinions are formed and the behavior of individuals is directed", internally and especially externally, as in the *peer group*, but everything in the staff comes from sharing a purpose, a mission, a vision.

In a staff there are rules, as well as in the *peer group*, but these rules are created specifically to win the same game together. In a staff the rules are not found, but chosen.

In summary, the *peer group* is an animal organism as behind the word group, while the staff is a team. In a team, there are hierarchies, roles and scores to perform to achieve the common goal *all together at the same time*. We must all obey to something greater than the sum of individuals.
Then you can also become a group, but only after. So at least I think, and in this I'm a hardliner: the team first, then the group.

In my opinion, the staff is *a team of evolved people*, where the evolution is the choice: the choice of the vision, of the mission, of the purpose, of the attitude, of the aim to be achieved, of the action plan, of the structure, of the roles, of the rules and, of course, of the components, which in turn choose to join.

My personal development is choosing to share with you my treasures in Staff Building, *all together at the same time*, so that you may enjoy it too. I think that's the best way to explain the process of building a team and *to create value by bringing up*.

This novel is a bridge between emotions and experiences in which Gianni, Piero, Federico, Roberto, Giuliano and Renato are the stars with you.

I've dedicated a part of Staff Building to each of them to give an order and a form to content. You'll find reading that each of them is *team spirit* (Gianni Caprara), *ethics and values* (Piero Monestier), *specific skills* (Federico Bisazza), *planning and results* (Roberto Oliva), *attitude* (Giuliano Vantaggi) and *leadership* (Renato Padoan) at the highest level. These friends of mine are really *a lot of stuff*.

I'm a lucky guy because they gave me the world and because I met some extraordinary human beings with whom I have experienced something wonderful. I won a lot, really a lot, but my treasures are not my titles, they are the people near me and my emotions. As Filippo Inzaghi, legendary goleador, I am ready to give it all back to start all over again. This does not mean that it all went well in my life, indeed. I ended ko a lot of times, I took a myriad of doors in my face, I made plenty of mistakes and who knows how many mistakes I'll make again. But I'm still here.

In life I experienced excruciating pain and immense joy. I did not miss anything.

I maybe miss a relationship with a Russian trapeze artist of Circus Orfei, and after that I've tried everything: I see myself dangling upside down twenty feet above the ground, without a net, while I give my exciting proof of love like a gigolo sloth. Wonderful! Got it Got it Lack.

My "circus" hope is that these *friends of mine on the track* can inspire, motivate and entertain you as you look, listen and feel the show from the stage.

Enjoy! At the exit you can pick up a *souvenir*.

2. WHAT IS YOUR CHALLENGE?

> *Be the change you want to see in the world.*
> GANDHI

One thing is certain: whatever your challenge is, you need a *team of evolved people* at your side to win it. You need your staff! We know that alone in life you go nowhere because nobody is extraordinary in everything but all are extraordinary in something.

To grow each of us needs *to get help and trust* from others and *to give help and trust* to the others. Growing means exchange. Then, together, we all need to believe in the beauty of our dreams.

This *team of evolved people* can be made by family, friends, co-workers, employees, business associates and others. However, these are human beings, with qualities and faults, dreams and needs.

Whatever the field you want to make a difference is, you will be successful only choosing the right resources, aligning them towards the same aim and living passionately with them all the way to the goal.

In sport, whether you want to win the championship or save yourself, besides your need of right players you need help to get out of them all that is needed to turn them into a real team. You need your technical staff!

In politics, whether you want to be mayor or senator, however you need trustworthy and competent people close to you, because of their strength will derive your strength. You need your electoral staff!

At work, whether you want to become department head or C.E.O., you need to build the right atmosphere around you to motivate and promote the resources that you can use, so that they may help you reach your goal. You need your company staff!

In volunteer work, whether you want to enrich an existing organization or create a new one, you need to use your passion to involve the people willing to invest their free time and energy along with you, for the cause in which you believe. You need your volunteer staff!

Very well. After the catchy slogans, a secret: no matter what you do, you will always be your own biggest challenge.

When undertaking any project, the first and biggest task is always the one in your head, building a system of convictions and thoughts that will make everything smoother. In fact, to bring out the best in someone, you need to think the best of them. This passage is about your challenge with yourself. You need to *see to believe.* You need to go first. The secret to success in staff-building is to value one's own men and women above all else.

The X-factor that makes a difference in the Staff Building process is what you think of your staff, whether hand-picked by you, or chosen for you by someone else. No matter how, this is now your *team of evolved persons.*

You can change your team up to the last day of the draft, but when the transfer market closes, you start. No matter who's in and who's out. This becomes your only horizon to look at. Now, it's about concentrating on *how* to look, to bring out the best in everyone by giving the best of yourself. Everybody knows, the eyes are windows to the soul.

How do you look at your team?
With admiration or contempt?

How do you feel inside?

Let me explain with an example. When during the first official press conference at the F.C. Internazionale Milano someone asked José Mourinho if he was happy with the team that the company had set up, he replied: «When I was at Porto I always thought of coaching the best team in the world. Now that I'm here I think it even more». Wow, when I heard him I thought that's why they call him the Special One! This man is a great leader! In fact, in two years Inter became the strongest team in the world doing the treble: Champions League, Scudetto and Italian Cup in the same unforgettable season, 2010. Thanks to this belief that the coach conveyed to everyone: coaching staff, players, officials and fans.

Of course, every team is a living organism, and it may change in some components. Whatever needs to change is the positive and enthusiastic attitude and enthusiastic towards your men and your women's team. That depends on you. You can give confidence to others only if you trust in your skills. You can give responsibility only taking your responsibility for everything, and with the responsibility I mean the response-ability, ie the ability to respond. This does not mean that you have to do it all, indeed. It means that you have to feel good at answering whatever happens and make sure that problems are immediately dealt to be solved. Rumors said that in a big company like Disney all feel adept at responding, regardless of the role they have, and they work to find solutions, though not from them directly. This is the winning mentality to build in every staff: *collaboration, cooperation and responsibility.*

To accomplish all this and successfully begin any new venture, the only belief you must have in your head and in your heart is the following: "We are lucky! We have the best staff in the world! We have the best *team of evolved people* in the world! Let's do our best working together until the desired result. Now!". This is the thing to communicate and to do this you have to believe in yourself first. The big challenge is right to convince yourself deeply about this and when you do it, everything becomes possible. People in your staff will give the best they can with you and so you become a true *team of evolved people*, oriented to achieving a shared purpose.

Otherwise if you still have any doubts and consider that a person is worthless or non-adapted for the function or has temperamental limits or weak competences, that would be faced immediately. First of all you must deeply accept that every thought, conviction, idea you may have towards anyone will be perceived by everyone and by that specific person, even if you have not expressed it formally with words. There is communication everywhere and it goes through the stomach.
It is impossible not to communicate; thus, it's better to take the bull by the horns and be coherent, transparent and brave to communicate explicitly one's uncertainty when we are not able to overcome them, in our minds and hearts, or to potentially change them into a conviction.

To begin with the broad picture, if plan A doesn't work or if plan B is more inspiring for you, then this B plan should be acted immediately.

For me it's so much better to call the person aside and tell her: «I've tried by all means to take someone else in your place but I just couldn't do it. My perplexity came from this and that and that (you must be absolutely specific). However, right now there's no time to be perplex but only to write – together – a new story with a happy ending. I believe in sincerity, transparency and hard work. Team work. So let's work together. My wish is to be able to say one day that you are the most beautiful human and professional surprise of my life. That day depends on you. I will give my all and do my own side of the journey with the greatest extent of commitment and enthusiasm. I know that you will do the same and we will meet each other. I can see it in the way you look at me now (perhaps at this point you should touch the person to build an anchorage). You are the welcomed one (sincere smiling). For anything that may come, we both know how to find each other (assenting with the head up and down). Have a great day!».

Certainly this will work better than hypocrisy or conspiracy or to get by skepticism that will sooner become reciprocal for communication is a both-way trip. If you are in this sort of situation, do as it's said! Use the provisions from your own backpack. I am sure that person will surprise you and will appreciate you at any rate for how you and your staff live your values.

In short, what is your challenge?

1. Whatever your challenge is, you need a team on your side to win;
2. Whatever your challenge is, the real challenge lies in you;
3. Whatever your challenge is, there is nothing more beautiful than to win together.

Have fun with Gianni Caprara's story!

3. WINNING TOGETHER: GIANNI CAPRARA

There is nothing more beautiful than winning together.
GIANNI CAPRARA

The first time I met Gianni Caprara it was in December of 2001. I still remember it very well. He was in the stands, anonymous, watching the game of the team of which he would become the new coach. In sports you know how things go: the first to pay is always the head coach, sometimes it's your turn, sometimes not.

At the time I was an assistant coach of the women's volleyball team and I worked as a head coach in the youth team of Johnson Matthey Spezzano, a village in the province of Modena, the birthplace of the Italian volleyball.

Gianni had just won the championship with Reggio Calabria and was called to replace the person who, just 4 months before, had given me the chance to realize my dream: becoming a professional volleyball coach, by inserting me in his coaching staff as assistant coach: Gianfranco Milano.

It all started at 2 pm on a beautiful afternoon in July 2001. My cell phone rang when I was on the terrace sunbathing during the lunch break and dreaming of California. Officially, I was an architect in a study of Belluno, but in reality I spent most of my working days preparing the training of my women's volleyball team under 13 and drawing green attack patterns.

My mother had her dream: having a graduated son immediately at work, close to home and in a renowned office. She saw me going out in the morning elegantly dressed, coming home for lunch to eat the dishes that she prepared with so much love, returning to work and coming again home in the evening, where other cooked with love delicacies waiting for me on the table. She smiled, and I was dying inside. Surely, not for her sublime dishes.

In office it wasn't long before I had to face the hard reality of property speculation and my first professional disappointments which increased my sense of unease. The first project which I "signed" was for a Belluno businessman who wanted a new office which would make him stand out from the others; a place which was different, unique and special.
Well, I designed him a spaceship, suspended in his premises and coated in the same material as the Guggenheim Museum Bilbao by Frank Gehry. Crazily cool, perhaps overly space-age.

In fact, the only ones who thought the spaceship stunning were those of us on the project. In behavioural psychology this is called *confirmation bias*: a damned distortion which leads you to self-nourish your idea in a way which is entirely partial, overriding every criticism. We were so sure of ourselves that we even went on a road trip in the boss's black convertible Mercedes 500SL to Permasteelista, the Italian company which created the coating for the Museum Bilbao, to discuss feasibility and costs. We were ready for anything and wearing a hefty pair of blinkers.

I will never be able to forget the look on that businessman's face when he saw the plan for his new office. After ten minutes of gazing blankly, in silence, he said: «Well, it's a little bold... Thank you, but I don't believe that I will ever be ready for something like that!».

Excellent, likewise. Likewise I will never be able to put up with someone who sells themselves as something they're not. If you are only prepared to stick up a couple of partitions in your warehouse then don't fervently request a sensational architectural project which could change your life. Blinkers aside, at least a minimum of consistency is necessary.

I was devastated. My boss – who loved the project – killed himself laughing until, seeing that I was feeling low (so low that I was five floors below ground), offered me a drink to pick me up. Between one *prosecco* and another he recounted his own professional disappointments to boost my morale. Unfortunately, "a problem shared is a problem halved" has never worked for me. Not only does it fail to make me feel better it actually pisses me off. Knowing that you have taken a kick in the teeth as well doesn't fix mine and it doesn't ease the pain.

Once I had resurfaced from the centre of the earth somehow, I was confronted on my return home with yet another terrible ordeal: my mother. «Well dear, how did your project go?» she asked with a broad, toothy grin. «Wonderfully well, mom, really great!» I said, though I felt like diving out the window head first. She felt so fulfilled that she didn't notice my pain. This sometimes happens to humans.

What is a dream for some, can be a nightmare for others.

I felt my life was somewhere else, in another dimension. My mind and heart were all into volleyball and every day I dreamt of becoming a professional coach like the mythical Julio Velasco. I must have wanted it so much that this opportunity actually materialized in the most wonderful telephone call in the world that I received at 2 o'clock PM on that summer afternoon. I was not aware of the existence of any Laws of Attraction, but I sure knew how to make them work. Sometimes you don't need to know something to make it work.

«Hi, I'm Bocca, Giampietro Boccanegra, volleyball scout. We haven't met but I know who you are and I've been keeping an eye on you. I know you want to go pro. There's a vacancy for second coach in Emilia, in premier league. The seat was offered to a girl but she shat herself and refused it. You have 10 minutes to decide, take it or leave it, but remember that there are trains you can catch only once in a lifetime». Wow, I thought, this guy goes straight to the point!

«I don't need 10 minutes, I'm on! When do I start?» I answered, thrilled. My dream had come true, the opportunity that would change my life had just materialized in that phone call from the man who would become my volleyball scout, a raving lunatic and the best person to have by your side to help you build a career.

Sometimes dreams come true, as long as you *truly believe they can*.

I hung up and started jumping up and down, shouting, thanking God. «It's my destiny calling! It knocked on my door, well... it called...» I said to myself, bursting with joy. I was so madly excited that I quit my job at the architect's firm that same afternoon, keeping as a memento of that experience the habit of writing with a green pen, like the boss . He didn't take it too well, he was fond of me and couldn't get over the fact that all those flutes of sparkler had not served the purpose.

In the evening I completed the work by communicating it to my mother, and she fainted. The pain was so strong for her that she fell like a cooked pear on the Persian rug. She never recovered completely, the carpet was never cleaned and she fell in a cosmic depression. I began to laugh again and she began to cry. There had been an exchange of roles.

After a month or so of anxious wait and prayers to the God above, I was called back by the destiny impersonated as the "devil", alias Bocca, asking me to go to Spezzano and see the property. I still remember the journey, an indescribable thrill. You know the feeling when you leave a place knowing that you'll never come back... *strong stuff.* I got lost, as usually and I arrived to my destination dreadfully late, but with a smile on my face and self-confident as few in the world. It certainly strengthened up my nickname "Toni the Compass". By that time, I was able to get lost in any circumstance.

I remember one time, with *The Shaman* and the mythical Gigi Tres, it took is 3 hours to arrive to Spinea from Mestre by car, on our way to visit a girl that I've met in the Galassi refuge. The distance between those two towns is a 15 minutes drive. Each time I turned a corner, I was saying "here we are!", but we were never there. We were dead-beat, but since I was the one driving and we were already going to the dogs, we had to get there without looking at a map and without asking anyone for help. It was an odyssey. Jack Keruac wrote *On the Road*, I would be the author of *On the Wrong Road.* Sometimes, your nickname marks you forever.

The encounter in Spezzano took place in a small room at the Bursi Junior High gym, in the presence of the President, his wife and the Team Manager. Everything went as well as possible. «If the Head Coach Gianfranco Milano says yes, you'll be our new assistant coach», affirmed the President in a triumphal voice. Bocca was even paid on the spot and so he improvised, as a naïf way of saying thanks, a shocking tribal dance, inspired loosely by Fred Astair. Inspired very loosely. I didn't know whether to laugh or cry, because everyone was appalled. He is even crazier than me, Balotelli and Mino Raiola together. Sometimes you can become a legend by dancing.

And so, as soon as the practice of the first team was over, I met Gianfranco Milano and we went to dinner in the team's den, a tavern on the hills above Maranello, in the Salse of Nirano natural reserve. Every team always has a meeting place where to grieve over the defeats and celebrate the victories. Going there becomes a habit, because you feel protected, at home. The walls and the innkeeper know everything about you. They know when to speak and when to remain silent, especially the walls. It was a wonderful evening, humanly speaking there was a great feeling between us.

For firsts we had double cream tortellini, *Gnocco and Tigelle* as second and vinaigrettes as sides. We drank a bottle of Sorbara Lambrusco each and talked about Volleyball all evening. It was fantastic. Towards midnight we parted, me and him both high. «Alessà, we start tomorrow. Come at my place next week, I'll fix my special pasta with broccoli for ya!», said Gianfranco in Apulia dialect. It was like we've always trusted each other. In a couple of hours he had opened himself to me and had say yes, like the *Maestro* a couple of years before, making all of this possible.

While we parted, with him on his gas blue Lancia Thema, I kept a British composure. As soon as the car vanished into the woods however I started dancing like Bocca, moonwalking on the gravel of the parking lot. Pure Joy. Endorphin, Serotonin and Dopamine running high. Since that day I always commemorated my successes with a dance. I do it for me and me only.

I did it! I had become a professional coach. My fate was sealed. Done deal. «Ok, ok, ok, here's the Ferrari, all you have to do is drive it, easy money for a guy like you, who's been at the wheel since twelve years old. Thanks Dad, everything comes around after all». I kept repeating that to myself, euphoric. «Err… how do I turn this on?».

As a driver I had incredible enthusiasm, not much experience and a lot of desire to learn. I knew nothing about tracks, neither about squads, nor *Serie A* Sport Arenas. It was all new to me. I didn't even have the license to watch from the sidelines but I was in nonetheless. This is the demonstration that limits are only something one makes up in his head. They exist because you create them. If I hadn't proposed myself because I lacked the *Serie A* coach card, I wouldn't have been taken in. Instead I wanted to succeed so much that I dove into it and went through. Sometimes you really dance on top of the world.

During the matches I followed the game from the stands filming the encounter with the camera and giving directions as I could. Four exciting months for me. As I'd finished the work with the first team I changed the gym to train my young team. The salary was 800 EUR per month for 10 months, plus the apartment. A pittance compared to the gain prospect I had as an architect, but this was the life I wanted and that I had always dreamed of. It was a mess, with bread and volleyball. I had so little money that I ate potatoes and frankfurters.

Unfortunately, the opponents were much stronger, because thins at Johnson Matthey didn't go well. The most talented athletes were injured, and the results were slow in coming. We started in order to win the Serie A2 and in December we were fourth from bottom in the relegation zone. Bocca called me on the phone, he was worried: «What the fuck are you doing, are you stoned? Look, you'll get fired!». In fact he was a good prophet, in sports the head coach always pay. Gianfranco Milano was discharged and returned home, but not before teaching me, by example, with what style and class a professional goes away. No controversy and a nice word for everyone: great Gianfranco, thanks again for everything!

In those days, my heart was broken because the person that cooked the "*orecchiette con le cime di repa*" for me and that had confidence in me had just been kicked. Someone better than Gianfranco Milano non doesn't exist in the world. I was devastated. My relationship with him was wonderful and I would do anything for him.

I remember that was the Sports Director to communicate the thing to him in the shower. He was very sad, too. A river of tears flowed with the water.

When you're discharged you haven't time to do anything and you have to disappear immediately. You have to take your things and get out. Especially, they don't want you to talk to anyone to avoid emotional and difficult to manage aftermath. So you put everything in boxes and go away without looking back. Never release statements on the spur of the moment. Cooly, try to find a good word for everyone. Style, class and dignity are the only goal in these cases. We are professionals and life goes on.

I remember that night we went out for a pizza together for the last time and I did not know what to say, I could just weep. He was the one who soothed me, as only the greats can do. A couple of years later, he would name his first son Alexander. This stuff thrills you. *A lot of stuff.*

I do not know why the company decided to keep me, certainly Bocca's hand was in it, but that was the second best chance of my life in volleyball. *I'm a lucky guy because they gave me the world*, as the pop song goes.

Still wrecked inside, I go through the first match after Gianfranco best as I can. On the bench sat our General Manager, the legendary "Pincio", an egg producer. We lose 3 to 2 but we fight until the end. When I walk up to the stands to turn off the camera, I run into Giovanni Caprara for the first time. Impossible to forget the confident and resolute expression on his face.

He approaches me aware of being a well-known face in the Italian volleyball scene. «You're Alessandro, aren't you?» he asks me holding out his hand and looking straight into my eyes to see what sort of chap I was. «I'm Gianni, pleased to meet you. Finish off your job, I'll see you tomorrow» he says, dismissing me and lowering his voice in a tone of command as to let me know that there would be loads of work to do with him. *Work work work*, that's his adage. If you've got time left: work.

I was speechless. Black down jacket, brown corduroy pants, dark shoes, piercing eyes, Big Jim's hairstyle. "Thick shoes, fine wit" I thought of him heading back home. He must be a tough, rough and very practical guy. Fast, smart and aggressive like few others. Perfect outline.

Gianni had taken along his deputy Mauro Masacci, with whom he had won the league title in Reggio Calabria the previous season, title which was not awarded by FIPAV because of the typical Italian-style bungle. The first impression was shocking, watching them as they worked together. They were synchronized like Swiss watches. They spoke the same language to the athletes. They divided the sports ground into two. When Gianni moved into Mauro's court, the latter would change of place immediately so that there was always one coach per court. The players were never alone. It looked like a tango, Caprara was a dancer in an Armani's tuxedo and that "plague" of Masacci a fat and lustful midget peasant straight out of a Fellini's film. Such was my dream one night because of too many potatoes and frankfurters.

On the Thursday six on six, Gianni coached the first-string team and Mauro the substitutes, to which male sparring players were added to increase the game level. Often, I'd play too and Gianni would always cheat me out of some points to support the team. He's worse than the Artful Dodger in that. Right at the most crucial moment, he'd invent something to prevent the first-stringers from losing the rotation and to keep the pressure on right until the end. His speciality was invading the camp with a jersey while you were turned the other way and you couldn't see or hear anything. The team is sacred to Gianni and it gains confidence by winning, so if he has to swindle a point or two he doesn't hang back, seeing as he's the match referee and supreme commander.

Sometime after, the scout Carmelo Borruto from Reggio Calabria also arrived at Spezzano and contacts with the previous season's trainer Giuseppe Azzarà became more frequent too. Gianni was piecing together the staff that he could rely on in order to win again. "Wisdom sometimes walks in clouted shoes".

Come to think of it, in the (almost) *new team of evolved people* of Gianni Caprara from Medicina in Bologna, there was a "useless" deputy coach from Romagna (Mauro), a "calafrican" scout, son of an African and a Calabrian (Carmelo); a "tortellino" trainer from Modena (Giuliano) and a "Calabrian salami" trainer (Giuseppe); a specialist in physiotherapy and osteopathy "pig's trotter" from Emilia (Massimo); a coach assistant "northerner" from Belluno (me). Regardless of the different cultures, proveniences, ages, religious beliefs, sexual attitudes and inclination to eating hot chili peppers (terribly strong in "calafricans"), Gianni knew how to keep us all in line and we'd often get a right bollocking.

Once Carmelo and I made it late to training, a minute or so, because we caught heavy traffic by bus and then we even stopped to have breakfast at the bar (crazy! I take this opportunity to do outing). Bad idea. We didn't even have the time to get in the gym, that Gianni immediately took us aside and told us, «Next time you're out! Do not make me talk to society!». Evidence procedure of Gianni Caprara: none! Practically, a single wrong move was enough to arouse his immediate bloody reaction. In private he could be very tough, but in public he defends his team until his death, taking all the blame on himself if necessary. You felt protected and stimulated at the same time. This bow-legged super hero with stonelike scuplted hair, like Javier Zanetti, had a way in doing things. A sharp minded, big hearted bastard, more prepared than an astronaut in a space mission.

For Yuri Gagarin Caprara the team was, is and always will be the most important thing in the world, a bit like a spacecraft. Nothing can come before the Vostok 1. «The individual comes later. First there is the team», he continuously repeated. You win and lose together, who's inside the spacecraft lives, who's out dies.

Let's go!

We went as missiles. In a short notice we learned to travel in space like him and protect our spacecraft as he does. No one could approach the athletes without permission or in a wrong way for that matter. If someone in the pre-race was going to stop the heating of an athlete just to have a friendly chat, he was practically dead, no matter who he was or what he represented. It could have also been the Pope, had done the same end of the others: placed in a Gulag and shredded in goulash.

In particular, it was legendary that time when we had a nice visit from the Financial Police interrupting team training to interrogate all present on our space mission. I will never forget. It was a blitz worthy of Mario Monti in 2012: rigor and tax compliance all across the board. In fact, ten financiers in civilian clothes suddenly entered in the field in the legendary Bursi middle school hall, what Gianni called the classic "crap" because there was only one way out: the entrance. It was a massacre.

But before our taxpayers were butchered like a piece of meat, especially the few taxpayers within the organization, Gianni ran the risk of getting arrested and put in jail. In his mind, team practices were far too important to allow any sort of interruption, so he went straight up to the pirate who was boldly leading the crew on board. Unaware of the personal risk he was taking, he had walked onto the parquet floor, waving his arms while the ball was still in play. A crazy, reckless daredevil.

None of us staff members had managed to stop the pirate in time, just as none of us managed to stop Gianni's primordial instincts in time.

«What the hell are you doing?» Caprara thundered at the plainclothes intruder. «Get off the court immediately, we're working here! What do you want? Sit down and wait until practice is over!». The inspector paused a moment, and without backing up one centimeter he looked Gianni right in the eye. While we feared the worst, he said: «Perhaps you haven't understood correctly. I'm a captain of the Financial Police and we're working too. See, this is a subpoena, this is my badge, and from now on I'm in charge here. No one leaves until we've finished the interrogations. Is that clear?». «Very clear» responded Gianni, with his tail between his crooked legs. After all, who can leave the "pigpen" if the door is blocked?

Only Irina can get away with "back-talking" Gianni, so we savored every juicy tidbit. How we laughed before that fiscal slaughter! But that's how Caprara is - he can't help intervening to protect the team, regardless of the cost. The team means everything to him, and no one can interrupt a practice without his permission or a subpoena.

Knowing our head coach's less than delicate methods and his reputation as a hardliner when defending his team from any external attack, if someone without a badge ventured into the wrong place at the wrong time, even in good faith, we staff members would go explain to the person that it really was not a good idea to continue. Working on Caprara's staff is like being a Blue Helmet for the UN, you're charged with taking " such action by air, sea, or land forces as may be necessary to maintain or restore international peace and security" (Charter of the United Nations, Art. 42).

This task can save many lives because a "retaliation" by Gianni is unforgettable for decision, immediacy and roughness. It is unforgettable to see too, let alone to suffer. "Your little ass squeezes immediately". But he is like that: true, tough and badass. He always says everything directly, with maximum transparency and no turn of phrase. Take it or leave it. It's impossible not to estimate him if you have a little brain and personality enough to survive. Of course, you have to be tough too, otherwise you don't get up from the knockout and you are taken out horizontally. Then, for how good he is professionally, coming after him is like having sex after Rocco Siffredi. It's hard to do better.

After a chain of space missions and volleyball-orgasms, we were about to become one thanks to him. We worked a lot. I remember that he made me do a report on our team after the game. In practice, to do it well, I jumped the day off and I didn't sleep two nights, but on Wednesday morning, that notorious dossier was punctual on his desk. Gianni, as a great leader, had realized how much I need to feel involved and to learn the job. In the reports I produced good things and monstrous "crap" that he corrected with grace, patience and determination.

Over time I understood also his method of Coaching, because to study our side-out I had to dissociate myself, I had to watch it all from the outside as a spectator. From the inside you don't realize it all, especially when you are emotionally involved in the everyday. That's what a Coach is. By training like a tactical to study the video of our game actions divided and merged into six stages, I became very good at recognizing situations during games. In fact, the race is missing Rewind button, you have to decide quickly and well. That work helped me a lot to grow professionally because you can build the training right from the game analysis. In sport you always start from the end to go back.

How much he really needed those relationships? I think less than zero. But he did it to grow me and I will always be grateful for this, because after a season of nights spent in front of the video I had become a sort of astronaut too. I remember one day, in a closet of the "pigsty," he said in my presence: «You can say what you want, President, but this guy is committed always to the maximum». And I felt more and more proud to be part of his staff, despite having limited liability, indeed, in honor of my little Riki "circumcised". «Dad, when I grow up I want to have the cabrio-willly like you» he told me one day while we were playing naked on the bed. Memorable phrases, such as certain moments with Gianni.

Every day with him I always had more desire to learn and to work to improve my team. With this spirit that united us all, inside and outside the field, we began an incredible comeback that led us to win the last available place in the play-off, for set difference.

I remember we were in the bus, returning from our match, and we were listening to the radio to find out what had happened to the other team in the race with us for the fifth place. If that team had won we would have been out. The tension was cut with a knife. The air was thicker than the creme caramel of the restaurant "La Bolognese" in Vignola.

This didn't depend on us but we believed it so much. We had made a crazy comeback and we knew that if we got in the playoffs we would go direct to the moon. We were all crossing our hands and praying. There was an incredible atmosphere, what could be called a religious active silence.

When the news we were waiting came, we jumped for joy and began to sing the Gospel. I remember a sensational party, made of screams, hugs, tears of joy, thanks to Heaven. Pure magic. How beautiful! Thank God for the thrill of that moment!

So, from the relegation zone we got to the play-off promotion. Now it would depend only on us and we knew that we could make it. In the gym there was a special climate, now no-one would have stopped us. It was like being on top of the Lagazuoi since the air in the "pigsty" had become so fresh and crisp. Caprara had made the miracle.

In the semifinals we eliminate Firenze in two penalty kicks of the match. Gianni gave me one of the biggest satisfactions in the pregame of the first competition, when during the technical meeting he used the same words that I used talking about the tactic to use in a certain situation of the game against their strongest player, a Russian player. He did this sending me a look of complicity that I will always remember, those gestures that will remain in your mind and that reveal to you /remind you the initial plan: *develop your competencies because they will help all the team.*

This is what they say about promoting you own staff

You would be dead for him. I loved the way he called the time-out, the way he rose his index finger to draw attention, saying: «Children, this is important...» and to think the game with several moves in advance, better than Kasparov. It was a little like playing, knowing where the ball would go. "Good, you like to win it easily?" like in the advertising with scratch and win. Our players always knew what to do and how to make pressure on the opponent / adversary with the wall-defense. We loved to win easily/without effort. We went on "smoothly", to use a typical expression of Gianni.

I loved even his shirts. Johnson Matthey Spezzano was a small company and during the training we could dress freely, because we didn't have always a sufficient number of mute training to be in uniform all week. Thus everyone put on the shirts they liked most: Carmelo the one of the successes of Reggio Calabria, Masacci the one of the legendary Teodora Ravenna, me the one of the glorious Pallavolo Belluno and Gianni the one from Russia. A visionary.

In particular she had a red, white and blue sweater which drove me crazy for how beautiful she was and for how proud she was wearing it. It was a present from his beloved Irina, that Gianni had met when he was the second of Bonitta, in Bergamo. She is simply "The Divine" Kirilova. A beautiful lady and of a different category than any other. Like draws to like.

One day, seeing him walking radiant and dangling like a cartoon because of his crooked legs (if they were straight he would be six feet tall), I said: «You look just fine. That shirt is in your destiny». I was prophetic. After another year together in Sassuolo in A, Gianni returned to Bergamo as head coach and in two years he won it all. Then he was called to the leadership of the Russian national team and he brought it back, needless to say, on the roof of the world. Winning the world championship, he changed his nickname from Che-Caprara, being a left-wing revolutionary freedom fighter like Che Guevara, to *the Czar of all the Russias.*

There was no history, it was fate.

In the final, we won 3 to 0 in Pesaro and in the second leg at home we celebrated the feast of our promotion winning 3 to 1. On the local newspapers you can see me in a photo jumping in the field as I've never jumped in my entire life as a player and not even in my experience on the trampolines. That is the documented evidence that I can jump a meter high.

That venture was amazing (I mean jump a meter high) and united us forever *all together at the same time* in the realm of emotions. *The Czar* took a myriad of water balloons and ended up all the clothes he had for the press conference after the race. As soon as he was changed, we showered him again. He was tired of changing wet clothes just worn, but we continued to shower him with our joy and gratitude in liquid form, also because we were enjoying a temporary immunity. Gianni was turned blue as the ghosts of Pac-Man, and we could eat him before our supreme leader came: "Natural Director, Big Scoundrel, Wolf Man, Piece of Shit".

What a great party! We had dinner at Salse di Nirano and I danced again on the gravelled parking. How nice! Among the first ball of the season with Gianfranco and the last with Gianni light years of emotions.

Still, when it happens to encounter some of the components of that wonderful adventure, time never seems to be part of the past. Just a look and you take the time machine from Back to the Future. You are older only outside. Inside you live instantly the same emotions of that time.

Winning together is difficult, much more difficult than winning on its own. When a *team of evolved people* can magically build a Team that becomes a wonderful Group, then nothing is impossible, everything is possible.

As the Czar says, "there is nothing more beautiful than winning together."

4. WHO DO YOU WANT WITH YOU?

> *No big deal. Just three stories.*
> STEVE JOBS

I want righteous, fair and consistent men with me.

Yes, I want it all, because there is always time to settle. Given the choice, in my *team of evolved people* I want human beings with character, strong attitude and ethical values with which I agree. Am I asking too much? My answer to this question is always no. Who seeks, finds.

What leads to great results, in fact, is always the result of an alliance between human beings, of a complicity of various levels, of a choral action, of a service in order to contribute to the creation of something precious, unique and important which will become the common heritage and the vehicle of the success of the entire staff.

The first secret of the great dishes is the quality of raw materials that compose them. In this, great chefs are extraordinary, they know what they want, how to choose on the market and how to use the trash can, i.e. cut out the ingredients that are not up to their desires.

It's always the people who make the difference in a team, so in my mind I want *all the best* and, when I build a staff, I always point the arrow to the moon. In case it goes bad, I hit the stars however.

To explain myself better, I borrow three stories. Then I return them.

The first story is about *righteous Men*.

In Jerusalem there's a wonderful place called Yad Vashem, which means "a place and a name". It is accessible through the Avenue of the Righteous and in this place every tree bears the name of a gentile (non-jew) who helped and saved Jewish lives. You know, in the Talmud, "Who saves one life, saves the entire world".

The trees are 2,000, but almost 16,000 names are engraved on the wall, as many men and women to whom the "Commission of the Righteous" has awarded the honor of "Righteous among the Nations", according to the four main modes of hiding, transferring, changing identity and ultimately protecting children.

People awarded the title of "Righteous" receive personally (or through the heirs in case of death), a medal, a diploma of honor and the engraving of their name on the wall of honor in the Garden of the Righteous. This is beautiful, even if none of them did it for this.

One of the presidents of this "Tribunal of Good" was Moshe Bejski, a Polish interned in a labor camp at Plaszow and escaped from Auschwitz because he was included in the now famous "Schindler's List". In Spielberg's film he is the child who's saved from the most desperate situations thanks to his cunning and will to live, witnessing to the world the horror of Nazism.

Just the committee chaired by Bejski, many years later, had the honor of proclaiming Oscar Schindler, the man who saved his life and that of many others, "Righteous Among the Nations". The ceremony was touching. But who is a "*Righteous*" man?

As stated by *the Master* Padoan, that of Schindler is the story of one, of two and of three, of the cross and of the whole medal, of a man who was Nazi, jew and a lot more at the same time.

Schindler is a "Righteous" man, because he knew to be three, because he knew how to interface in an extraordinary way with conflicting situations, because he was able to interpret all the way roles and moments, because he was able to really experience the highest values of life.

When I say I want Righteous men with me, I refer to those human beings (males and females) living with similar values as mine and having the capacity to be three, i.e. to interpret positively the world and their role within their staff.

Righteous Men know:

- to do their job very well;
- to achieve their goals through the achievement of the team to which they belong;
- to put a greater interest in front of their;
- to take their responsibilities to the bottom;
- to risk personally if and when it is needed;
- to maintain balance and determination in difficult times;
- to relate with others in the right way;
- to interpret their role in the staff very well;
- to read the moments and situations;
- to be an example for others;
- to live the shared values fueling the enthusiasm and the respect for life;
- to enjoy.

Moral? You don't need to be a hero to be a righteous man.

The second story is about *loyalty*.

In every life there are those revealing moments where you cannot really know the level of *loyalty* and *fidelity* of a person towards its fellow travelers, its employees, its business partners.

In those moments, the sirens of selfishness and opportunism play their music in the most seductive way as possible, to confuse and tempt, making one feel an immediate benefit for which the price is rather the sacrifice of the highest values and the noblest relationships.

You know, reputation is built in a lifetime and it burns in an instant.

In those moments, you play your credibility and your future, something that in my experience is directly proportional to your level of loyalty and fidelity to the given word, implicitly or explicitly, and to the reason you're in the world.

For the amateur golfer Francis Ouimet, incredibly in the final at the U.S. Open, this moment comes when the President of the Club, before the decisive holes, approached him and urged him to replace one of the architects of his success, his caddy Eddie, with a professional caddy who really knew the field well. Eddie was just a baby, but with a special gift: he was able *to believe in order to see* and he was motivated only by a deep and sincere passion for the game of golf. In fact he was Francis' Mental Coach.

The intent of the President of the Golf Club was to safeguard the label and, under the guise of a noble gesture of help, to destabilize the child of humble origins Francis precisely to prevent the success and the resulting uproar that would have been generated in a conservative and elitist environment as that of golf, reserved to the rich and the noble. Francis was neither rich nor noble.

"The Greatest Game Ever Played", one of my favorite movies, tells this story in the following way:

«Young man, we were just talking about it. Club members believe that today you will need help» the President says to Francis.
«What kind of help?» Francis answers.
«According to the Regulation, the caddy is the only person who can give you advice. A person who truly knows our field» the President resumes.
«Eddie is doing a great job» Francis replies.
«Oh, for heaven's sake, Ouimet, these are the U.S. Open, not a championship for amateurs» the President urges.
«Did you say it to Eddie before talking to me?» Francis asks.
«You cannot reason with a child like that. We will make up a collection and will reward him generously, as far as I know his family needs it» the President insists.
«Do not let them doing it Francis, please!» Eddie intervenes crying from the other room.
«Hey, hey, hey, sure? You know I cannot pay you» Francis answers.
«I wouldn't do this even for $ 10, not even for 100!» replies Eddie bringing out his passion and values.
«You thought I'd replaced you?» Francis asks Eddie still upset.
«They told me you wanted to do it» confesses Eddie revealing the dishonest subterfuge.
«It doesn't matter, it doesn't matter, you and I are a team. It is not up to them to decide, okay? I'll meet you outside» Francis reassures him.
And while Eddie comes out proud and happy with his bag on his shoulder, Francis turns to the President of the Club closing the story with these words: «Don't speak to my Caddie anymore!».

As in all the legendary stories that encourage you to dream, Francis wins, and he wins thanks to Eddie. So, when he's carried in triumph by the cheering crowd, the new champion addressed his first thought to his little friend who helped him realize his childhood dream: to win the U.S. Open.

«Pass the hat for Eddie .. Pass the hat for Eddie ..» screams Francis to collect the offers that come abundant, thanking his friend with facts.

Loyalty, gratitude, friendship: *all together at the same time.*

This is the first real gain of Eddie Lowerie, which will become a multi-millionaire, thanks to his ability to live his passions and values by putting them in front of the profit.

Instead, Francis Ouimet will become a respected businessman and, simply, the most admired ambassador of the game of golf in the world. Mythical Francis!

Francis's father, always hostile to the fact that his son was playing golf instead of working risking to remain disappointed and with nothing more than the bat, in the course of the tournament will understand the greatness of his son's passion and he will put his few money in the hat for Eddie, recovering in this way the most valuable asset: the relationship with his son.
"The Greatest Game Ever Played" is a beautiful story, a story of true friendship. Also Alessandro Del Piero's story is beautiful. On 5th September 2012 he chooses to play again, in another continent, in Sidney, becoming the ambassador of football in Australia. A beautiful story of life, loyalty and love. Love towards his family, his team Juventus, and the game that made him famous in the world.

Moral? Loyalty is important in sports, in business and in life.

The third story is about *consistency*.

Long ago in India, a mother decided to take a very long journey with her diabetic child to reach the house of the Mahatma and ask him for help.

This woman wanted it to be Gandhi to tell her child to stop eating sugar because she was convinced that her son would have listened to him. So she left her village with her child and walked for three days.

Gandhi received her, listened to her, and simply told her to come back after three weeks. Such was the confidence in the Master that the woman took her child by the hand and returned to the village.

Three weeks later she knocked on the door of Gandhi who received her and listened to her again, but this time he turned to the boy and told him to stop eating sugar.

With great respect and disbelief she asked the Master because he didn't say the same thing three weeks ago, saving her and her baby another long and expensive journey.

Gandhi looked at her and said: «Woman, three weeks ago I was greedy of sugar too!». And even from this little anccdote we understand what kind of leader was Gandhi!

Certainly he knew how to adapt his communication on the lens he wanted to achieve starting right from the final result and then coming back and thinking about *how* to make it happen.

How can someone greedy of sugar convince someone else to stop eating it? How can it be credible? Also Italian politicians should know this story about spending review and taxes...

To be effective, the first step is to ensure that our map of the world is truly consistent with the message we want to communicate. If not, we have two possibilities: change it in the facts or avoid sending that message, because however it'll happen something that will make it ineffective.

As well explained by Richard Bandler and John Grinder in their thesis "The Structure of Magic", "..if there are any conflicting parties, none of them has the upper hand, but each carries a sabotage on the efforts of others to achieve what they want".

The fact that in a person there are conflicting parties requires the presence of at least two incompatible maps or models of the world that, as a guide for this person's conduct, make them inconsistent.

For the principle that everything is communication, as well explained by Bandler and Grinder, "the term congruence is used to describe a situation in which the communicating person has aligned all its output channels so that each represents, transports or convoys the same message or a compatible one.

When all the output channels of a person (posture and body movements, tone and pace of voice, words) represent the same message or compatible messages, we say that the person is consistent.

The experience that others have of a consistent human being is usually described in terms like these: he/she has a distinct personality, knows what to say, he/she is charismatic, dynamic and a slew of other superlatives.

The term incongruous designates then a situation in which the communicating person has a set of messages sent by his/her output channels, which are inconsistent, incompatible; we say that this person is incongruous.

So the others have a confused experience: he/she doesn't know what he/she really wants, he/she is inconsistent, untrustworthy, indecisive."

What we notice is that the step to define a person as incongruous as his/her communication is very short. And this precisely because of the lack of internal alignment that is explained in the outgoing message.

"Not to practise what one preaches", in communication and in life, determines an immediate negative effect with loss of esteem and confidence. As Carl Rogers said, "I clearly realized that behaving as if you were different from what you are, it doesn't produce any fruit in the long run, in interpersonal relationships".

Moral? Better to be congruently themselves, you gain time.

After reading these three stories that I have just returned, you must be wondering: but are there *righteous, loyal and consistent Men*? And if so, how many of them are there? And I can find them along my path?

Well yes, they exist! They're Staff Building's protagonists. And in my life I've known many others. Of course, you will find what you want and similar characters attract each other. God makes them then couples them. What you don't know is when this all turns out. As you may be ok in understanding the people and therefore in choosing your staff, you never know who is with you until the first real difficulties.

In this regard, many pray that everything always goes smoothly, I think instead that the difficulties are necessary to complete the process of building a *team of evolved people*. Every team, in fact, is formed through the overcoming of higher and more demanding obstacles. Sometimes certain setbacks are indispensable.

You can enjoy victories but they can teach you anything, someone very wise said. Only in times of trouble you can find out the truth about yourself, about others and what you're together. Only in those moments you can really know how much your staff is joined and what the value of your *Men* is. Only in those moments you can feel the bond is there. Only in those moments you can find out who is *righteous, loyal and consistent.*

Enjoy the story of a *righteous, loyal and consistent* man: Piero Monestier.

5. RIGHTEUOS MEN: PIERO MONESTIER

Free people, get the ideas.
PIERO MONESTIER

According to Piero Monestier, women are the *righteous Men*. In Certottica his staff is almost entirely female, an extraordinary team for skills and group spirit.

One day, as we drove along the Belluno-Venice highway in his mythical gray Toyota Corolla with two cowboy hats on, I asked him: «Piero, why is your staff almost entirely female?».

«Look, kid ... » he begins to answer with his calm and decisive voice, « the Monestier exist since 15 generations in these valleys. If my son Roberto doesn't hurry to give me a grandchild, our last name will vanish because there are only women on my brothers' side. Patience. My grandfather committed suicide because he had debts and didn't know how to do. My grandmother was widowed, paid all the debts and raised 4 children. That's why I want women in my staff.

One day I came home from school with a rubber in my pencil-case that wasn't mine. I don't know how it ended up there, but my mother, when she saw it, wanted me to bring it immediately back to its proper owner. I had to ask all my elementary classmates because I didn't know who it belonged to. Luckily we were just a few in the classroom at that time. The rubber belonged to the last I went to knock at the door. He had put it inside my pencil-case as a joke. I had to excuse myself with him, with my mother who followed me for all the houses to make sure that I did what I was told to do. In your opinion, what values I grew up with? That's why I want women in my staff.

Women have a higher gear and sacrifice themselves for the family, you just have to be careful they don't destroy it all due to fights between them. After me in Certottica there will be a man who knows how to handle women just like me».

Piero is one of the best leaders I've ever known. His communication is soft and direct. Ibrahimovic in his biography "Me, Ibra" tells about that time José Mourinho walked over to his Swedish partner and whispered in her ear: «Helena, you have only one mission with Zlatan. Feed him, let him sleep and make him happy!». Well, Piero is like Mou, he always says what he wants and people follow him. «This man gives everything for the team, and then I want to do everything for him, too. He had this quality, after listening to him you wanted to kill for him» Zlatan told about the Portoguese. With Piero Monestier from Belluno it works the same way, but no violence.

We met for the first time on October 19th 2011 in Certottica at Longarone, in the industrial area of Villanova under the famous Vajont dam. The secretary at the entrance announces me and after a few minutes a 60 years gentleman come to pick me at the reception. He is confident and moves slowly, with large salt and pepper colored eyebrows that frame a piercing and decided look. Those eyebrows seem to me to cover the headlights of the "Crazy Love Bug". At his feet light and fluffy loafers. He wears a dark gray tailored suit with a classy blue scarf.

We climb the stairs and enter into the main meeting room, the legendary "Fridge" room, from the name of a Certottica historic director. Just next door, there's the "Washing Machine" room (that's a joke!). We settle at 45° on two chairs around a wooden oval table with 16 seats. I tell my life and my desire to do something for them. I'm there to offer myself. We come out after half an hour with nothing done. He greets me shaking my hand: «Send me something… ». Enigmatic and challenging.

My luck? Listen to him and take his words. I leave Certottica repeating this phrase: «If you stop at the first door in your face, you're nobody, remember Ale! Head up! Send him something!». And by the time I sit in the car to go home I start to use my head to produce that something. Something special, curious, motivating, which induces him to take me to work with him. I don't know how to explain it, but I felt that my life would have gone there. And I always listen to my feelings. So I stay up all night and early in the morning I send him an e-mail.

E-MAIL TO PIERO MONESTIER

Subject: Coach Alessandro Vianello: Shell Longarone Miami

Good morning Mr. Monestier,

as a result of our conversation yesterday, coming home from Certottica I got the idea to propose to you a particular training that you may not have ever made in the terms that I'll explain.

The source of inspiration consists of two experiences:

Shell's head, a global leader in the mining and marketing of oil and its derivatives, decided in 1967 to implement the strategy of the analysis of multiple scenarios, forcing their managers to think about winning strategies in the long term (2000 year was the name of the project) based on extreme scenarios, far away from the situation of the late sixties, when the oil price was very low, or the raw material was over. Only thanks to this idea, the company found itself really ready when in 1986 the price of a barrel fell to 10 $. Shell had a scenario to $ 15 barrel in 1984 and so was able to react to the structural crisis better than all the other companies in the sector. The value of this idea lies not in the results, but in the process of thought and communication on the future that puts in place: flexibility, decision-making skills, practical developments in managing risks, open and successful mind.

At the beginning of his career as a trainer, Richard Bandler realized a course of training to develop the communication and relational skills for a period of 5 days. This course was to be held in Washington with a detailed work program for each day. In fact, at 9:00 am on the first day, everyone was given the following communication: «See you in Miami in 4 days at 9:00 am, those who managed to arrive, will explain to others how they did it. Then we will develop the program based on this experience. If you want to participate, you have to deliver everything you've got, sign a consent form and get on the road because you'll have only a telephone token and an identity document. The goal is to get to Miami with the token still available to you, because you'll have to use it only for emergencies. Have a good trip communicators, see you in Miami».

The idea is to create a training practice starting from an imaginary scenario, extremely negative or positive, requiring participants to rethink their lives completely out of the blue, pulling out their talents, developing their communication and relational skills, one working in the service of others, all with the support and guidance of a Coach: Alessandro Vianello.

The result of all is to exorcise the fear of tomorrow increasing confidence in themselves and in their wealth of knowledge and skills, so they can use them in their real life.

What do you think? We can put it together and start it up?

Thank you. All the best,

Alessandro

PIERO MONESTIER'S ANSWER

Yes, not in Certottica, in the Open Club for all those who want to take over their lives.
Let's think about how to structure and promote it.
Grateful.

Well, that's something, I think to myself. Then I don't hear about him for 20 days, untill another call, like Bocca's one, that suddenly changes my life: «Good day to you! I'm Piero Monestier. The course is ready. The participants are 25 people looking for work because they have lost it or have never had it. 4 days in a row, 8 hours a day, from 9:00 am to 6:00 pm with one hour lunch break in between. I want you to work on internal and external communication. On transmit them confidence and desire to get involved to restore meaning to their lives. I can give you only 50 EUR per hour, you agree?».
«Yes!» I reply firmly, mentally trying to write down all the things he had said to me earlier.
«Well. Thank you for accepting. I need the course program for tomorrow! The training days are from 29 November to 2 December 2011. Grateful. Bye».

Well, these are Piero's phone calls. Fantastic! With him, everything must be ready since yesterday. Roberto Oliva is another one like him, I'll tell you later his story. With Roberto things have to be prepared the day before yesterday. With Gianni Caprara, of which you've already read if you followed the order of the chapters, things are required to be ready before he asks for them. You have to anticipate his wishes. I love this kind of people! They claim they give you just as much and, indeed they always give you something more than what you expect.

The course of my debut goes very well. On the third day Piero surprisingly enters the classroom. It's 4:00 pm and he rightly wants to see what I do and what atmosphere I created among the participants. He enters during a magical moment, when we were having fun working on the preparation for job interviews. I was unleashing on the concept that *the economy changes, but friends remain*: «The most important asset of all is the reputation. You can tell everything about me, that I'm tall, short; thin, fat; black, yellow; heterosexual, gay; nice, nasty; but you can't say you don't trust me! Trust and loyalty are everything in business and in life!» as another great teacher of mine taught me: Claudio Belotti, to whom I owe the start of my Coach path.

However, I am white, tall, thin, heterosexual and nice (at least I hope so). And while I was saying all this, I saw that Piero was nodding, sitting at the bottom of the room, quivering from the desire to intervene in support of my thesis. In fact, unable to resist, he gets up and asks my permission to speak, and in a flash he begins to expand my idea in his unmistakable manner, in front of the students.

Initially it's a thin embarrassment to me, but immediately it turns into a great pleasure. And so it is my turn to nod with non-verbal moving my head up and down. Piero is one of the few people I would like to be always with me while I'm training. We are in perfect harmony and when he is there, I grow. With Piero I learn a lot of new things about training and life. Forty years of experience are *a lot of stuff.*

To celebrate the last day of the course he invites me m'invita to take a coffee in Martyrs Square in Belluno and while we're waiting in the arcades the other professor, Dr. Paolo Latini, says to me: «I have good news: I can give you 10 EUR more per hour. Congratulations, you've done a great job, the feedback of the participants are all excellent». I remain speechless and thank him sincerely.

But surprises don't end there. At the bar we order three spritz, the typical Venetian aperitif, and as we're toasting to the success of the course moving up our glasses, Piero begins to say: «I want to form a team of salespeople for a company operating in the renewable energy sector. I've been already contacted to do so. Alessandro, you build the team and teach the boys to enter into relationships with others. Paolo, you develop the process of selling and marketing. I coordinate everything and follow the boys on the field. Are you with me on this project?». I almost choke on the chips due to my emotion.

«Of course Piero, I'm with you! Thank you for this opportunity!» I say a little shaken as I try to recover from a cough, amidst the laughter of the others.

A few months later we find ourselves in the classroom to educate our sellers. Piero gives the ball rolling with a rap: «I am on the market since 40 years; I've nothing to repent of; I've helped more people than I could; people trust me. Here we want to build real sellers; not some fleeting crooks. We want to stay on the market all life long; just so you can be successful. For you, we put our faces in this project. We're here to help you; to teach you a beautiful job».

What to add?

Piero's strength is direction, reputation and creativity.

The direction because it gets inside you before you know it. You get distracted for a moment and it's already browsing in your belly, in your unconscious.

The reputation because it has values that are not for sale, which it lives every day. He challenges you to find out what you're made of and if he can trust you.

Creativity because it is a volcano of ideas. An active volcano. A generous volcano spouting lava: his experience, his ideas and his enthusiasm.

One day, sitting in his office at the *"Circolo Cultura e Stampa Bellunese"*, where his staff is made up of women (needless to say), while we were preparing the topics for negotiation on renewable energy, he begins to tell me a story to inspire me and give me some gemstone of his enormous and volcanic experience.

«Once I had to sell timeshares in Venice and I didn't know what to do. Then I have an idea. I choose ten customers and send them a letter, containing a thousand lire bill, on which I write:

First I wanted that you felt the thrill of receiving something unexpected.

Second, I wanted to make sure you got to the bottom of this letter.

Then in the body of the letter I explain that when you make an investment it is important to understand the use you can get from it. By purchasing a timeshare in Venice you can experience the atmosphere of a magical city and you can travel the world.
If this is not a deal ...
Do you know what happened? I sold 2 timeshares in 3 days» he says smiling and satisfied.

After this story our topics born fluid and our relationship enters a new dimension. There is trust, exchange, estimate. We have a lot of fun comparing our personal growth courses and planning higher education. At the *"Circolo Cultura e Stampa Bellunese"* born *Brainstorming* and *David's Sling*, tools to get better, ways to get out of the crisis, meeting places for young people in and out.

During each meeting Piero always manages to surprise me for wisdom, intelligence, balance and generosity. A real mentor to which it is impossible not to become attached. "If you do something to please someone you've built your chains. *Free people, get ideas.* I can be wrong, Men can make mistakes, people can betray. Get ideas and take them forward, without binding yourself to anyone. Get the beautiful in the world and do it for you", he told me this one day.

I will never cease to thank him, he made me understand many things, making my relationship with my son even more beautiful and free. I would put a signature to get to his age with the desire to play as a child, with the lightness of a butterfly and the *mental mobility* of a contortionist. *A lot of stuff.*

As stated by the legendary networker Keith Ferrazzi, "generosity is the single currency of relationships". As for trust: to trust in someone you must first trust in yourself. That's why it is so important. To be generous with someone you must first be generous with yourself. In generosity there is the pleasure of giving and the security of having what is given. "I have what I have given" is a motto of Gabriele D'Annunzio Monestier.

My friend Giuliano Vantaggi, I'll tell about him in regard of attitude, would say that "those who have the ideas, will always have them", so why keep them for yourself? The best thing to do for yourself is to give your ideas to others and change the world for the better *all together at the same time.*

It was impossible not to write a book about my friends!

I SELL MY SELF

I quickly do another inventory, disassemble the cabin and go away,
I change area, route, my address is madness!
Wherever you go, there's someone unhappy.
I want to broaden my customer,
I sell wishes and hopes in spray.
(Mi Vendo – I sell my self)
RENATO ZERO

Piero is a super seller because he's a super person.

Many mistakenly think that sales techniques make the difference, but those come later, very later. What matters is the value of the person, always keeping promises, honesty, the desire to do and the pleasure of helping others. With this way of being, Piero knows how to accompany the customer to purchase in a simple, clear and safe way, without leaving him alone. "It must be a bargain for all", he says and does this.

With Piero you feel protected, it's like having a *Marine* by your side: you know that in one way or another he'll bring you home and you can trust him.

What makes a Marine a deadly weapon is not, in fact, the rifle or the technological equipment, but *Body Spirit*, *Ethics* and *Values*. Those humans have been through so much to become Marines that they considers their brothers and sisters people like themselves, because they had to overcome the same ruthless selections, the same hard trials and the same grueling training, without exception. For this reason they are a family and bring one another an eternal respect, regardless of age. They're always *all together at the same time.*

The Marine Piero Monestier is "Semper Fidelis", lives with Love, Ethics and Values and he doesn't sell himself.

6. WHAT ARE YOU LOOKING FOR?

> *If I were fire, I would burn the world;*
> *if I were wind, I would bestorm it;*
> *if I were water, I would drown it*
> CECCO ANGIOLIERI

If I were *the Marine* I would say: immediacy, honesty, strive, skills. To these qualities I add energy and exchange.

IMMEDIACY

Because you cannot wait for two days to have an answer. You need to be ready, you need to be smart, clever and quick. Fast and painless. Firm and careful. In one word you need to *be there*.

You cannot send the cenotaph of yourself ahead, times have changed. Nowadays a 3 months old camera is obsolete. While you're hanging out for a drink, comfortably kissed by the sun, a kid in a garage on the other side of the world is troubling your business. Internet has changed everything.

The current reaction times of the world are enormously faster than that from the past. You get distracted for a moment and Bolt is already signing autographs with his new world record. Back in the day a letter took dozens of days to arrive. Well, I think that hasn't changed much.

Back in the day there was the payphone. I remember when I used to go out with three pounds of stinky iron scrap in my pocket. Now you won't find a payphone in a thousand miles. And I'm not a hundred years old! I'm still perfectly healthy.

When they're seven, kids already have a mobile and a tablet. "A phone because you never know, if they need it, they can call you and we know where they are". But since modern parents are a bit ashamed, they give to them those prehistoric models 2.0, pulled out of their "forgotten by God" drawers, where you can never find the right charger.

I mean, why? They're so old that you don't even remember how to switch them on, you cannot even text with the T9 and you give them to your son? Why would you do that?

Then the tablet. Well, you need a tablet at school, damn! It's absolutely necessary to grow up healthily. So modern parents, in order to avoid buying an iPad, they give to them those ugly small steel and glass boxes which don't even work well, just covered in your finger-marks on the screen and there's no way you can slide on an App. And all this because it's important that your kids grow up with tomorrow's language?

"I mean, dearest modern parent, damn, why do you wish to be sympathized at all costs? If your kid can use an iPhone better than you, why do you give them prewar carbon fuelled models? What's the use? You want to keep fast and beautiful things only for yourself? What if they want to listen to some music? Would you give them a walkman they have to drag with a cart? It's as if your father or your mother, fifty years ago, gave you a stone and a broach to write: "Here, honey, your new diary: an amazing and extra-light Istria stone… We thought about the pen, too: a cast iron 5 pounds Montblanc with its tip freshly frosted". Does it make sense to you? I feel like asking.

You might criticize me on this, you may put a poster of me in Piccadilly Circus with "here's a true dumb father" written on it, but my little 5 years old Riccardo owns an iPhone7 and an iPad5, retina retinous display! Or else who would teach me how to use them at their best?

HONESTY

Because without it you're dead.

In the times we live in, busting travels on optic fibres. It takes a whole life for you to build yourself a reputation and in the blink of an eye you may destroy it. Internet has changed everything. Nowadays the world is interconnected on every level and the consequences of a misdeed are immediate, amplified, globalized. With no values nowadays you won't go very far because you won't last. You get blown away by a click. And this counts in every field in life: sport, politics (maybe not in this one), business, volunteer, love. Yes, I put that too because to me everything is love.

So, as the great mountain climbers say that "it's the mountain that lets you climb it, it's not you climbing it", nowadays it's the world that lets you entrepreneur, it's not you doing it. As we learn from Arthur W. Page, "in a democratic Country, all the businesses born out of the community's permission and prosper thanks to the public's approval". Here's where the world has changed. Nowadays you cannot even think of being on the market without having the consent and the approval from the community you belong to. It was like this back in the day as well, what has changed is the community's dimension. Today you cannot be the dumb of your district, today you automatically become a "world dumb". And everyone gets to know it, be sure of that.

They magnify a jpg picture of you and project it in Piccadilly Circus, and you don't even know about it. And when you walk down the street and you see other people pointing at you, mumbling something like: "look, that dumb from the poster" and they laugh at you, please don't be dismayed. As we learn from Giampietro Vecchiato in "Crisis Management", reputation becomes a certification that comes from the outside, connected to your identity and to your image. Hence connected to the perception of yourself.

Would you still do business with who wants to bust you? Well… if it were Marilyn…

Would you still enter the staff of a person you don't trust? No, not this.

STRIVE

Let's start with some bad news.

I've got two. Some things hurt but you better learn them straight away, or do you prefer finding out when you're 60 that your wife or your husband has been cheating on you for a lifetime with your best friend? I guess not, you better never get to find it out and live blissfully like a moose in the wood or finding it out straight away, so that you may at least retire in a Tibetan convent that will be soon destroyed by the Chinese. With you inside it.

First bad news: strive is no longer a requirement. So you better don't mention it in your resume or in a business interview. If you go to an interview saying that you strive they will laugh at you. You will hear laughing from miles away. The world has changed. If someone wishes to be part of your staff and tells you that he strives, let him be dismayed and pass to the next candidate.

Rumour has it that people who have nothing and who comes from unemployment have 400% more possibilities than the average class American citizen to make the American dream come true.

Rumour has it that on the Earth there are young human beings who are willing to do what you cannot even think anymore.

Rumour has it that a huge number of people is willing to do everything to conquer for themselves a place in the world: yours!

It's sure that, while you're lying on the sofa watching your favourite TV show nibbling nuts, an infinite number of people is striving to reach and exceed your level of wealthy and to come and switch your TV off.

Let's talk about the good news.

Recently I've had the pleasure and honour to teach a training course within a "project for the valorisation of the territory" in Tambre, Alpago, in the Belluno province. A wonderful place, you have to visit it at least once in your life, even for its sexual customs. It's commonly known that Alpago women are as beautiful as determined. If they decide that you're the right man, they take you and there's nothing you can do. They do all by themselves and it's fantastic. If you're a sissy instead, be aware that when I was young the Alpago was known for its percentage of well-hung men. "They make 4 feet in three", they used to say in Belluno. If you ask around maybe you can still find some interesting item.

Anyway, in my classroom there were about twenty young men, the older was 26. Surprise, surprise, among them I found 15 years-old boys who were extraordinary bright, motivated and well-prepared. If I think how I was like when I was 15 I just quiver. I used to play with my toys. These boys would have wiped me out in a second.

Luckily the crisis, besides the tragedies, dramas and economical troubles, also brought something good: new generations think differently from the old rag dolls. This is great news!

Someone says in Italy a generation got lost and unfortunately, maybe, they're right. Even if it's hard to admit it and it hurts. There have been such fast changes we weren't culturally ready, and they have determined a devastating castling on positions that were useless. Nevertheless, such positions are as dead as our political class. Dead inside. Without even the dignity to keep on playing music while the Titanic is wrecking.

We held on to something that no longer exists. Not even as a shipwreck down the sea. Now we need a new mentality, which luckily nowadays kids prove to have. There's a beautiful hope! They're alive and smart! They have what we need! Let's help them!

Let's also help us to realize that times have changed once and for all. What was once sufficient now won't even take us to the tenth day of the month. We need a new strive, that will guide us to the immediate building of skills, in a fast, safe and funny way.

Nowadays you cannot be amazed by anything. It's like when you're running and you already cannot take it any longer and Linus runs by faster than you with Nicola Savino on his shoulders talking bullshit. And you think «Hey, where are you running so fast? Didn't you work at the Radio?!». Well, if you have such thoughts, you're a dead man walking. Not even running. And this is the second bad news: if you waste more time to feel amazed by something, you'll stand behind.

Running, I learned 2 things:

1. There's always someone running faster than you, unless your name is Rudisha. There's always someone hungrier than you. So be ready and start running, running fast like Forrest Gump, because "life is like a box of chocolates, you never know what you're gonna get".

2. Would you like some free cuddles? Go running in the most unusual hours, you will always bump into someone crazy like you that will say hello without knowing you. They will identify with you and this is all it takes for them to be happy. Generally they raise their arm and their eyebrow. Sometimes, if they're really fit, they move their mouth a little as if they were chewing some broth. If it's your lucky day you can even hear "Hello!". Take a look, because if he's tall and black, it's Rudisha.

3. *Do always some extra.*

SKILL

When I was four years and a few months old, at 10 am, on my third day at the kindergarten, I ran away in my light blue smock and blue slippers, crossing the city by myself (traffic lights included) and got home. Which skills did I acquire?

And which skills did the nuns at my ex kindergarten already acquired when they realized that I was missing, only when my mother, at 4 pm, went and fetch my shoes and my clothes saying that I wouldn't go there anymore?

Questions that will be left forever unanswered. By the way, thanks mom. I really appreciated it. It was wise of you perceiving my discomfort and keeping me at home.

Now everything's changed, schools and kindergartens have become unassailable bunkers. To pick up my son at the kindergarten they take my fingerprints and they scan my retina. The younger one then is under special surveillance: closed-circuit cameras that follow him wherever he goes and his iPhone 7 is under control. They even put bugs in his smock, they always know where he is. His father's guilt. We went from an extreme to the other, but in this case safety is never enough.

Now everything turns around skills. As I learned collaborating with Certottica, the European Union, in order to facilitate the internal professional redundancy, provided in the far 1989 the Certification of Skills and in 2005 the Project EQF, European Qualifications Framework.

The idea is simple. Who graduates in Italy in a certain school must have acquired the same basic skills of one who graduates somewhere else in the European Union. Who runs away from the kindergarten in Belluno must be able to run away from any other European kindergarten. Even from the German ones. Instead, if you attend a kindergarten in Switzerland you're doomed, because it's out of the European Union. You need different skills but you could make some money turn.

With this system, the school, the work and the educational world is renovating itself, because you no longer start from the contents but from the skills, as learning's results. Enough with frontal, theoretical and abstract lessons, where you would fall asleep after one minute. Now didactic has to be active and participative, with workshops, simulations and experiences. In short, it's a big planned chaos. At first you involve, you extract, you share and then you add your special contribute. As tests you get rid of multiple choice testing and at its place you do crosswords and rebus (joking!), that is complex tests that simulate the work reality, the tasks and the results to achieve together.

In fact, the term skill refers to "the ability to use knowledge, skills, personal, social and methodological skills in working or studying situations and in professional and/or personal development". In other words, learning by heart a poetry is no longer sufficient.

If I were Ale, as I am and was,
I would get the most beautiful and graceful women,
And leave the filthy and cripple ones.

ENERGY

Because everything is energy. We're made of energy. We're magnets attracting the same kind of energy we give off. The Universe just obeys to this law called Law of Attraction. In the past years it has been revived with "The Secret".

Because our mental universe determines our material universe, if we think about the lack of something, we will attract it, because each of us attracts in his/her existence what he/she focuses his/her thoughts and emotions on. So, watch out! Basically, our thoughts and our emotions release an energetic frequency in the Universe and all that casts at the same frequency will be attracted to our physical world.

A good question is: what do you cast?

Prosperity and abundance, that are the dreams of many of us, are states of mind. The more the emotional energy with which we combine our intents is intense and the faster the materialization of such desires will happen in our world.

A dear friend of mine, Modena's notary Aldo Barbati, has everything big because he has a big heart and thinks big. Family, house, garden, cellar, office, car, dogs, belly,… everything is Extra Large in his life like his XXL generosity.

EXCHANGE

Because it's the first form of love.

Love for oneself and love for the others. It's a bit like with the stickers: if you do all by yourself, you will never fill the album. You just waste your time and your money. What you're looking for someone else has it, maybe double or triple. Like you may have a double or a triple of something he lacks. It's just a matter of getting together and exchanging your stickers, because getting together our skills, our experiences and our talents, we fulfil ourselves.

This is the way to make new friends and to experience new emotions. Who stays close in his world will never grow up, as beautiful and rich he may be or look. Like the legendary Pat Riley used to say, "if you don't get better, you get worse!". If you don't move ahead, you're moving backwards.

In this first part of my life I realized that to make our dreams come true we need to share them, to build a staff around us and to exchange our stickers with the world.

Got it got it lack.

7. SPECIFIC SKILLS: FEDERICO BISAZZA

> *In the swing, you need to grab your club under the hypothenar eminence!*
> FEDERICO BISAZZA

This story is about an oak and a man in a red jacket.

Like the wise man says, every person has his tree. My tree at the Modena Golf & Country Club is the oak at the border of the training court. It is the tree that I've always drawn since I was a child, the tree that has always been in my imaginary before I had even seen it. Nevertheless, It has always been there waiting for me and, judging from the width of its log, it was waiting for me before I was even born.

Sometimes it happens with people too. When you feel you know someone since forever even though you just met him, because emotions are timeless: we're always *all together at the same time* as we learn from the quantum physics. It's just a matter of realizing it.

So, one day in February 2010, destiny decides it's time to meet. I was browsing the Net looking for something new and on the Modena Golf & Country Club website I read an advertisement about a promotional golf course. I suddenly decide to subscribe to those 10 group lessons. Until that day I had never grabbed a club besides those of the mini-golf at the beach, all marked and ruined as if they were involved in a war. Golf, the real one, I just followed it on TV and I was fascinated by the Majors and by the Ryder Cup, wishing one day to work with some player, since I had already won as a Mental Coach at track and field, at volleyball, at tennis and at soccer.

Then I like doing strange things, maybe because I am strange. New things, apparently far from my world, because I learned that those very activities, which bring you far from your comfort zone, make you grow up, enriching you with fundamental experiences. This is method to me, a life style, a way to challenge myself always.

Said and done. Let's play! On a Saturday morning at 10 am I find myself in the Club House at the Modena Golf with a dozen other beginners in jeopardy. We look at each other bewildered and we become friends right away because we share the same fate and the same unmistakable outfit of civilians inside a military camp. It's very easy to recognize a newbie. In golf the ethic and the etiquette, and by that I mean the totality of the rules, customs and habits passed on for centuries, are an essential part of its charm. And so you need to respect them and make them respect. The great master of ceremonies at the Modena Circle is the Director, whom I will always be grateful to for his warmness and his willingness to explain to me how to stand in a golf court and what to absolutely avoid. Precious suggestions in order to be easily introduced in a new environment with no risk of reject. Initially I thought he was a "lemon water-ice", instead he's just a Jedi, in love with his job, with the Club and with golf.

Once his general grounding ended, with the same effect of a Mentos, "the air fresh maker", we drop by the Caddie Master to take the clubs in order to go straight and with composure to the training court, where a teacher would have taught the first lesson. Cautiously we step into the crypt where they religiously keep the players' relics - pardon me, their bags. The atmosphere is ascetic. The temple guardians are two nice, soft and kind guys called Gaetano and Mauro. They make ourselves at home in a "Kung Fu Panda" style, they give us the "weapons" and they explain us the way to reach our "arena", located three hundred feet from the Club House. Excited like babies we start walking and mumbling, with the same stealth of inspector Clouseau waiting for an attack by his Chinese butler, Kato.

Everything is new to me, like the feeling of grabbing the mysterious Iron 7, with which in golf you start learning how to swing and to hit the first balls. It's my samurai sword. I almost put it in my belt. I'm ready to fight. *We're ready to fight till death, Italy called*, I don't know why I hum the Italian National Anthem inside me. Maybe I sensed it, but at that time I would have never thought it was the day that would have paved the way to a great friendship, new titles and an experience with the Italian National Golf team. But the unconscious knew it all, you just have to listen to it, carefully interpreting its messages.

Besides "lemon water-ice", it's still winter. The weather is cold, it isn't even 15° C. At the sides of the small street that leads to the training court there are still some snow traces. The entrance to the new world is a opening between 2 hedges that protect the hitting cages, isolating them acoustically and visually. I go through it holding my breath, drowning the respiratory system like Genoni (what a fool!). Under me dark wooden boards make a little ramp, slippery like the base of a soccer game that is soaped because it has being raining and it's humid. Three fins and I'm in. So beautiful! So excited! Once I re-surface, I look around like inspector Gil Grisson on a crime scene, collecting as many information I can in the time unit. In this I'm a Manassero myself.

On the left there's a harmless wooden house where you take balls from the automatic dispenser. Baskets are conic and they're sweet. You feel like picking some flowers for a garland and to hug someone singing Abba's songs around the fire. I wonder which may be the firm who has produced them and which is the industrial site. I would go there immediately. The noise of the balls that rolls in the dispenser is similar to the gurgle of someone who's swigging a beer. I feel like having a cold beer.

Suddenly it seems like I am in a German gas station. Full tank, please. Could you please also check my tires? That dark wooden house where balls come out must be fantastic for dessert, because it looks like the witch's home in the Grimm's tale "Hansel and Gretel". Yummy, delicious dark chocolate roof. Delirium of the senses.

In front of me, "there's a wide green lawn where hopes born, which you call boys, the great lawn of love", like the great Gianni Morandi used to sing. Such grass sweep is covered in a million balls, already hit, that are collected by a man inside an armoured vehicle. Judging from its fender benders it must have been one the practitioners' greatest fun. Everyone knows, when a game is forbidden it becomes the most desired. And, in fact, I'm day-sleeping too. I dream of hitting and wrecking from far that moving cruiser, with a strong, low, straight like a needle torpedo. I see myself, while I aim and shoot. A perfect shot. I can tell from the impact and I already know that I hit the spot, like the real players. Who am I, Severiano Ballesteros?! As I finish my movement, I see my ball aiming relentlessly towards the armoured vehicle that is unconsciously riding in the other direction. I hold my breath and pray that it keeps with the same speed I calculated my rifle range and in the same direction. Here, a few meters more... a few instants more... and bang! The music of success plays in my ears. Go go go! The cluck of my bullet on the shell is like a shoot. Scared birds fly far away. My ball bounces on the roof like a stone on the water surface and at the same time I see the scared driver flinching, and then gesticulating in the armoured vehicle swearing against the bastard who hit it. At that point the other practitioners turn to me, to that bastard who all of them would like to be. My sense of guilt is a drop of shame in a sea of satisfaction. It's such a pleasure to hit the spot! I enjoy it. Then I figure myself lifting my hand, with my head down to say sorry, sad for that serious, accidental and involuntary accident, that unfortunately starred me as the protagonist. Inside me, instead, I gloat over satisfaction. I feel like screaming my happiness but I have to keep my cool. The power of the creative imagination.

With that feeling of invincibility, after a long sigh, I turn to my right and I see It. We recognize each other right away. At the bottom of the semicircle with the cages, there's my oak, my tree. I'm enchanted by its beauty and its perfect proportions, of a nature model, 36-24-36 like Sophia Loren in her twenties. I cannot take my eyes off of it and I miss a good part of the teacher's initial lesson.

And yet, in a golf court, there are many trees! But It is special indeed. Impossible not to notice it when you walk the crescent-shaped hitting cages in the training court, because It is at the bottom, like Marilyn Monroe's mole: irresistible. Walking towards right, in fact, the cages go from uncovered to covered and then closed like boxes in order to assure more privacy and tranquillity to the practitioners, conveying a Rossinian crescendo in importance that leads to It, the natural wing of that stage.

In what it seems to me like a magic kingdom, populated by fairies, gnomes and pixies, right in the first of the two last private cages, a red spot catches my attention like an iron magnet. I take a better look and I realize it's a red jacket, worn by a tall and mighty man. My eyes on there, inevitably, like on a beautiful woman's cleavage and a well shot ball down the hole. My oak looks like an enormous flag that waves among the green and that man in a red jacket looks like the professional who's about to get his putt. Spaces of pure poetry.

In the meantime my group lesson has already started from awhile and I missed a good part of the introduction on the game's basics, absorbed as I was in my thunderstruck thoughts. Basically I do what one may call a handicap-start to take the handicap.

I don't care much, after the theory I missed with my feet off the ground as in school, we get nicely located in the uncovered cages, near the opening between the hedges. Practice starts. Each of us has a basket of balls to try hitting. I said to try. The training method must be "Swiss", and by that I mean that they give us a club, a ball and zero know-how. The know-how, that is the essence of the swing, is denied for now. This way, everyone does what he can. Our cup of - stale - tea. I look at such embarrassing scenes. Hitting that "fucking" ball isn't easy at all. I'm part of that group disaster, even though after a while I'm able to send the ball a hundred meters away with some sort of perseverance and from time to time a presumed feedback gets to me, like "bravo", "here, now you did it right", "great shot!". After thirty minutes of vain attempts and of comments that sounded like mocking, I suddenly see a light at the bottom of the tunnel.

From the covered cages, the man in the red jacket steadily walks towards us. I follow him with the corner of my eye because I'm fascinated by his firm pace. When he gets to me, without saying anything, he stands in front of me, he puts my club between his legs, he places my hands on it [in golf, you call this adjusting the grip] and says to me: «In the swing, you need to grab your club under the hypothenar eminence!» which translated for the human beings means that you must not let it pass long the life line, like I was mistakenly doing for thirty minutes without anyone pitiful enough to tell me, but long the fortune line, because this way the movement is blocked on an articular level.

Incredible! With that small great *feedback* my swing takes off: I hit it farer, more straight and most of all I start having fun! The movement becomes fluid, there's harmony, naturalness, ease. That man in the red jacket has to be quite experienced. Thinking about this I see him going back to his privileged cage near my oak. He must be friends with It. It must have seen all of his lessons and by now it must know about golf just like him.

Here, what that man in the red jacket gave to me is what I call a Feedback with a capital F! "Bravo" is not a feedback, it's a little perfumed fart exhaled from the mouth. And as fanatic as I am about feedbacks, I can hardly consider it as a positive backing at all. "Bravo" is too trivial, uselessly generic and headed to a low level. A wink or a pat on the back is much better. At least I think so.

Enthusiast about golf and life I hit a basket of balls in the blink of an eye. It feels so nice when you hit a ball in the right way and it flies straight like a spindle! The first two hours of lesson with the "Swiss" method were about to end and the man in the red jacket passes by again and with an immense gratitude I smile at him.
«You have some good coordination skills» he says looking into my eyes.
«Thanks. And you're good at teaching!» I say to him very straight forward.
«Well, I can humbly say...» he tells me pointing at the Golf Italian Federation badge on the red jacket. A big group laugh follows: that red jacket is the uniform of the Italian National Golf team's teachers! What an ass I had been! I was the only one who hadn't realised it. Everyone knows, when it comes to approaches I'm the best: I graduated at the Blooper University.

But that far from nice approach proved to be the sparkle between us and it was a sudden empathy. We have lunch together and the next week I go with a 200 EUR yellow-brownish banknote in order to integrate my training with 10 individual lessons with Him. *The prepayment always works*. I recommend it, most of all because you get more involved. Great choice!

I learn at the speed of light, although I missed the introductory lesson with the "Swiss" method.

Having worked with trainers who won everything, I know how to recognize right away the "good" ones from the others and this time too I hit the mark like Jessica Rossi in London 2012: 99/100, Olympic Record, World Record, Golden Medal (need some more?). The main difference between the "wannabes" and the *number 1s* is here: the *number 1s* do not do what they do for convenience or because they have to, they do it because they love their job. What urges, in fact, a professional who's busy with his lesson to walk 30 meters in order to give a feedback to a perfect stranger about how to grab his club? He could have ignored me, after all He was not my teacher. But no, he couldn't help himself and he came to adjust my grip. Great Fede!

The answer, for everyone, is simple: Love.

Thanks to love and sacrifice, *Number 1s* develop that combination of skills that makes them special, unique and precious beings. Number 1s are humble, smart, determined. They make the difference in their behaviour. Their great ability, when they build a staff, is to have around people who are better than them at something, to trust them and to orient everyone towards the achievement of a common goal. *Number 1s* forget their ego. They don't need it. The "wannabes", instead, show off. Margaret Thatcher used to say that "Being powerful is like being a lady. If you have to tell people you are, you aren't". That means: the boss doesn't have to say that he is. He is, full stop. Those who shout out how good, handsome and nice they are, you can be sure that they are not. Sure enough they're not as good as they think they are. Leadership is something that you gain on the field.

Federico Bisazza, the man in the red jacket friend with my oak, has won everything on the field, first as a player in the European Tour then as a Coach, becoming one of the most respected coaches of the Italian National Golf team.

Seeing in action *the Specialist*, "the links number 1", is a mystique experience. I think he's one of the most multi-tasking man in the world. In this, but just in this sense or else he would get angry, he's a female. Maybe he has the same callous part that links the brain's right and left hemisphere as women, since he manages to keep under control the swing of twenty golfers, to have a sandwich and to get a phone-call.

And I still ask myself how the hell he could see from 30 meters away that I was holding my club in the wrong way?! To Him this is easy like tossing Prosecco. He knows where to look and when to look. With one look he reads your grip, your movement, the ball flight and even what you're thinking, because he's a game psychic. When he goes with you on the court it's even different, being trained to compete and to pass on his game experience. Of course well-adjusted.

Federico's lessons are a blast: you laugh, you joke and you're terribly serious with the club in your hand. My oak saw them all because Federico's cage sheltered champions, professionals, amateurs on each level. Now it's my turn to put on a show! I'm the one who's looked after: an ex volleyball-player who's tough like a log, who tries to find the best harmony in the gesture but never succeeding!

Once I even fully hit it with a "skull" (those balls flying very low hitting whatever they bump into). Who knows what he thought about me. "Ungrateful". Nevertheless, I should be inspired by the pictures of Ernie Els' swing that are all over Federico's cage, a champion who's currently winner of four Majors.

Ball by ball, correction by correction, "skull" by "skull", laugh by laugh, Fede and I become friends and we get to know each other very well. Both of us have a little son who we love more than heaven and earth together. Both of us have had a troubled life. Both of us know how to enjoy. Both of us love sport.

After less than a month that we hang out together, in late February 2010, Federico introduces me to his two best boys with whom I start working. *All together at the same time*, one afternoon we walk all around the Modena court, designed by Bernard Langer. It's my first 18 holes, I'm in my white Prada training shoes. I look like Piero Chiambretti in his TV show "Chiambretti Night". What a wonderful memory! Biso, Federico's nom de guerre in the Italian team, explains to me all he can and shows me the various hits, leaving everyone speechless. He's still a phenomenon. I collect information about the mental dynamics in the game which according to Him affect the result for 70%. A huge percentage.

After just two months we are working together, I start feeling satisfied. Riccardo "Melman" Michelini amazes everyone but us and surprisingly wins the Italian Match Play Championships at Garda Golf (my first prize in golf) and the next month Cesare "8" Turchi, called "the Killer" in a friendly way, gets to the tie breaker at the "Città di Milano" tournament, a very important national competition. Things are running so smoothly that we think about making our collaboration official by starting the *Flow Golf Team*, a partnership between a Golf Coach and a Mental Coach, working together for the amateur and professional athletes. Our motto is "Up and Joy". Our philosophy is very simple: "your best results with work and fun together".

Federico and I always believed in this, even before we met each other. Who works hard without having fun will never express the best of him/herself because the state of best performance is linked to the fun. Same way, who only thinks about having fun will never express the best of him/herself because success is old-school agriculture: without hard working and sacrifice you cannot improve those details that are essential to the achievement of the great result. *Nothing comes out of nothing.* The Flow Golf Team (FGT) manifesto is a video that we shot under our oak and that we uploaded on YouTube for the joy of our friends. In this distillation of ignorance there's us, with black shades like "The Blues Brothers", with all our enthusiasm and our specialistic skills. "Two donkeys", like Giuliano Vantaggi - about whom you will soon read - would say.

After 7 months donkey's ears pop out just like Pinocchio and we start working with our first professional FGT player. In mid-October 2010 we're in Rome, following him on the court in the Challenge Tour's competition. While we walk around the Olgiata's court (this time I'm wearing some Adidas white golf shoes) Federico looks at me and says: «Ale, do you realize that just 8 months ago you didn't even know what golf was and now you're here following our first FGT professional in an international tournament?». As a matter of fact time flies when you feel good. Universe likes speed. When you get the chance, carpe diem, no doubts, no second thoughts, just act! Down the hole! Get down in it! Jump in! Fire! (I guess I made it clear).

There are people and trees with whom it's love at first sight. People you only need one look to know that they will enter your life and that from that moment nothing will ever be the same, not even your grip. *The Specialist* is my oak, a real man I love.

8. WHAT MATTERS?

> *Try not. Do… or do not. There is no try.*
> YODA, Star Wars

Think about the bigger picture, plan and act.

THINK ABOUT THE BIGGER PICTURE

One day, while I was flying to London for work, for a soccer player client of mine I was helping to prepare his press conference for a Premier League's Londoner team, sitting next to me there was a family that consisted in 2 kids under 10, Italian mom and English dad.

Right as that family was composed, the two kids were used to fly and perfectly knew the times and the procedures, almost better than the flight attendants. When they grow up, the boy will be a pilot and the girl will be a hostess.

Those kids knew when they could finally move, when the sneak would arrive, when they could stop playing, when they had to put their seatbelt on and when they had to start preparing for the landing by keeping each other's hands and praying. Fantastic!

The take off and the landing, everyone knows, are always magic and exciting moments, especially for kids, because it's like the outcome of the whole journey would focus in these moments: after the take off, you only wait for the landing. And in the meantime you can have fun by asking the permission to go in the cockpit. For those who smile at life, everything is easy.

When the airplane landed in Heathrow, the two kids started applauding and celebrating, because this time too they were safe and sound, and according to the air-traveller's etiquette, pilots are professionals who are used to do their job and as such they should be considered, hence one should avoid applauses and stadium squalls when they land, because it's not a miracle, but the natural consequence of their skills. But everyone knows, enthusiasm is contagious and the other passengers joined the liberating applause too, big smiles, handshakes, pat on the backs.

Everyone's celebrating except the mother. She was sitting next to me and was keeping the same tension of the previous minutes. She reminded me of a "lemon water-ice" and I was wondering why she was so glacial.

Noticing I was curious, me being transparent like glass, she explained to me politely that «being landed to me is not enough. From where we are you cannot tell much, you cannot tell where we're headed and, for what we know, we may crash into a wall, or another airplane is coming in our direction, right now while we're talking. (Nonchalantly I start to touch myself). I'm used to chill out and to celebrate the good outcome of a flight only once I walked down the plane's staircase and I'm walking in the airport with my luggage».

Whoa, this great Italian lady knows the secret of success: *think about the bigger picture*, or at least the flights. And she knows how high is the possibility that the air-companies lose your luggage.
«Also for me, Madam» I replied winking to the kids who couldn't wait to get off.
«Let's go down to take our luggage, it has been a pleasure flying with you and your family. Bon voyage» I said to her, showing off all the languages I know beyond Spanish and the international language.

If you forget, in fact, about *thinking about the bigger picture*, it might be dangerous. It's like starting with just the idea of starting a firm. This is a good way to fail straight away. You better start with the idea of starting a firm and of carrying it to the success for 50 years, and then leaving it in good hands. *Thinking about the bigger picture* prepares you to all you need.

If you train your soccer team to play for 90 minutes, you're training to lose a lot of games in the extra time. A team has to be trained physically, technically, tactically and mentally to play for 100 minutes in a terrific way. Furthermore, the really good ones train their team to cope with the post-match communication, in order to avoid problems with the opponents, with the supporters and the medias.

PLAN

A terrific genius at the transformation of a bigger picture in a numeric-operative planning is Roberto Oliva, about whom you will read soon. He thinks alike general Eisenhower, by not considering useless plans, only the essential planning. With his collaborators he makes a very simple reasoning.

«How much do you want to earn monthly in commission? 5.000 Euros no taxes. Very well, then you need 8 A contracts (A=250 Euros x 8= 2.000 Euros); 4 B contracts (B=500 Euros x 4= 2000 Euros); 1 C contract (C= 1.000 Euros). What is your percentage when you close a deal A, B, C? A 60%, B 35%, C 10%. Very well, then you have to do: (100:60=x:8) 13 meetings for A contract; (100:45=x:4) 9 meetings per B contract; 10 meetings per C contract. And hoping that God helps you. What's the percentage of phone-calls to set a meeting for the A, B, C contract? A 70%, B 50%, C 40%. Very well, then you have to do: (100:70=x:13) 19 phone-calls per A contract; 9x2=18 phone-calls per B contract; (100:40=x:1) 25 phone-calls per C contract. And always hoping that God helps you. To sum up, in order to get 8 A contracts you need to have 9 meetings and 19 phone-calls; to get 4 B contracts you need to have 9 meetings and 18 phone-calls; to have a C contract you need to have 10 meetings and 25 phone-calls. What can you notice? You suck in the C contracts. So, work hard! In the time left beyond what you need to do in order to earn your living, let's work straight away on the deal for the C contract, with the goal of doubling the percentage of well-ended deals, and on the related phone-call from where it all starts. And then again why do you wish to earn just 5.000 Euros per month?».

One can't argue with this reasoning.

There's always a 20% of what you do that brings you 80% of the results. It's called Law of the 80/20. Then if you double that 20% you'll get 160% of the results. Pretty easy. To do it you have to challenge yourself and get out of your comfort zone, moving your focus on the most profitable, gratifying, demanding and complex activity. Or else everyone would be like Forrest Gump, richer than Davy Crockett. Too often instead I see people spending their time tidying their desktop, cleaning the office glasses, polishing the telephone, doing whatsoever but that one phone-call that may change their life. Obviously you need to know who to call, first. That's the first step. The second one is to pull yourself in the right state. Third one is to dial the number. Once you located your 20% that brings you the 80% of the results, you only have to act.

Just do it!

ACT

Fire, fire, fire.

Nowadays no one aims before shooting. First they launch their products and then they adjust the target with a feedback by who bought them. This strategy made Microsoft a world giant and Bill Gates a billionaire. When he was fined by the Antitrust it was already too late because he had already conquered the world. It's been a bit like closing the stable once the cows had already run away. I'm not saying to shoot randomly on the crowd, there are already too many criminals who do that, but to be firm and to feel yourself free to be mistaken. Yes, you got me: *free to be mistaken*. Who does nothing is never mistaken. A characteristic of the Successful men is that they make a lot of mistakes, always different, until the result they craved. Act fast, be mistaken fast, learn fast.

"No mistake no progress", Bruce McLaren used to say, the founder of the McLaren stable. "Do, be mistaken and learn fast, correct and apply", this he used to say to himself and to his collaborators. Talking about the two wheels, Soichiro Honda used to say that for each successful project there were 999 wrong ones. But without those ones you wouldn't have the right one either. The secret lies on making always different mistakes, on learning from them and to never give up. You have to be *perseverant and creative*, like Soichiro.

The famous Deming Cycle, used today in the firms for the quality control and for building a continuous improvement of the productive processes, is inspired right by this mentality. It's not accidental that Edward Deming was called by the Japanese firms to extract a strategy that would grant continuous improvements. The very Lean Production was codified by the American researchers Womack and Jones, by studying the Toyota productive system. Basically, the Japanese used to do these things already, but they needed external consultants to name and codify them. Who's inside cannot realize what he's doing because he's so absorbed in himself, so he doesn't have an external point of view from which he can look at himself in order to improve. That's why you need a Coach. The Coach is outside of yourself and is not emotionally involved like you are. So he may help you to see yourself, by becoming your favourite mirror. In order to grow up you need somebody else's help and a definite strategy. You cannot go anywhere by yourself. Not even to pee. Especially ladies in bars.

The Deming Cycle, P.D.C.A. for the specialists, is a method based on the iteration of 4 phases in a circular way:
P = *Plan*, where you define projects, priorities and the action plan;
D = *Do*, where you execute your plan in a definite and close context, the equivalent of a simulation in a statistic sample;
C = *Check*, where you collect and study the results and the feedbacks that are coming from the execution of the plan;
A = *Act*, where you act to improve the process and/or the product based on the received feedbacks applying such improvements in every field.

Hence Plan, Do, Check, Act, and then again Plan, Do, Check, Act and so on endlessly.

Soichiro Honda surely made the Deming wheel turn with the hamsters inside. Among the many stories you can find on-line that tell his fantastic life (November 17th 1906 - august 5th 1991) I chose to share with you the one I posted on my *blog* www.apertopercaso.com

Soichiro is the son of a bike mechanic. In 1938, when he still went to school, Soichiro Honda took all he owned and invested it in a small lab where he started elaborating his idea of the Piston Ring. He wanted to see his work at the Toyota Corporation, so he would work day and night, absorbed in grease up to his elbows, sleeping in the shop, always convinced he could achieve his Result. In the course of time, in order to stay in the Business he even pawned his wife's jewels. But when he finally managed to make his Piston Rings and he offered them to Toyota, they told him that they did not suit the Firm's Standards.

So he had to go back to school, where he had to tolerate the ironic laughing of his teachers and his mates when they would talk about his absurd projects. Still, he did not focus on the unpleasant side of that experience and Honda decided to keep on focusing on his goal. And in the end, two years later, Toyota offered to Soichiro Honda the contract he dreamt of. His Passion and his Perseverance had been rewarded because Honda knew what he wanted, he had acted, he had noticed what didn't work out and had kept on changing his approach, until he obtained what he wanted.

At this stage, though, he had to face another problem. The Japanese Government was accelerating the production for the War and it refused to provide Honda with the reinforced concrete he needed to build the Factory. Do you think he would have renounced? He didn't even think about it. Do you think he would have focused on the unfairness he suffered? That he thought this would have ended his Dream? Absolutely not.

Again, he decided to take advantage of that experience and he developed a new Strategy. With his team he invented a new system to make reinforced concrete and then he built his Factory! During the war it was bombed twice and a good deal of the Production Machines was destroyed. Honda's reaction? He got his staff together and together they collected the reserve gas cans that the American bombers had thrown away. Honda used to call them "President Truman's gifts", because they provided the Raw Materials he needed for the Fabricating process [materials that you couldn't find in Japan at that time]. In the end, after having overcome all these difficulties... an Earthquake razed his Factory!!! Honda then decided to sell the patent of his Piston Ring to Toyota...

Here's a Human Being who evidently had made important Decisions in order to succeed. He had a great Passion and he really Trusted what he was doing. He had a great Strategy. He acted with Decision and kept on changing his Approach, but he still hadn't obtained the great Results he was destined to. Despite that he Decided to Persevere.

After the War, Japan was left with no Fuel: Honda couldn't even drive to buy some food for his Family. Out of desperation he put a small engine on his old bike. Suddenly his neighbours started asking him to make one for them too of those "Engine-driven Bikes". One by one everyone imitated him, so that at a certain point Honda had no engines left. Then he decided to start a Shop in order to make Engines for his new Invention... but sadly he lacked funds. As he did already in the past, he decided to find a way... at any price!

He thought he could turn to the 18.000 owners of bike shops in Japan, writing TO EACH of them a Personal Letter where he explained that they could have contributed to the Japan Rebirth through the mobility that his inventions would have provided... and he persuaded 5.000 sellers to fund him with the Capital he needed!

Nevertheless his Motorbike was only sold to people who were really keen, because it was too big and voluminous. So he adjusted it a little and obtained a smaller and lighter version of the Original Model. He named it Superclub. Out of the blue, the Motorbike had a great Success and it was worth a Highest Honour from the Emperor. Afterward, Honda started exporting his Motorbike and selling it to the European and American kids, until the 70s of the last century, when he started making the Cars that have now become so popular.

Today the Honda Corporation's personnel counts 100.000 people, between United States and Japan, and it's considered one of the great Car Empire of Japan, it comes second only after the Toyota for the Sales in the United States. And all this because a Human Being learned the Power of a truly dedicated Decision and has Acted with Perseverance and Continuity, no matter the Conditions.

Soichiro Honda created with his firm wonderful objects that allowed people to live, to move freely, to see and get to know the world. Honda's power units have enlightened the Channel Tunnel during its building; the android Honda ASIMO robot is the most advanced ever created; the Honda mechanical prosthesis system gave back mobility to whom had lost it; Honda electric and hybrid cars paved the way to the diffusion of non-polluting vehicles in the world. And then Soichiro made my first motorbike, a wonderful yellow and black Honda 125, with which I started to grow up and ride the world.

It's so nice when you start being independent! The first day on the street is so exciting, followed like a shadow from my father in his car. I rode for hours, with him always behind. At that time I considered him an idiot and I would hope that he went back home. Now that I have a child I understand him so well and I thank him. As it often happens, you realize someone's value when he's not there anymore.

Maybe it's because of this too that I'm so attached to the memory of my yellow and black motorbike, the colours that the *Shaman* has chosen for the cover of Staff Building to be once again, someway, *all together at the same time.*

Thank you Soichiro, thank you Alberto and thank you dad... I miss you a lot!

Wish you were here!

STAFF BUILDING

9. THE RESULT: ROBERTO OLIVA

> *Living is made of people and emotions
> and only your heart can open to life.*
> ROBERTO OLIVA

Roberto Oliva is one of the most intelligent, surprising and funny people I've ever met.

He is a General Agent in the Ina-Assitalia, a big insurance company from the brand Generali. Together with his 50% partner Maurizio Masiello, Roberto manages the Vignola Agency (in the province of Modena), one of the best Italian agencies for the results it produces and for its attention on the customers.

Since a dozen years Maurizio and Roberto win every year their cup, which consists in knowing how to successfully adapt to the business conditions that are imposed by the group (more and more restrictive), to the market change according to the economical and financial situation of the Country (since 2009 we're in full crisis) and to the changing demands of the customers (the leading star of every action).

Actually, this is all just a cover.

Roberto Oliva is a *Secret Agent of His Majesty*, like James Bond. And little matters his childish attempt to hide this and pretend he cannot speak in English. This just confirms my thesis. For me, in the MI6 he's an expert of unconventional questioning techniques, that is not based on torture, but on listening, on the observation and the immediate understanding of human beings. In this, as he would say, he's "atomic".

I've never seen a better person at that. Once, in the Vignola Agency, in an office with glass walls, I was assisting, unwillingly, to an argument between a consultant, an employee and a manager. Right at that moment Roberto walks the corridor and, without stopping, just throws an investigating glance at our office. Ten minutes later, without me saying anything, he calls separately the three disputers, showing that he had perfectly understood what had happened and how that happened. I was amazed. Enchanted. His ability of calculating the context and the human beings is impressive, especially when he's negotiating as General Agent to protect his alias.

Do you have no time and you'd like to understand a group's dynamics? Would you like to quickly learn your opponent's hidden intentions? Would you like to get to know the reliability level of your collaborator? Would you like to know if your partner is cheating on you? I've got a phone number I could give you: Roberto Oliva's! Quicker than Tom Ponzi.

I don't know where his talent comes from, maybe from the study of the face micro-expressions like Lie to Me's doctor Cal Lightman, maybe from the Secret Service's training, maybe from a Master degree at the Mossad in Tel-Aviv, maybe from his experience in the field among human beings. What I know is that his talent at this is incommensurable and that you can count on professor Roberto Oliva. Always. In all senses.

Professor Oliva, in fact, comes from the sport world, having been a gym teacher and an athlete. Seeing him playing tennis is a prohibited to minors experience and has a negative influence since he destroys rackets and screams as if he had a finger squashed in the door. Still, besides tennis curses, when he was young he used to jump 80 inches high. *A lot of stuff.* And I think he was recruited by the Secret Service right at that time, during a track and field meeting in Geneva. There's in fact a strong link between intelligence, aggressiveness, competitiveness, mental alertness and nerve, a mixture that is desperately sought by the MI6 head hunters. Everyone knows, spies need to know how to cope with every situation, recognizing at the speed of light the hidden dangers and the opportunities that life offers.

As *The Specialist* is "number 1 at links", those Scottish fields between the beach and the cultivated areas where the golf is born and where you need to adapt yourself to the soil undulation and to the wind, keeping your ball low, Roberto is *number 1* at the analysis of the situation, at the choice of the right strategy and at the planning that leads to the result. When he looks at you with his clever eyes from behind his glasses, you know that he has already thought about a fight plan and that you're in it like an egg white. With Roberto the staff is always involved, sometimes consciously and sometimes in the deepest mystery.

Our first meeting was in perfect Oliva style. Part of the company wondered who I was, the other knew it very well because Roberto made a report about me. So, on that legendary April 28th 2010 at 10.30 am, all the Vignola General Agency's management was ready waiting for me: the HR manager, the account manager and of course the partner, Maurizio Masiello, whom I will probably dedicate a whole book one day, since he's a unique person.

Everything was planned in order to show what I was made of, even though Roberto would have been enough for that. His ability at putting a person under pressure is extraordinary. At this he's a cursed talent like Amy Winehouse. I realized that on that day, when his staff carried on this art to see how I would deal with it, humanly and professionally. In his mentality, who cannot cope with some emotional smack better stays at home, because this is no place for him. Life is hard and you need to know how to cope with pressure. Then not everyone can be recruited for the special missions!

Luckily, I've got a cursed talent too, at least that's what they say, that is at listening to people and then act consequently. "A Coach who cannot listen is not a Coach", says *the Marine*. I've always enjoyed listening, maybe because I don't talk much. And I've always loved collecting information before expressing myself. From time to time, in fact, Oliva gets angry and tells me: «You could say something too or you think that you get paid only to listen?». Ha ha ha, I love taking time before getting straight to the point! In that waiting you can gather your energies before the explosion and you draw the attention. Being silent helps to look smarter, even though you need to say something smart afterwards. Or else you're dead. They label you as an amoeba, a mono-cellular organism that continuously changes its shape in order to avoid answering. Man parasite.

So, after visiting the whole agency, after having registered all the manager's analysis who would prance by expressing their belief of being part of a top agency ("humbly", with the image of the peacock tale, was the current communication leitmotif) and after having taken Roberto and Maurizio's lumps, they promptly ask me how, according to me, I could improve the working environment, the collaborators' effectiveness and the company's climate.

I was driven to the corner, I was protecting my face with my boxing gloves under a punch storm. Remembering the proverb "the best defence is the attack", especially when the others have finished all their energies, as a big fan of Mohamed Alì, after they have beaten the hell out of me, I go straight to the chin with my uppercut: «I have a question: how can you tell that you're an excellent company?». In a second, silence falls in Roberto's office. I hit the spot. The quickest man at answers in the world, Usain Bolt Oliva, takes time, while the referee starts counting. Eight… Nine… Ten… KO! Incredible at the Vignola's Madison Square Garden! The NEW… World Champion is… The Coach Alessandro "Stone Question" Vianello. The championship belt goes to him. The audience goes into rapture. Photographers go crazy. The two twisted boxers finally hug and they congratulate each other for the match. And as it often happens after a great and hard match they become friends.

We have lunch all together, there's feeling and a mutual respect. Lambrusco and *tagliatelle al ragù* are waiting for us in the legendary trattoria "La Bolognese" in Vignola. Wonderful! A unique dish, and by that I mean that after it you don't have room for anything else, since it is the same overflowing portion they used to serve in the post-war, perfect for the Maestro Luciano Pavarotti who always ordered the second course and the dessert too. Everything is handmade by the chef, an 85 years-old lady who's more lively than Pippi Longstocking. In the room, a silent waitress, with two huge tits and two ankles that were big as an electric trellis, looks like the younger counterpart of the chef, a skinny and witty old lady, so funny with her customers. To me, speaking in the Modena dialect, she suggests the crème caramel: «Ssssir (she's got a sibilant 's' and screams because she's a bit deaf), we make the best crème caramel in Europe… how much of it can I bring to you?».

Fantastic! Just eating it I'm able to fully understand her joke. It's amazing, but it creates a semi-unconscious state for a couple of hours, having the consistence of concrete and the specific weight of lead. I think it's the only dessert that won't give you the spoon back, since it's so thick that it gets stuck and you need a crane to get it out. An old recipe, made with real eggs, from real chickens, from a real highlander. A delight and slightly heavy.

In the afternoon, after a favourable and redeeming walk in the historical centre, with the General Agents we already talk about the future together and I get officially in charge of supporting the manager staff:
- in the process of merging what they called "administration department" and "account department", the agency's load-bearing axis, crucial to one another but always opponent and fighting;
- in the building of a staff that would work together to achieve in the best way possible the company's goals;
- in the improvement of the company's climate;
- in showing off the agency's value.

A lot of stuff.

We quickly define everything and right from the next day I'm operative. Like, at 10.30 am I enter an unknown place, ignoring everything and I go out at 7 pm feeling one of them, with a super-challenging and immediately operative task.

Universe loves speed and slow food.

On the next day, with alertness, simplicity and clarity, we start working together. On my beautiful iPhone I add to Roberto Oliva's contact the ringtone "The Race". He is speed. Sometimes he's too quick for everyone and I have to shoot at his stacked Aston Martin's tire in order to stop him. He doesn't stand in front of the audience, he smokes it. In his car he does the same. Heavy footed, sport drive. "Anyway and anyhow", exciting.

To form the team I suggest to step in each level, following the logical levels of change by Robert Dilts: environment, behaviour, capability, belief, value, identity, spirit. It's not enough saying that I find a breeding ground. Basically I'm planting grapefruits in Jaffa.

In just three months we pick up these yellow and scented fruits.

ENVIRONMENT

We've changed the company's face, transforming the meeting room in a temple, making the entrance more warming, facilitating the internal walks for the collaborators and making the interpretation of spaces and services easier to the customers. In the meeting room and in the entrance open-space we exposed trophies, that is the agency's numbers, to remind us and everyone the difference between "toilette paper and silk", like the funny Masiello says. In the temple each collaborator has brought a picture from home.

Then we made the agency's t-shirts that we gave to each team member during a wonderful party (see Equipment chapter).

Then we took pictures of all the people that work in the agency, no one excluded, with our new uniform "Ina Assitalia Vignola" on and we printed and hang these pictures next to those they brought from home. This was to underline the passage to a different dimension: "now you're part of a team!".

We made the same folders for everyone, with a different colour according to the role they have within the company.

BEHAVIOUR

We defined once again, without taking anything for granted, which are the right behaviours to welcome customers and to have between colleagues. "Presupposition is mother of fucker", like Steven Seagal says in a famous film. (My cultural quotations are always high-standard…).

Some things, then, always have to be developed accepting ideas, cues, suggestions that comes from down below. This way everyone will feel involved in the building of new internal rules and ethic code, for which we have made a wise men committee, asking Dalai Lama an external counselling.

CAPABILITY

We have immediately programmed and started internal training courses for a better communication with the customers and with ourselves. Amidst the capabilities that we have wished to develop there are:

capability to welcome and make people comfortable;
capability to make a real expert advice to the customers, expressing the latent demands in order to find a shared solution;
capability to move positively towards the others;
inclination to always take responsibilities;
capability to work in a team or, if you prefer, in a staff.

BELIEVES

We have worked to build the belief of the social and cultural importance of the job as an insurance agent and of how you always have to live it proudly, because it may save people's life. The insurance agent has a mission, like Masiello says. A well given expert advice may secure an entire family, because the insurance company transfer on itself some risks against the payment of a premium by the customer.

It's a matter of taking the risk and in this in Vignola they're *number 1s*, Mauro, Simonetta, Mario and the other experts are above average when it comes to relate with the customer and understand what they really want. The insurance agent is a noble and fundamental job, especially now that we're globally experiencing a time of economical crisis and of incertitude on every level.

Let me better explain this with an *open letter* to Gigetto and Marietta.

Gigetto, you have 2 young kids who go to school, you're the only revenue in the family because your wife doesn't work, you have a loan, you have the car payment and you don't have a life insurance? Are you crazy? If you're gone what will your kids do? How will they go on? What are you waiting for to protect your family in case you suddenly kick the bucket?

And you, Marietta, with the new Monti-Fornero reform you'll retire much later and you gain much less. In Italy we all rely on contributory from now on. This means that every human being will have a retirement gap, that is will have to deal with the big difference between the last wage and the pension fund. We're talking 40% less if you're lucky. So, if you gain 2.000 Euros per month your fund will be 1.200 Euros per month. Is this enough? It all depends on how the Country system is. Low GDP = Low fund. A party! In Spain things don't go better. In Greece they already have one foot in the grave. If it goes on like this we're up for harsh times. We better think about it right now. When we'll be old we'll have to spend more, certainly not less. What about the nurse for your husband gone gaga, who pays for that?

My question is pretty simple: Marietta, what are you waiting for to build yourself a social security? Do it right now, now that you have the energies to work and save what you need to cover the gap and to avoid to lean on your kids one day, they will already have lots of things to think about.

When I got in the Vignola Agency, although I had the culture and the mind to understand, I realized that I was acting like an ostrich. I used to put my head under the sand hoping not be seen. I didn't want to think about it. Thanks to Roberto, to Maurizio and to all my consultants friends in Vignola, I realized how important some securities are. It doesn't take much to live happily, protecting yourself from any dramatic event that unfortunately might happen in life. And if you have little financial sources all this is even more important. You better go out at dinner less often and sleep quietly forever.

Dear Gigetto/Marietta, don't act like an ostrich like I used to do, get informed and then chose the best for you.

Trust me, it's better in all senses.

VALUES

We have located in honesty, transparency, respect, meritocracy, cooperation, will to put the customer first, the values that lead us and every long term strategic choice.

These values are written in our ethical code.

IDENTITY

Everyone knows that identity goes through the name and the nickname.

So we got rid of the terms "administration department" and "commercial department", that would just create distances and make positions and arguments more radical between the two company's axis: administration and commercial, two opposed teams under the same roof.

The first ones, open-ended contract employees, should mainly do a bureaucratic, legal and administration job at each insurance deal. Actually they're also crucial in the relationship with the customers.

The second ones, commission free lancers, should stipulate insurance contracts to the customers. Actually they also are crucial in the administration and legal management of the company.

Hence we started the process of building a *team of evolved people* beginning from the very name: we have all become insurance consultants.

SPIRIT

We have worked on the climate, on the building of an entrepreneur spirit in all the staff members and on the definition of the *leadership affirmation* of the Vignola General Agency:

"A team of insurance consultants who listen to the customer's needs and dreams and make them come true. With our professionalism we take care of your future".

This is essential to make good decisions in the course of time and to know how to move in the present time.

Vision, mission and goal are useful for this, for being the constant landmark of a leading star.

All roses?

Absolutely not. There have been moments of great tension and difficulty, but we overcame them more alive and united than before. Among smart people you always find a solution, especially when you crave the same thing: love for the company, the people who work for it and the customers.

The great challenge to me has been sensing the right moments to do things, by choosing what to do first, what to do afterwards, what to post-pone, what to push, what to slow down and most of all how to do it. During these three months I lived like a tightrope walker, constantly walking on the rope. A wrong move and I would have crashed on the ground, losing another life.

Luckily, at the Vignola Ina-Assitalia Agency I found a group of people I got really close with and which I root for. They're good people, hard workers and professionals who do all they can for their customers. Surely they don't live on air, like any of us, but what I've seen doing in the interest of their customers is incredible. When you work in a team for such a long time and on such a deep level in a company, you get to know everything and you find out if the values that are written on the ethical code are fully experienced.

I found in Roberto Oliva a boss, an entrepreneur, a guide, a friend, a life mate. Or how he says a "brother".

Nothing that has been realized would have been without him. He made everything for his staff: he organized concerts and legendary parties and he's been so crazy to let me do some unforgettable *team building*.

Once we took everyone out of their comfort zone in a gym, in tracksuit and training shoes, where among "circus initiation", "carwash", "monster pass" and "silly games" we broke every communication barrier among us merging together. Another time we rent a whole villa, making teams that would challenge each other to theatre improvisation and in the kitchen. Wonderful moments when we laughed *all together at the same time*, the secret to become a successful staff.

What I found in Roberto has been the trust, the collaboration, the willingness to go himself first where he was needed, realizing what was essential to keep on being successful. *The Secret Agent* has always been the first to not play safe and to have fun. And this is such a terrific quality.

In good or bad, Roberto is one who always gives himself away. When he's angry you can tell, when he's happy as well. Sometimes he wears out his collaborators by practicing the "theory of elasticity", a psychological submission technique he learned at the C.I.A., according to which he pulls, pulls, pulls and when he lets it go you find yourself in a different position. Hence you're closer to where he wants you to be. He's a Sorbonne lecturer at this. Sometimes he throws chairs and makes the doors shake with a shout. Sometimes he's like Freddy Krueger. But always, "anyway and anyhow" as he says, when you really need him he's there and shows you an uncommon human sensitivity.

Roberto taught me how to take care of myself. To plan. To look far. To trust. I learned that when you deal with a real boss you have to let them have the last word. First because he deserved it, or else he wouldn't be a boss, secondly because they decide and they feed your family, thirdly because they know what they're doing. Roberto is a real boss. He knows what he wants and he knows how to always be ahead of his audience.

With him I never had to sign any contract. I never had to remind him of his commitments. I never had to remind him of paying me. Quite the opposite. The characteristic of the *number 1s* is that they always surprise you even at this and they gratify you in advance, beyond what you would have expected. In this the General Agent Roberto Oliva is on another planet. With him never a problem, just the pleasure of working together for his company, *all together at the same time.*

10. WHAT DO YOU REALLY NEED?

> *Creativity is arguing, refusing, transgression.*
> MICHELE TISON

A *Shaman*, to stay young, to find the right way and to laugh out loud.

Luckily I have one since I was 11 and I keep it close like a teddy bear. My *Shaman* is called Alberto Bogo and we're pals since forever. I can tell that Alberto has been my first friend in a chronological order, the one I started playing with in the yard, hanging out at night, and going after girls. And most of all laughing out loud. I will always be grateful to that teddy bear because he initiated me to the passions of the world I live in, making me become what I am. Without the *butter Shaman* my life would have been totally different and it wouldn't have been so fun.

But let me start from the beginning, because shamans have their own way to introduce themselves. In a summer afternoon, while I was playing with my ball in the yard, I hear a big noise. Threatening, shouts, screams, crying. One minute later a boy called Alberto comes to hide in my yard; he had just beaten the crap out of another guy in the street. Big Alberto is massive and when he gets angry he turns into "Fury the Brave Stallion", he neighs and kicks. So, while he leans on my garage's door all aching, sweated and sighing like an ox after having dragged a cart all day long, I kindly ask him what happened. Surprise surprise, instead of thanking me and politely answering me, he says *I can beat the crap out of you too*! Terrific! At that point I burst into a contagious laugh and the both of us start laughing, laughing and laughing and we couldn't stop. The best thing is that from that day on we've never stopped laughing together.

That sparkle of unstoppable comedy could happen because someone instilled in his mind the "law of the jungle", where the strongest one wins on everyone. But he was like an atomic bomb in Mister Bean's hand, it couldn't work out. "The big fish eats the small fish. It's the law of the jungle!", he said proudly. But this belief, which he tried to implement, clashed with his peaceful, sensitive and humoristic nature. Such contrast made me laugh so hard. It was impossible taking him seriously. So that *I can beat the crap out of you too* out of which our friendship is born, has turned into our first big hit that we would repeat every time we felt like laughing or mocking each other. Together we've always been two total jackass. Especially him.

What I've always loved about Alberto is his being a child and that unique, magic and precious ability to find the funny side of everything. With his wide sensitivity he put me through worlds that were unknown to me, worlds that then have become my worlds. Alberto has always been an extraordinary networker and since I was a child I suffered because of this talent of his and I wanted to be his exclusive best friend. I wanted him all for me. In the course of time I realized that the shamans live on another dimension. Their mission is to go with us discovering places, people and experiences that will become a fundamental part of our life, leaving to us the task to live them. They open the door, we go and see what's in there.

THE COMPUTER

In our district Alberto was the first to grow keen on computers and on the technology world which from that time on would have changed everybody's life. When I used to go to his place I would often find him on his computer where he pretended to be interested in the PC's cultural potentials, but actually he was only interested in video games. In this he has always had a crazy talent and still now we challenge each other on the Play Station, on the Wii and in the arcade, where he always wins.

At that time he had the legendary Commodor VIC 20 and me, after an exhausting negotiation with my parents, the Commodor 64, at first bought for the school, but that we would use almost exclusively to play. At that time you loaded games with the "tape player". Still no disks, no CDs and most of all no software to download on the internet. Different times, even though it was not that long ago. The screen was still the TV. It was the 80s.

Our soccer and basketball games are legends also thanks to a special characteristic of my computer. While we were playing locked in my kitchen, alone and in the middle of a big storm, a lightning caused a blackout and so it caused some permanent troubles to my Commodor 64. Basically the games would crash if we didn't keep pressed the Command button. Total desperation.

How can you handle a joystick and at the same time always keep a button pressed?

It's crazy. We had to find a solution.

As it always happens when your willingness to play goes beyond your physical limits, "every law has its loophole", we thought of putting a weight from my antique scale on that damned button so we could focus on our challenges. That looked a bit ridiculous, a new computer that was perfectly working thanks to a brass artefact from the past century.

Shamanic intuition, mix of genres, fusion of objects from past times, lateral thinking.

What would usually happen then is that, eager to play, when we scored, for the joy or the rage, we would tear the joystick from the table and let the legendary weight fall and hence interrupting the game. How we screamed! It was so exciting! Good old times.

Alberto then initiated me to the Apple cult. Our personal computers from that time on have all been Apple and still now we have the bitten Apple sticker on our cars, being absolute worshippers of the brand.

As I often say, "the iPhone is not a mobile, is a way of living".

VOLLEYBALL

In the Saturday and Sunday afternoons, during summer, my computer had become just a fallback since all the guys from my district would meet in the yard of Alberto's apartment house to play volleyball. Instead of the net there was a rope, pulled from the gutter to the railing, that never made clear whether the ball passed underneath or above.

That's what the net is for in the volleyball.

The borders of the game's court were made of a little wall that was open on two sides and, here too, a thousand arguments happened to decide whether the ball was in or out.

That's why you have lines to delimitate the court and the instant replay.

When I would see them playing I would start wandering around hoping they would invite me, but since I couldn't play they didn't want me. They were big kids who went to high school and they all knew pretty well how to hit the ball. The only one who would let me try was Alberto who at that time had been playing for a year in the mythical under 14 Belluno volleyball team. So, after many afternoons spent looking at them playing, when school and training started again, *the Shaman* "stone hand Al Bertoli", honouring Franco Bertoli, legendary Italian volleyball player, invites me to go with him to try in his team. So exciting! I'm welcomed like a promise. Everyone knows, being tall counts in the volleyball and I was growing very tall.

That was the youngster department of the A league, *a lot of stuff*.

After one year of trainings with people better than me, summer comes again and my level was already so good that older kids would let me play with them. I finally become one of them. This is what is called social integration process through sport.

The following year, instead, what is called social disintegration process through sport happens. In fact, having grown pretty tall, I experience the same fate of the previous year but for opposite reasons. Ostracism of return. First those guys didn't want to let me play because I would lower their level, then they didn't want to let me play because I had become too good and I would hit the ball too hard.

Alberto and I, at that stage of our sport evolution, needed other pals and opponents to keep on having fun together and growing up, so we moved the match to the Nogaré park, a district near Belluno, that suddenly became our second home. There was a rectangular net there, space around the court and red painted lines. We only lacked the instant replay that was substituted by the ball print on the dust. At the park we would play for the whole day, challenging in 2 vs 2 and 3 vs 3 other volleymad, with whom we became friends even out of the court.

Since we were addicted to volleyball, and since Belluno looks like a Scottish city for how much it rains, one of those days we couldn't go out playing because of the weather, we even turned my room into a rink, using the door as a net. I would serve a sponge ball to "stone hand Al-Bertoli" who would jump and spike the ball on the bed. On that day he was loaded like a spring because when "his vein gets stuck" he always turns into "Fury the Brave Stallion". I don't know what happened, but at the end of that sequence of perfect serving and spikes just as perfect from Alberto, I hit the ball in a wrong way and *the Shaman*, in agonistic trance, hits with all his strength the corner of the door and he crashes his hand. I don't think I've ever laughed so hard. I was lying on the floor and couldn't even breathe while Alberto was crying for the pain with his hand under the water in the bathroom. The more he whined the more I laughed. I couldn't take it anymore.

What wicked genius does it take to hit the door instead of the ball?

And I couldn't take it anymore, but for opposite reasons, that day in my living room when I smashed my hand against the sofa's wooden headboard, while I was exercising by myself "Mila and Shiro" style. I smashed the ball really hard and it would go far destroying everything that was on its way: Chinese Ming vases, silver frames and even the Murano chandelier. On that day I didn't laugh at all when mom and dad came back home: they grounded me and took the ball away from me forever, my beloved white Spalding which I used to bring in my bed too.

Sleeping alone is not easy when you're used to a sweet leather presence next to you.

Besides great pains, volleyball gave to me what a sport can give. Emotions, friends and a love out of which my son Riccardo is born, the greatest gift I've received in my life. It just wanted in exchange my right ankle's ligaments and my right knee's cartilage.

That sounds fair, doesn't it?

THE LIBRARY

Before the *Shaman,* I didn't even know that such a place existed, because in summer I used to do the shepherd with the sheep and during school I was locked at home pretending I was studying in my room. Luckily, in an autumn afternoon during the pimple era, Alberto came to me with a face that said it all and tells me: «Come on, let's go to study at the library». Very well. I grab my books, throw them in my backpack, I say bye to mom and I go with him.

Too bad in the library we have never actually studied. And it's not all our fault.

Let me better explain. The library, as institution, is a cursed place, because in the study rooms it's politically incorrect to mess up and, as if it weren't enough, females are in there. To be more precise, in the library you cannot do anything, you can just read silently (without playing with the pen's cap), talking quietly (and only when you really have to), walking gracefully like butterflies (the parquet often squeaks at every step preventing every wish to move), breathing (but not too much, or else oxygen finishes and then you start yawning, which is contagious).

Particularly, at the Belluno's library the rules are so strict that the Mafioso in the maximum security prison in the close Baldenich could do many more things. The very Adolf Hitler must have written those rules, as an appendix to "Mein Kampf", because the librarians were real SS. In such an environment, for two dumb kids with crazy hormones like us it was impossible resisting the transgression's call.

In fact, after a very short time we seemed aligned to the jail system we started going to the library only for fun and to draw the attention of the girls we liked. It was the system asking us to do that! "I'm not bad, I'm just drawn that way!", Jessica Rabbit used to say. You know, "who owns the means' structure also owns its content", my friend Michele Tison says, creativity teacher. On Facebook you do something, on Twitter you do something else and in the library something even different. So we were destined to perdition, I really want to say this for my family and for my reputation. It was impossible not putting on a show of extravagant idiocies, we were forced to do it! I blame it on the means' structure.

Alberto's special treat, which in the course of time has become his *must* with me in every public crowded environment where people are devotionally interested in something else (cinema, theatre, shows, meetings, conference, etc.) was getting closer to my ear in the general silent, pretending to be damn serious and to have something extremely important and vital to tell me, and then, alternatively would:

- say some monstrous bullshit;
- not say anything and start to laugh while punching me;
- clear his voice like an ogre, making the library's walls shake;
- shout "SO WHAT!" deafening me and getting every human being's attention in one mile. He's such a jackass!

At that point I challenge everyone not to laugh. It's basically impossible not to burst! The more you try to restrain yourself, you start sweating, to moan and to bend for the cramps in your abs. It's useless trying to hide your face or pretending to look for a rubber under the table or biting your lip to pull yourself together through the physical pain. The more you try not to laugh the more you laugh.

You may figure the result of all this: a collective *giggles epidemic* which together with the rage of those who are there to actually study (all serious and outraged) makes the situation even more irresistible and hilarious.

Much less fun was the librarian's reaction, already librarian in the Auschwitz extermination camp - she really didn't like our twaddle. I think we still keep the incomparable record number of banishments from the Belluno's Library. Too good and embarrassing at the same time.

It's like at the funerals, when you cannot laugh, in the attempt to restrain yourself, you have the best laughs of your life. With this I'm not saying that I go to funerals to laugh, it was just an example.

Anyway, is there anything funnier than laughing when you cannot laugh?

ARCHITECTURE

"Anyway and anyhow" like *the Secret Agent* says, but I'm not any less and I wish to retaliate at that slightly embarrassing twaddle from Alberto. So, my specialty, which in the course of time has become my shtick with him, consists in pretending to be his lover and in public, right when he doesn't expect it, I make a scene of Neapolitan jealousy or a declaration of love with strong sexual innuendos. Alberto, for some aspects, is "a damned fucking puritan" (excuse my language) and seeing him blushing and pretending he doesn't know me just drives me crazy.

This Star Wars saga started in the first year at the Venice University I.U.A.V., where I enrolled, go figure, thanks to the *Shaman*, since I didn't have any clue of what I wanted be when I grew up. Looking back at myself now, I got it perfectly right, even though in the course of these university years everything has happened.

One morning, in fact - and I always blame it on the system that tickled Alberto's twaddle - we were about to be banished from the math lecture of the well-known professor Troi. Among 500 students stuffed in the room, he caught us laughing, interrupting his lecture. Then we ended changing that course because it was impossible going to the oral exam after what had happened on that day. He would have certainly asked us the proof of the algofuckingrithm.

So, still angry for the worst impression ever that cost us at least one out-of-course year for pure goliard, the day after I serve to Alberto my cold dish of revenge. It was 7:30 am and we were waiting for our bus at the bus-stop, far from each other since we were still angry. When the 18 arrives, overcrowded as usual, I get on from the front, and once on the bus I walk all the way to him and pretend to meet him accidentally. We're really stuffed, impossible to reach him.

When we get on the bridge between Mestre and Venice, where there are no more bus-stops and no one has to get off, I barely see him 7 meters away from me and I start calling him among the people like a tranny in love: «Honey. Honey. Honey hello! Hey, it's me, I'm here. Don't you recognize me? I'm your sweetheart...». Alberto, who cannot believe his eyes and his ears, blushes and pretends not to see me and turns his back at me, hoping no one will notice. And this very desperate gesture ratifies his end, because I start one of the most hysterical and embarrassing scenes of jealousy in the history of cinema. Golden Globe as best leading actor and Oscar nominee!

«What, now you pretend you don't know me? After all we went through the other day? You're a bastard! (I scream like a cat in heat). Excuse me Sir, yes I'm talking to You, could you please call that disgusting worm next to you for me? (pointing at Alberto, with a bewildered face)». In the meantime you could see on the bus many different and opposite reactions.

I needed a Candid Camera.

- One lady says to me "men are all the same" and that I didn't have to be offended (I was about to weep for desperation).
- Another man says that we are pervs and that we only need to be ashamed of ourselves. «Honey, you would love it too, trust me. My sweetheart, that fucking liar, may give it to you too! He's such a beater, he may *beat the crap out of you too*, you know» I say to him to keep my role until the end, making Alberto turn purple until he starts laughing and insulting me.
- As if this weren't enough, an old man near the obliteratore publicly proposes castration for "faggots", hence ours. I start thinking to myself that the situation is slipping through our hands.
- Other guys laugh and don't know what to do and how to behave. It's a mess and Big Alberto is panicked.

Finally we arrive and as the doors open people fling out like Champagne from the Alonso's bottle when he won the world cup. «Here, now we're even, Sweetheart...» I say to the *Shaman*, who was wrecked and sweated in such an uncommon way, a few steps away from the bus, as I even squeeze his ass. What a show! We have fun like this.

I have to say that these *must* are still dramatically living, and by that I mean that we still do it every time we can, especially when we're in places where nobody knows us. I think that life's beauty lies here, on living a different part of yourself with each person. You know, by changing your partner you also change your way of making love, of behaving, of talking, of playing together. Each relationship is special for a matter of chemical, complicity, binds, moments. And you cannot repeat it.

With the *gay Shaman* I do things that I don't do with anyone else, luckily. And he does the same with me, luckily.

GIRLS

In front of our house lived a girl from Naples called Giuliana Sacchi, the best B side in the city. We were crazy for her. She would walk in tight jeans, basically hardcore vacuum-packed, and in white blouse opened on her breast. Slightly provoking. Slightly.

When she would go out on her terrace and we were playing basketball in my yard in front of her house, we would turn into Magic Johnson and Kareem Abdul Jabbar to impress her. And it was suddenly "Show Time": no-look passages, strikes and Balotelli-like poses after his goal against Germany at Europe 2012. You know that testosterone increases the physical performance but you lose a bit of mental clarity. Maybe right because of this the *Shaman with the stuck vein* proposes me an encounter of the third kind: «Come on Ale, let's go and ring her bell, by now she knows who we are».

It cannot get worse than this.

His logic was tight, exactly like Giuliana's jeans. *Said and done*, no problem. In the blink of an eye we're in front of her door, dressed up in such a way that defining it embarrassing would sound like an euphemism. *We looked like Fantozzi: GIL t-shirt, high waist underwear that we closed with a pin, massive racket 1912, an elegant green peak with the writing Casinò Municipale of Saint Vincent;* green briefs with yellow flowers, Trussardi orange polo shirt, Superga white shoes for me; *Filini's outfit: white culottes from a rich aunt of his, Lacoste pure white t-shirt, leather sneakers, tartan socks with garters, double liberty racket for badminton;* purple briefs with a burgundy stripe, white t-shirt with a sauce stain on the chest, yellow Espadrilles-like shoes for the *Shaman*.

Embarassing.

In front of the door we read "Sacchi family", scary and powerful family from Naples, in fact his father was the Belluno's vice-prefect, and he was slightly possessive when it came to his daughter. So, to chill down, we quote our favourite movie and I go on ringing, as it always happens between me and Alberto: he paves the way and I walk it till the end.

I remember the sensation of the shaking finger on the bell. Pure emotion. After a few endless seconds a charming and *very human* voice says: «Hello?». Why did she pick up? «It's us» I say. And of course she says: «Who's us?» and me, stupidly: «Us us». Then I look at Alberto and we burst out laughing and we couldn't stop. In the meantime Giuliana hangs up and we're there lying on the floor in tears and Alberto keeps on picking on me: «I mean, could you be more stupid? Who's us? Us us! Ha ha ha… jackass!».

After thirty minutes we find the strength to go back and ring again the "Sacchi Family"'s bell, but with a better plan: when she would say "Hello?", I would have answered with a press release: "It's Alessandro and Alberto, the guys who play in the yard in front of your terrace and we would like to meet you". Of course who's going to ring the bell? Obviously always me. Another shot of adrenaline and other endless seconds before the same dramatic question on the buzzer: «Hello?».
«It's us…» I say promptly, marking such a stupidity! I mean, I prepared my press release and I say again "it's us"? What am I to do with myself? Unbearable emotion, my brain in neutral.
«I mean, it's Alessandro and Alberto, the guys who play in the yard in front of your terrace and we would like to meet you…» I say trying to fix it.

Endless pause. Panic. Disbelief suspended.

«I'm her grandmother!» the same voice answers freezing our blood. Good, keep on with the bloopers. Luckily the old lady felt bad for us: «Let me call Giuliana. Come up!» she says pushing for ten seconds the button to open the door. Maybe she might have thought: «These two are so stupid that I have to push the button longer, maybe they will understand they need to push the door to get in».

Like two idiots we rejoice and punch each other with no reason because we are finally in. Instead of taking the elevator, in order to find the courage to meet Giuliana we take time walking the stairs. So long. For the emotion and our mental idiocy, we push each other rejoicing as if we had won a cup with a breaking strike. Heartbeats out of control. Blood pressure 400-80. Zero saliva.

Finally we get to the third floor. A mind-blowing vision awaiting us on the door: her grandmother! With an unforgettable smile, maybe out of pity looking at us dressed that way, she lets us in and have a seat in the living room. Thanks grandmothers! Then Giuliana arrives, to die for: «It's alright grand, you can go, thanks» she says fixing her hair on a side and driving our hormones crazy. Whoa, it's a good start, we think, she even lets the old fart go.
«Guys, I don't have anything to offer. There's only some of my FATHER's whisky left, is that ok?» she asks leery.
«Very well, we always have whisky in summer at three in the afternoon!» I reply promptly to break the ice in the whisky. Ha ha ha, funny!

We spend a wonderful, fun and surreal afternoon, flattering that provocative creature, sitting on her father's human leather sofa, in green and purple briefs, and a Scotch in our hand. *More than jackass.*

From that day, I'm afraid, the "extravagant" approaches become my specialty with girls, a sort of embarrassing and funny side effect of this experience.

PARTIES

Being one year older than me, Alberto used to drag me in many situations and, among those, there is one that is history for two episodes, that everyone remembers, which star me as incautious protagonist.

We were at this girl's place, she thought it would have been nice organizing her birthday party, 60s themed in her garage, using the cellar as a VIP area. Better than the best disco.

Alberto, braggart as he was, knew everyone whereas me, the shy one, I would stand aside watching what was going on. At a certain point the *Shaman dj* decides it's time to heat the party his way putting on the music, another passion of his, and asks me to dance: «Come on Ale, what are you doing there, do something, move, let's leave our mark. SO WHAAAAAT!» he shouts in my ear. So, after his battle cry and some grooving track, I say what I'm told and think: «Hell yeah, I don't give a damn!».

Into the music and with an excess of vitality out of control, on the notes of the Bee Gees' "Saturday Night Fever", I take the dancing floor and make a senseless and rhythm-less solo. As if this weren't enough, I even slide on my knees like Tony Manero, but on the uneven and dusty floor of the garage.

The result?

Blooding knees and trousers I had to trash.
Alberto bent laughing, the others shocked.

Then, to keep leaving my mark, the host wants to get to know me better (she cannot resist my charm) and when in the VIP area she asks me "who are you?" in the angular posture typically seductive of a female, I rudely reply:

«I'm Rambo, I eat drink and humpo!».

How to end a relationship forever and quickly become the uncontested idol of my male friends.

Never invited again. Erased forever. Game over.

STRIKES

You need to know that *the Shaman* is also a great agitprop, that is a world renowned consultant at the "Department of agitation and propaganda" in the URSS, in charge of education (that is the against-education).

One day, to avoid the test at school and to keep his girlfriend from going to her classical High School, he literally made up a student parade out of nothing, involving all the schools in the city, mine included.

At this he's a wicked genius.

In the leaflet that he gave out everywhere, he wrote a sentence meaning all and nothing, with a terrible grammar mistake in it, showing that he could perfectly use what the NPL (neuro-linguistic programming) had defined "Milton Model", that is a skilfully vague language that goes straight to people's unconscious to heal them, persuade them and urge them to act.

And strike shall be.

Milton Erickson, maybe the greatest hypnosis therapist in the world, had been moulded a few years earlier by Richard Bandler first and then by John Grinder, to extract the linguistic models that could have been useful to everyone, Big Alberto included. You know, in our life we're always *all together at the same time*, it's a matter of universal energy and so the skills of the NPL inventors were available for *the Shaman* too.

The best part of that parade was that nobody knew what the strike was about. A communication shaman masterpiece. That Saturday morning was unforgettable for the total absence in the students of a direction, a shared idea, a connection between neurons and willing to study. They all had their brain in neutral, as if under the influence. "If you repeat a lie often enough, it becomes the truth", like we learn from Gobbels, minister of the Nazi propaganda. It's a whole different thing, but it came to my mind. Effect of the shamanic hypnosis.

And suspension shall be.

THE SHAMAN TODAY

Big Alberto, taking full advantage of his sensitivity, has become a versatile artist: respected photographer, graphic designer, communication consultant for fashion, webmaster, dancer and tango teacher of the greatest kind.

In my experience I think he's an extraordinary talent when it comes to catching what the right idea may be and to translate it into reality through current communication languages. He's fantastic at this. Of course, with no hurry, he's extremely kinaesthetic and lives out of time, in his shamanic dimension.

11. ENTHUSIASM: GIULIANO VANTAGGI

Smile at life and life will always smile back at you.
GIULIANO VANTAGGI

There have been times when I would feel "Tired and lost" like the character in the Vinicio Capossela's song. So "some stars shine bright among lights and shadows on my way, lost and lonely I cannot remember the sad notes of the eyes, the running after the moon, run away".

But this never happened to me while I was with Giuliano.

His will to live has always been very contagious and together we've experienced some magic moments that had in common the night, the car, the girls, the party, the laugh. In three words joy to live.

Giuliano and I belong to the generation with *uneven teeth*. And we're proud of it. We were both born in 1971. When we were young braces were just starting to spread or our parents chose not to put them on us who knows why. Maybe they wanted to save us the experience of having that scrap iron in our mouth during a critical phase of our childhood. Now you can hardly find a young man with uneven teeth like us; most of them have a perfect smile, commercial-like, with perfectly even teeth. Not us, we comb our hair with bombs (and by that I mean that we don't have much hair left because of the explosion) and we have a shanghai game going on in our mouth, where we have our teeth instead of wooden sticks.

We met at a volleyball match in the Belluno oratory though a common friend of ours, Roby Fufo Costantini. «Hello dirty dog (this is the cute and sweet way my friend Roby addresses to me), this afternoon at the oratory it's going to be two vs. two, beach volley rules. Me and you against Giorgio Cugini and Giuliano Vantaggi. Alright?» he asks me on the phone. «Of course Fufi, but who's Giuliano?» I ask. «A big baby like you (Sardellone), I'll see you at three. Hey, we have to cream them, I already betted a beer with Giorgione!» he explains to me before hanging up to get me fully loaded and determined at the match.

Giorgione Cugini is the man with the softest hands I've ever met. He can use them as an airbag by putting them on the steering wheel and hit his head on them and he wouldn't get hurt. Since we were invincible together, to make the competition more balanced, Fufo would always put us one against each other. Then, when we betted something, we would enter a crazy agonistic trance and we didn't leave much choice.

That's how it went that time at the oratory. Giuliano really was a big baby like me, 6 feet of idiocy and personality. We hit balls against each other, insulted each other, mocked each other during the whole match and in the end we've become inseparable friends. Similar people always recognize each other, without knowing anything of the other. And they chose each other instinctively.

In the course of time we came to realize that we both have behind a great pain: for him it's the early departure of his parents caused by an accident, and for me it's my father's suicide.

We did everything we could.

Still *uneven teeth* and family tragedies never prevented us from laughing and that's why we're friends.

We like having fun.

Among the *advantages* of our peculiar family condition I could mention not having to care about the time we had to go back home and the sense of responsibility we developed faster that many other friends of our age. Giuliano was the only friend of mine with whom I could stay out till late or go back home after two days without anyone grounding us. I used to say «mom I go out, I don't know when I'll be back but don't worry I'll be back» and it was ok. Saintly lady. He used to say more or less the same to his brothers. Saintly themselves too. Different times, no mobile and strong will to party and to get to know the world together.

Well, if I had to trace an essential profile of Giuliano Vantaggi I would start from these two steady points: Giuliano is one of the biggest party boys on earth and he's a living GPS.

PARTIES

In Budapest, after the school trip in 1990, everybody is scared that he may come back one day because he finished the beer stocks in every bar in the historical centre.
In Barcelona they're still looking for him because he shook the whole city during the Olympics in 1992.
In South Africa in his car he chased a rhino in the Kruger park and demolished a mall in Johannesburg.

In Italy he made even worse, possibly.

Only who's lucky enough to know him well like I do can understand what he's really capable of with his friends: he's been in trance, in tranny, and impossible becomes possible. The Tom Cruise from "Mission Impossible" is an amateur compared to him.

In order to describe Giuliano's wildness I'll borrow one of the most colourful expressions from the *Specialist*, referring to some guys from the golf national team with whom we've had the pleasure to work with, because "if you let them free they may even poop in front of a restaurant door!". Well Giuliano never pooped in front of a restaurant door but he's born *free in his spirit*.

Together we've had some *gypsy* experiences that have become legends, and when you tell them they don't even sound real. Like in the film "My friends" by Mario Monicelli, what matters in a gypsy wander is the joke, the friendship and the journey.

What's important is going away. You don't have to know where. You only need to be a little gypsy and a *big babie* (Sardellone) inside.

With this spirit we did so many things and 3 of these ventures are memorable.

THE FIRST VENTURE

Cortina d'Ampezzo, the pearl of the Dolomites, was often the place where we would finally get at the end of our *gypsy wanders*, especially during the Christmas holidays. You can hardly find such beauty all together anywhere else. Everywhere you look in Cortina there's beauty and you're left charmed. In the Christmas time the atmosphere gets even more magic and Cortina is crowded with tourists from all over the world. We didn't even think of not going, it would have been like asking a bear to give up his honey without the danger of being beaten by a swarm of bees.

That night we left Belluno at about nine in my old white Fiat 500 from 1968, *destination heaven*.

First stop "Snack al Check" in Tai di Cadore. We haven't been eating for a specific technical choice: so that we could nourish our fame of world record big eaters. In this picturesque pub we would order all the sandwiches on the list, making the owners glad, in fact they would welcome us like prophets. To them it was as if the President of the Republic came with the Prime Minister. In this delicious place every sandwich had the dialect name of a bird and we would turn into food ornithologist for the occasion.

Second stop Hotel Miramonti Majestic near Cortina, where we would drive by screeching in front of the entrance for at least three times, by pulling the breaks of my legendary staked Fiat 500 with the naphthalene in the filter and with the plate covered in snow so that they didn't recognize us and press charges against us. I still remember the adrenaline when we would switch the right turn signal and drive the turns up to the Miramonti, an emotion that is similar to the low flight of Maverick on the control tower in "Top Gun".

Third stop Corso Italia in Cortina, where we would walk smiling and saying hello to all the celebrities that we would meet, pretending that we knew them since a long time. «Hello, haven't we met in Costa Smeralda? How are you doing? God it's been such a long time since that time in Porto Cervo...» so fun! So fun sensing the discomfort in their eyes and in their shaking words. A nerve worth an Academy Award.

Fourth stop disco "Ippo", where we would flirt with tourist girls in Cortina. First we would take a quick look and then we would pick up the most beautiful ones. Goodbye shyness. Our motto was "if you don't ask the answer is no anyway".

So you better ask and go ahead smiling with your open arms.

Our approaches were legendary because we would challenge each other to who said the greatest funniest bullock. You know, girls: or you make them drink or you make them laugh. We aimed to the second strategy for them and the first for us. At that time our hair was gathered up by a coloured pin to keep our tuft in a shape similar to sumo wrestlers. Good old times, we could still afford that. With our smile with *uneven teeth* and our stylish hair we used to be quite successful and we would often have nice relations with the tourists.

That time we were dating these two girls from Milan, very cute, richer than Flavio Briatore and, as we would say, "very whore". After the approach on the dance floor we separately walked them to their humble places in Corso Italia: two 3 floors buildings which current values goes from 15.000 and 20.000 Euros per square meter. Such a humble thing.

Our meeting point was Cortina's Duomo where we would promise each other we would get at around 5 in the morning and then go back home. That night we arrived both late for due reasons. I still remember the hugs and the celebration when we met under the bell tower. So exciting! What an *atomic idiocy*, like Roberto Oliva would say.

The way back home was exciting too. We spent it mocking each other on how "whore" our girl was, and by that we mean loose.
«Yeah you surely got a big slut, didn't you?» Giuliano mocked me laughing.
«Yours instead was a nun, wasn't she?» I replied laughing with tears.
«Mine is a saintly lady» Giuliano said, «can you smell her perfume, can you smell how delicate it is, smell how pure it is…» he said making me smell the handkerchief he stole from her as a war trophy.
«Well, in fact, I can smell, I can smell her French perfume… Eau de grand cow!» I would joke. And laugh and laugh! Friendship is precious!

That journey back home was unforgettable also because we set a running record that you may hardly upstage on the mountain streets: Cortina - Belluno 69 km in 43 minutes. At that time some of the streets that now make it faster to get up there hadn't yet been built, it was extremely dangerous but wonderful to drive them fast in your car like James Dean. That night I ran in my car while Giuliano would GPS me, since he knew the way so well:
«Left 3 in right 3 long shuts 2 long shut, bump, deer on the left, 4 right, smell her perfume…» he would whisper as if he were high.

If Enzo Ferrari would have seen me… maybe I could have become the legitimate heir of Gilles Villeneuve: "Give me anything with an engine and I will push it to the limit".

In Modena, in the Museum dedicated to the Canadian legend on wheels, there's a plaque next to his fantastic blue Ferrari 308 GTB with written: Montecarlo - Maranello 432 km in 2 hours and 25 minutes. Gilles in fact has set with his Ferrari the speed record still valid on the Italian highways and we set it on the mountain streets in that magic night. But no commemorative plaque for us, just the good chance to tell this story to everyone.

We're two lucky guys, many times we've been lucky that nothing happened. Maybe they owe something to us, maybe a sort of immunity because of the past pains.

THE SECOND VENTURE

One night we decided to go to a party at the disco "Il Drago" in Lignano Sabbiadoro, where we felt at home since we went there so often. We left Belluno right after dinner in my "Oil", my fantastic metallic grey jeep Nissan Patrol 3.3 turbo-diesel, nicknamed "Oil" for how much I used to hit it.

The party was a celebration of the 60s we took part in a "flower power" look: white suit with tight trousers with flairs, black shirt with a high collar left opened on the chest, tight jacket, black shoes, same pin on our head. We got changed in the car, excited like kids during the school recite, and we made a triumphal entrance with black shades on.

"Il Drago" was charmed.

The night was unforgettable. Everyone dancing on the tables and we were crazy on the German ladies who usually fill the Adriatic beaches during summer, becoming object of desire of the big babies made in Italy like us. We ended up partying on the beach, taking a bath in the moonlight with two "fun and very whore" blond German ladies of whom I cannot remember the names. Slightly high alcohol level. Slightly high testosterone level. Stupidity - well I'm not even going to mention it. At dawn fulminating departure like Real Madrid 2012: Khedira steals the ball, Ozil serves, he passes to CR7, who scores under the goalkeeper's legs. Italian big babies (Sardelloni) 1, Germany 0.

After a reviving pasta at the "Key West" at five in the morning, I hit it in my car like Gilles Villeneuve until we're home again. Giuliano had to be in the bar in front of the Belluno hospital at 8 in the morning and I had to be at the shelter up on the Nevegal, Belluno's hill, by 9 in the morning.

Sadly "Oil" is "Oil". At 7:27 am in Fadalto our car runs out of gas. Life is life.

«No, I cannot believe this, it's dead, we ran out of gas!» I say incredulous to Giuliano.
«A Ferrari would need less gas! How much does this do? 4 Km per litre? And now how are we getting to work?» he says desperately.
«I don't know, but did you see how I was driving? Who am I, Gilles Villeneuve?» I add still high on speed and not only that.
«Yes, bravo, ask Luca Cordero di Montezemolo if he may come pick us up in his helicopter, dumb ass!» he replied totally panicked. So fun!

As we stopped laughing, we quickly find the solution: let's stop a car in the middle of the street like the agents from Alarm for Cobra 11 – The Motorway Police, they drive us to the next gas station and we fill the emergency tank always there in my gas thirsty beast.

Toss down, "Oil" takes it all and says thank you by burping a black gas similar to the King Lion's roar and more polluting than the Exxon Valdez.

We look at each other like two idiots, we countdown with the engine high: Three.. Two.. One.. Go! They turn off the red lights and we get off again like the good old Schumacher and arrived at work in a coma.

"Lucid and effective", this is our motto.

«Good morning, a cappuccino with lots of foam please» the customer asks.
«Good morning. Here's your tonic water. No ice you said, right?» we replied lucidly and effectively!

Good old times.

THE THIRD VENTURE

This time no "Oil", which would have been very useful in the *gypsy wander* that I'm about to tell since it was an off-road vehicle, but instead we were in Giuliano's compact car.
«Come on, let's go with mine today!» Giuliano says in my parking with the same will to discover new places.
«Ok, and where are we going?» I ask curious.
«Well, I wanted to take a walk on the Dolomites and visit an area I've never seen...» he says with his dreamy gaze.

Giuliano has always loved our mountains and he visited them all. There was just this middle of nowhere on the Agordino which he decided to visit that day with me, in his hunter green Fiat Uno. One of the ugliest car I've ever been in.
«Great Marco Polo! If you're sure about it let's go. Bye "Oil" we're going to miss you!» I said addressing to my jeep in the parking lot. The most self-realized prophecy ever.

A couple of hours later, as we passed by San Tomaso Agordino's saddle, Marco Polo Vantaggi, with such a genius idea - I would say Leonardo couldn't have done better - drives on a dirt patch and ten minutes later we're stuck in the mud in the middle of the wood, with no telephone, in the rain, 20 km away from the next urban centre. The only positive thing was that we still had gas. Too bad we couldn't get out of the mud with the hunter green cart.

But we were camouflaged.

Attempt by attempt, it gets dark and cold. We're in jeans and t-shirt, soaking wet, full of mud, totally isolated. Only wolves were missing. Panic. We think we may walk down the valley to ask for help but Giuliano disagreed:
«No, we cannot leave it here! We have to bring it back home».

As a matter of fact you cannot leave your ship stuck in the rocks in front of the Isola del Giglio like captain Schettino did on January 13th 2011 with the Costa Concordia! You cannot betray what has been your partner in many ventures!

So, with big pride we get ready to make one last extreme attempt, like the special corps in the army when they get ready for a blitz to free the hostages.

We clean once again the wheels with some branches, we insert some pieces of wood under the driving wheels and we get the way out ready for at least five meters with blankets, pebbles, branches, a boar that was passing by, hence everything that would assure that the car didn't get stuck even worse, from mud to quicksand.

When everything is ready we hug and we incite each other like before the match that's worth a cup: «Come on now! Come on we can make it!» we shout, and after the Haka we hug each other tightly in a way that only athletes and real friends can really understand. Then *Giuliano Mud Vantaggi* gets at the steering wheel, soaking wet, phlegmatic and determined, while I go behind, like a rugby third line, to push in the mud turning into David Campese.

Three, two, one, go! We start with the second gear like on the snow in order to avoid that the wheels would slip which and they finally move towards safety. I remember that Giuliano wouldn't take his hand off the horn, so happy whereas me, leaning on my knees exhausted, I see the green Uno going away. Pure adrenaline. Giuliano gets off and we hug each other, we scream like crazy "Yes!" as if we fled from prison and we were finally safe.

We made it together. Once again together.

LIVING GPS

"Hey, do you want me to take a look at the maps on my tablet?".
"I'm Marco Polo! The GPS asks information to me!", "Marco Polo" says before falling down a cliff, in a popular TIM's TV commercial that revives the history of Italy through funny episodes. And this line could have been played by *Marco Polo Vantaggi* as well, and by that I mean that he knows the Dolomites area like nobody else, and not because he has been reading or watching about it on books in some documentary, but because he's been there in person. Even falling down some cliff.

Giuliano knows every centimetre of our land because he visited it and when he tells you about a place you suddenly feel like getting into a car and go there straight away, such is the passion and the love he conveys when he describes it. I think that currently he can be proud of having a great photographic archive of the Dolomites, besides an immense patrimony of knowledge. I mean knowledge of places, of stories and of people, because having partied all over the places he's got a net of relations that is bigger than the one of a life senator.

Here's the networking secret: to make people have fun and enrich them every time you meet them. This way you will be remembered and they will always love hearing from you.

«Belluno is the city of love, kisses and fountains. But do you remember Ale what kisses at the lion fountain below the Duomo? And at Santa Maria dei Battuti? And on the bench of Santo Stefano? What wonderful declarations of love in the moonlight on the Torrione! With our fantasy we had it all, we ran up in Via Le Scalette like Rocky on the San Francisco staircase and we sneaked at night in 3 atomic shelters under the city, like American spies fleeing from enemies. But these beauties, who knows them besides us?» he asks me strolling on the *Liston* in Piazza dei Martiri.

His attitude, curiosity, *mind mobility*, love for the land, *warmness* and his love for the people who live there is the reason of Giuliano's success as a communication, marketing and training expert for tourism.

He is the *Enthusiasm*. The only thing we really need.

Vantaggi, and the very word says it (it means 'advantages') is a terrific touristic guide, because you feel like you're there, in another space and in another time, and you realize you're watching the world through his loving eyes. Like D.K. Berlo affirms, in the communication "meanings are in the people, not in the words". What makes the difference beyond the what always is the *how*. And the *how* is linked to the *who*. To the identity and to the spirit.

Quoting Virginia Busato, international marketing expert and cultural mediator with China, "remember that *enthusiasm* is the only thing they cannot copy from you".

Giuliano Marco Polo Vantaggi always had in his heart the Global Positioning System and he would give it away to his friends even before 1994, the year it became fully operative even for civilians on the dashboard of their car.

Knowing the way is not enough, you also need to know how to tell it.

That's why now everyone can customize their GPS' voice pretending it was a human language, that talks to your heart. We live in the world of friendly interfaces, where we can become familiar with the technologies by customizing the welcome message on our computer, on our mobile, on our oven and on every electronic device.

The human factor always makes the difference.

When I do training in the classroom, I often ask provokingly to the participants:
«In your opinion, in order to build a world successful company, how much enthusiasm and money in proportion do we need?».
In the answers, statistically, money wins: according to the majority of the interviewed the right mix is made of 70 money and 30 enthusiasm.

What would you answer?

Once I asked this to Giuliano who answered like *the Marine*:

«*Enthusiasm 100 of course!*».

You don't need money if you don't have the right ideas and the enthusiasm to bring it to the world. Luxottica and Ferrari are an example. Leonardo Del Vecchio and Enzo Ferrari started their firm from nothing, with no money and full of debts. They had a vision, many ideas, 0 capital and 100 enthusiasm. And right with that they managed to persuade the funders to give them money, the collaborators to work with them giving their best and customers from all over the world to buy their fantastic products. With the *enthusiasm* they get everyone involved in their vision, changing forever the perception of the glasses and of the car in the world, transforming them into luxury goods.

Quoting Sun Tzu, like *the Maestro* Padoan does in the preface, *men are moving stones only if they stand on the top of a cliff!* And it's exactly *the enthusiasm* that allows you to build that leaning board where they can travel and convey emotions.

About this, my GPS has Giuliano's voice because it reminds me those night spent together, "where the car was hot and it would drive you where it wanted". Like Ligabue sings, "those night where the street is not important, what's important is feeling that it goes.

Gipsy wander by gipsy wander, "some nights you're just as happier, greedier, more naïf and more dumb as you can be. Those nights are that addiction I never want to quit".

Thank you Giuli, love you.

12. WHO ARE YOU?

> *Everything rises and falls on leadership.*
> JOHN MAXWELL

I don't know who you are, but I am a Coach. My job is to believe and to go first, firm and creative.

I'm going to tell you the story of three soccer coaches and about the definition of leadership that I do *Like*, to put it with a Facebook language.

3 COACHES

On October 4th 2009, in the locker room of the Olympic Stadium in Rome, after one more defeat of his soccer team, the words of Aurelio De Laurentiis, Napoli team's president, spread. Somebody asked him whether he still trusted the coach after only 7 points in 7 matches. Here's what he replied:

"Donadoni? It's an important life experience. He's a lovely person, very deep, well-mannered and he has good qualities. He remains a piece of my soccer experience, whatever might happen tomorrow, in a month or in a year, because it will still be an extraordinary encounter with a person who has given and is still giving what he can to the Napoli team".

I thought to myself: he has already exonerated him. Donadoni is doomed, done, finished. Game over.

As a matter of fact, on October 6th 2009, two days later, president De Laurentiis discharges Mr Roberto Donadoni with the following official statement: "A fundamental decision to let the Napoli team breathe fresh air in the new season and for the next five years. The society thanks Roberto Donadoni for the work he's been leading during the last months, and sincerely wishes him all the best for his future career".

Moral? Nothing is more important than results and not only in the soccer world.

So it's not important being lovely, deep, nice and well-mannered. What truly counts is how the boss, helped by his team, can take all the qualities out of his players in order to produce tangible and measurable results on the field.

Hindsight, De Laurentiis made a great decision. In only two years Walter Mazzari's Napoli team got qualified in 2011 for the rounds phase of the Champions League and in 2012 he rewrote the sport history of the SSC Napoli.

The Napoli team was placed in what was defined as the death round for the presence of great teams such as Manchester City, Bayern Munich and Villareal, played some extraordinary games that made possible qualifying for the last-sixteens where it would have met Roman Abramovich's Chelsea, trained by Villas Boas "Special Two", who worked for the Porto team, acquired for the modest price of 16 millions Euros.

To get things more complicated for the Neapolitans, Mister Mazzarri was disqualified for two turns, because he had pushed a Villareal player in the last crucial match of the round. "I wanted to push my players" he said in a press conference to justify himself in a funny way. As a matter of fact, he would have skipped the two most important matches of Napoli's recent sport history and of his career as a coach.

How would have the team reacted without its inspirational coach on the bench?
How would have the training staff behaved without him?
How would have the chief Coach behaved?

Many times I have assisted disqualified coaches being even more present than the times they were sitting on the bench. Headset, SMS, tablets, spokesperson, notes-person, etc.. Sometimes it doesn't change much, because many Coaches hold on tight no matter what happens. This is my ship and I sail it. Formally they have to be away but actually they have a thousand eyes and a thousand ears on the field. And they still take every decision.

But if you were the vice-coach of such a chief coach how would you feel?
Would this situation increase or decrease your respect for your boss?
Would the consideration of you from the players increase or decrease?
Would the staff as a whole grow stronger or weaker?

While the tension was rising, the heat got even worse when reportedly a note was found, handwritten by the trainer André Villas Boas, with the strategy and the formation of the Chelsea against the Napoli.

Truth or wise red herring?
Who would have played as striker?
Torres or Drogba?

What's doubtlessly true is the miserable impression of the five stars Naples hotel that was hosting the English team. Like: how to lose in the blink of an eye a life-long reputation. Personally I wouldn't want to be for a second neither the person who gave the note to the journalists, neither the hotel manager. As to me, they are both responsible to have caused a huge image damage to the business they work for, to the Neapolitans and to the Italians. Especially the manager. I feel like asking them both:

Who's the client for you?

For all these reasons February 21st 2012 was becoming such an interesting day for the sport and human topics enthusiasts, like me. The anticipation for this first match of the last-sixteens, which would have been played at San Paolo stadium in Naples, was huge. Pop-corns like there was no tomorrow, rivers of beer and free burping.

As an enthusiast of sports and leadership I couldn't wait to know how Walter Mazzari would have behaved in this fundamental match for his team and for his own career as a coach. Around 7 pm, from Sky Sport 24 channel the verdict arrives: "the team has arrived without Walter Mazzari who stayed in the training camp in Castel Volturno to watch the game quietly".

Well, greatly done! I'm excited too, this man is a great leader and his team will play a good game. I say this to everyone, tonight the Napoli is going to win, I'm ready to bet whatever you like. *Said and done*. It ends 3 to 1 for the Napoli and a few days later Villas Boas got exonerated because he was demolishing his team. At his place Roberto Di Matteo, the vice of that Special Two which was sent home. A self-realized prophecy, since being special at arriving second is not an identity you can be proud of.

Abramovich's choice of denying himself and of sending Villas Boas back to Portugal changes everything and gives a hope to the Chelsea, a team of great champions that André wanted to get retired too soon. John Terry, Petr Cech, Frank Lampard, Michael Essien, Didier Drogba, they had won everything but the Champions League, losing at the final match against the Manchester United at the penalty shoot-out under the Moscow rain in 2008. It was the very captain of a thousand battles, John Terry, who wrongly kicked the match point. So it was pretty clear that those champions wanted a revenge and they would have done all they could to play their last chance of crowning their sport dream in the Chelsea team: winning the Champions League. That was the very last train for a whole generation.

Hence, Di Matteo starts by changing the team's strategic asset aiming it all to the Italian-style concreteness and trusting his *senators* who, though not that fresh, in a blunt match could always make the difference. Needless to say, the Chelsea, with an incredible match, closes the gap with the Napoli eliminating it for 4 to 1. Scores by Drogba, Terry, Lampard and Ivanovic during the extra time. Drogba is elected MVP of the match, simply out of this world.

In the quarterfinal the Blues band gets rid of the Benfica by winning either home and away, starting to build a solid and scrappy mentality, which they need to face the strongest team of the world in the semi-final: Pep Guardiola's Barcelona, another great leader who had "invented" a new way of playing soccer.

Chelsea FC - FC Barcelona 1-0. The Blues confirm themselves as unstoppable in Stamford Bridge: the Ivorian decides, two goal posts and several occasions for the guests.

FC Barcelona - Chelsea FC 2-2. Two goals under and a man at Camp Nou, the Blues close the gap and eliminate the Barcelona: Ramires and Torres respond to Busquets and Iniesta. The Chelsea will play the final with the Bayer at the Munich Allianz Arena.

From the summary of the UEFA website to the summary in the post-match statement of Roberto Di Matteo in Barcelona, the new Nereo Rocco: "I'm not a supporter of defensive tactic: it's just that I don't like to get goals. There was no other way to face the Barcelona". No need to add anything else.

The rest, as wittingly reported by Roberto D'Agostino on his website Dagospia, is just common sense. The common sense of getting in the locker room as "the plumber": you are the hosts, I'm just passing by to lend you a hand.

The *number 1s*, in fact, know how to talk to your heart and to your head and forget about their egos to let the players' *team spirit* and *self-esteem* grow.
"I had to fuel with trust a group of confused players" this is what the young warlord tells after the venture that takes his team to the final, 4 years after the Moscow disappointment.

For one who does my job, press conferences always are a way to find out the values, the hidden structures and the beliefs of a team. Specifically, those of the Champions League follow a classic protocol: the chief coach and a player always have to participate, even if they keep a press blackout. Catching hidden information in such a context gives the same satisfaction of climbing a wall with no handholds until the top. No one wants to give any advantage to his adversary and the risk of sliding over a classic fallacy like "we will do our best… we have 50% possibilities of winning…they're a very strong team…" is very high.

But this time it's different, because above the talk there's also a little walk. Frank Lampard is the one:

"The Chelsea wants to win the Champions League and must believe in it till the end. Di Matteo's future? The society has to deal with these decisions. I'm not going to talk about it with Abramovich, but I would be happy if Di Matteo stayed there. Results talk for him. He's a capable and energetic person, he gives us a lot of strength. He's straight forward and brought along a lot of trust. We have to win, we owe it to him. We're happy we're here again, only a few months ago we would have never thought this would happen".

After these few words I already know who's going to lift the trophy.

"Moscow memories are bittersweet, but what's stuck in our minds is the defeat. We needed time to recover, but we're confident looking towards tomorrow's match. Only by winning we will be able to heal that wound".

Here, now I am a 100% sure that the destiny is offering to a generation the chance of a lifetime to close that loop that was opened 4 years ago by John Terry's mistake.

The Chelsea great top-notches are aware of that destiny, written inside of them: after an extraordinary painful match they will be finally able to kiss the Cup with the big ears, closing that wound forever. In my head I was only waiting to discover *how* the Chelsea will win the match, maybe to the penalty shoot-out, with a goal by Drogba at his last match with the Blues. *Said and done.*

I think knowing how to instil confidence and to keep believing that everything is possible, overcoming those difficulties which proves necessary to a *team of evolved people*: this is a great quality of the *leader*. Sometimes you just have to keep working without ceasing to believe in it. This is the only way to get an opportunity for another chance.

If you give up, you erase yourself in the waiting list of the dreams, in the soccer and in your life.

Roberto Di Matteo never did, quite the opposite he insisted with all his energy. He was born in a small town in Switzerland where his parents emigrated looking for a better luck from the Abruzzo region, when he's 23 he wins the Swiss championship as a foreigner with the Arau, and he says no to the Swiss national team in order to keep an Italian passport in soccer too.

At the life buffet food never ends.

When Sacchi calls him in the Italian national team he says:
"I would have kept my Italian nationality even only to work in a factory".

After a sensational career as a midfielder with technique and ideas, in Italy and in the Chelsea team, a severe injury breaks his leg in several points and forces him to quit. After a bad surgery he even risks of having his leg amputated. A few dark years follow without soccer, but he keeps on telling to his sight-impaired sister about the matches.

He studies to become a Manager and starts his new career as a coach in England, with a small team at North of London which he brings to the third league. The following year he gets exonerated, but he arrives at the West Bromwich Albion, which he gets promoted to the Premier League. The rest is still recent history, with the opportunity of going back to the Chelsea as a vice-coach, a team he had been playing in, winning twice the English Cup and even hitting the decisive goal in every match in Wembley.

As Chelsea's chief-coach, with modesty, perseverance and creativity, he revives a team that everyone thought was dead; he eliminates the Napoli, the Benfica and the Barcelona; he wins the English Cup beating the Liverpool; he wins the Champions League beating the Bayern at home to the penalty shoot-out, even though fundamental players were not available, starting by the captain John Terry.

In your opinion, is Roberto Di Matteo a Manager or a Leader?

LEADERSHIP

The definition of *leadership* that I better *Like* combines the gothic meaning of the term leader, and becomes: *a relation that creates value while rising*.

First of all *Leadership is relationship*, it's not a power that comes from a role. That might only give you a little more time, but afterwards you have to become a leader or else nobody will follow you, because that kind of relationship is conquered on the field with communicative, personal, strategic, relational and systemic thought abilities. If the manager is who manages *things*, the leader is who aligns *people* around a common goal.

Between things and people is the difference between a manager and a leader.

Secondly, in the gothic sense of the term, the leader is *who creates value while rising*, where *leader* comes from "laeder" which means 'ladder' and *ship* from "shappen" which means 'upper warehouse', that is the precious place where they used to put the work tools that were fundamental back in the days. Only afterwards, with the arrival of the Romans, the meaning has become: the one who dictates and later the one who leads.

Nowadays, the true leader is the one who creates other leaders around him.

The real star is the one who makes the others shine.

13. A LEADER: RENATO PADOAN

You are free as long as you think you're free and act freely.
RENATO PADOAN

Renato Padoan "saved my life in every way a person can be saved". We did not make love in the Titanic's hold, but to me he's had the same importance Jack Dawson has had for Rose in the James Cameron's colossal.

What you are reading now is the last story I wrote in Staff Building, even though it's in the middle. Till today I didn't know what to write about *the Maestro*, I only knew how important he's been for me, without deeply realizing the reason.

Other people explained everything to me, in the most simply and affectionate way possible, with a phone-call, with a caress and with a soccer game. Three hints make a proof and I realized I had learned myself a little that way of living of which Renato Padoan was *the Maestro*.

His story is my story, the one of a *improntitude*, of a desperate journey and of a door that was found opened. Without that 'yes' to me, nothing I am would exist. I finally realized it now, writing this book with the yellow helmet on my head.

When you write you dig. You dig in yourself and in the others. Maybe that's why Staff Building has become a necessity, a point of inflection, an event to indulge my will of starting everything anew keeping my emotions and giving away all the rest, like a message in a bottle.

I start from myself, from my will to live and to thank all the arms that have been holding me making me become what I am. I still want many hugs! Staff Building is my "Canzone del Sole" (an Italian song), the reprisal after the half-time of my life as a free man. A freedom I started experiencing thanks to the help of those who trusted me.

Everything starts from there, from an open door.

The first hint is a chased phone-call, I mean a missed phone-call on my iPhone, which was followed by my missed phone-call on his iPhone. We were both working and finally in the evening we got to talk to each other. We hadn't been seeing and hearing from each other for a couple of months.

«Hi Ale, how are you?» and I said «Very well thank you, it's good to hear you! And how are you?» and he said «Fine thank you, here it's like being in the defence line, whenever you drop by give me a call, we can go for a coffee, is that ok? I mean it…pass by some time…». It takes Hemingway to explain what was in his tone…a mix of *I miss you, I love you, thanks for trusting me.*

I love chased phone-calls.

The second hint is not a phone-call, but a chased meeting with a colleague of mine, who I highly respect, in a bar in Belluno. She's ok, a kind of person who always know how to hit the spot. I mean, she's the kind of person you think you already know while you haven't actually seen anything, not even a small bit. She might seem superficial, but digging with the help of avalanche dogs you find out that she's got a whole world inside, which she keeps in the shadows like a snow mountain.

For a living she's a marketing consultant of great skills, freshness and immediacy, the ideal professional with whom you might want to talk about Staff Building. We meet at 6.30 pm of a late September 2012 Thursday, in the parking of the bar she chose. She comes from work, naturally sparkling in an elegant formal attire that suits perfectly with her long black hair. Like, you know those women who can dress with the dumbest item and still look amazing? It's easy to figure how she looks when she's dressed a bit preppy: continents move, emotional earthquake!

I just finished running, with my light blue Asics gel training shoes on, blue shorts and a Nike orange t-shirt. Not at all sweated, just a bit frozen because the weather is starting to be cold. In my headset "Let's dance" by Bowie warms my heart.

We make such an impression, well mixed, given the outfits. We go in fiercely and we sit on transparent plexiglass chairs around a transparent plexiglass table, that kind of table that allows you to see all the movements of her legs, of her ankles and of her feet: sexy. You suddenly think of the Thousand shades of grey, black, red and all the colours.

To match the furniture we order some water, no gas no cold with lemon for me, sparkling no cold with lemon for her. They're been served in two glasses, also transparent, which the waitress put close to each other as if they didn't meet since a long time and they had many things to tell. Classy sensitivity.

In the water two lemon slices of the same lemon look into each other's eyes holding their hands and smiling. We toast, because we have always said everything to each other, fearlessly. The lemons take advantage of the situation and kiss each other...

«I get struck by those short sentences that you can tell in every event of your life. Make a presentation where you can project yourself on a page as if it were printed, where you take a few excerpts inside a specific context, where you can leave something... A couple of hours and no longer, even though with you I could spend 24 hours non stop without getting bored for a single second...». Thank you, I say going back to look into her eyes and taking a break in writing down her illuminating ideas on my wrinkly paper. Thank you so much.

«Value your belief, your energy» and while I sit like a Disney character, absorbed, I stare at the square and sparkling chandelier in the bar, and a caress touches lightly my right hand that was on the table waiting for it, unaware. Our hands agreed on it without saying anything.

Before I go I move once again my glass towards hers to let the lemons kiss for the last time. Those sudden kisses, like hugs, they leave you speechless.

I love chased meetings.

The third hint is not a phone-call, is not a meeting but it's a chased ball. He runs, he kicks harder than before, he doesn't miss a ball. For a hour and a half he never stops and tries to do what I do: the keepie-uppie, the bicycle kick, the curl, the tiki-taka. He's still very young but he does all his best.

In this he's just like his mother who, when she played volleyball, she would take all the balls for fear they would end up on the floor. She would make a big mess, but I fell in love with that very will of keeping the ball alive, of playing freely and always doing her best. That's how Cri is.

I start running too like a madman after every ball, showing off all my repertoire and my joy for that magic moment together. We're alone at the oratory, it's just me and Riki, thanks to that priest who opened the door for us although it was closed. Nice opening.

There's no such thing as the time for the emotions. While I look at my son running happy after a ball I see myself in a gym training her in Spezzano, just the two of us making bumps against the wall.

«Come on Ale, let's play volleyball now! Look what a bump I make...» says our five years old wonder as we were all watching the same movie, *all together at the same time*.

I love chased balls.

With *the Maestro* it was all a chase, and it goes without saying that it all started because prompted by the *Shaman* who had discovered the existence of an optional course of Scenography whose professor was a fool who used to go around the university with a white ab coat on, he would project films that were hard to find, and every year he would change the subject going from Mickey Mouse to Detective Columbo and would challenge his students in every possible way. We were freshmen and dreamt of being already senior in order to attend his course, with that eccentric character who was so far from the idea of professor we had in our mind.

Along my path I realized that I have unconsciously found the motivation to cope with some exams only for the fascination of finally experiencing some others. In this Padoan has been magic too, because he represented a comet in the imaginary of many students who couldn't care less of Math, Statistic and Building Science. We simply had to cope with those exams to enjoy some others and get to the finish line. Years later I still remember with great pleasure just two exams, although I passed 30 of them: Staging and museology (full mark with distinction) and - obviously - Scenography (only full mark no distinction).

My access to the world of *the Maestro* has always been somewhat special, because he would make you use your heart and your brain, sensing an emotion and most of all he would force you to challenge yourself. To attend his course, with a compulsory attendance, you had to write your auto-biography first, the only interesting thing to him. Renato knew that doing it for him meant doing it for yourself, so you would have gotten prepared to a course that would have changed your life.

I don't even remember what I wrote at that time, I only remember that I told everything about me, from my cheerful childhood to being a shepherd in Nevegal to my father's suicide. Basically a Quentin Tarantino's script:

«To me death is cold and hard, as cold and hard as my father when I found him stone dead in his car in front of the graveyard. I tried to shake him, to call him, but I couldn't even move him of a millimetre. That sweet man who had got to know me, who had cuddled and caressed me with his big hands, who had taught me to drive at twelve years old and who I loved more than anything had turned into marble. From that moment on I have been talking to a gravestone».

That November night was a real tragedy, with a full moon I can hardly forget. It took the thunder of a supersonic fart to bring me back to life, making me burst into an endless laugh. That big ass of my uncle Palato, while attempting to take my mother out of the car (she was overturned and desperately hanging to my father's corpse screaming "I'll warm you up! I'll warm you up!"), in that devastating effort he farted in the biggest and most sounding way I had ever heard.

I owe my life to that ginormous flatus!

Well, try to find someone else who was saved by a fart...

My surgeon grandfather used to say that farting is good. And he was right. When I was a child, to make me laugh my ass off, when we would take the elevator from our sixth floor of our beach house, in the exact moment we bumped on the ground floor and the doors would open, granddad would make a breaking wind at will.

Doctor Vianello was a nice character, a patriarch of other times who knew the whole world, with a taste for humour and love for the beautiful women. He would always dress elegantly with his suit on, his golden watch in his pocket. Other times, other sense of space. He had been a fascist, but he had saved many people from the Nazis and helped everyone he could, because first of all he was a doctor. He had really believed in Mussolini, always listening to his own conscience.

I remember a day when a fifty years old lady came on our floor, with lots of jewellery and with aristocrat gestures. In the elevator we stood tight because it was an old four passenger elevator and then granddad with his big belly would take half of it, so we were stuffed. As we got on the ground floor, granddad Alessandro, so used to make that monstrous flatus at will as the doors would open as if it were a CR, he forgot that there was the "countess" on board and made a sensational breaking wind.

He made everything shake, it must have been 47 decibel at least, dead man talking (from the *Smorfia*).

The lady's face is unforgettable: outraged, horrified and smothered, like granddad's face, surprised himself for not having thought that we were not alone. We broke in a crazy laugh.

I ran and I reran. At the top of that havoc of that tragic night I burst in a laugh for the same reason and in the same way, like Demeter seeing the nudity of Baubo. The slave wanted to bring the goddess back to life and she caught her lifting up her dress and showing a male face drawn on her womb, where his eyes where her nipples, his mouth was the belly button and his beard was her pubic hairs.

When I heard for the first time the story of the Demeter's laugh from doctor Spinotto, alias Leonardo Spina, at the Clown Doctors course, I realized I was at the right place. This is my story, I was saved by a laugh as well. Maybe that is why I am now a Coach and a Clown, but you look at the bigger picture only by looking behind, like Steve Jobs used to say.

You can realize the importance of some unforgettable farts only afterwards, when a lot of time has passed and a lot of gas in our bowels. Until that moment you have to keep up, stay strong and overcome the dark moments when you feel alone and you don't know where to go.

Sometimes talking to a gravestone is not enough.

What's more devastating about a suicide is that it drags you in like a vortex, it swallows you, it kills you for the pain. A terrible sense of guilt is born out of it, because you cannot rest for not having been able to realize it on time.

Being able to forgive yourself is the biggest challenge.

The attempts are praiseworthy, because you might start by helping the others - since you cannot help your closer people and most of all yourself. Inside you, you think that it won't happen again and you become a good listener, you develop the ability to catch the hidden signals, to read between the lines and to be in someone else's shoes. You train yourself very hard hoping to acquire those skills that might allow you to save the life you were not able to save, as if you could turn back time and change the story's ending.

All this is praiseworthy but it's just praiseworthy.

All this is just not hitting the spot, it's a good way of taking time and not to face the real matter: yourself. Everyone knows it, helping the others is way more simple than helping yourself and the people you're emotionally involved with. From this side there's no prophet in his hometown and we all always need help to make it: to ask for it, to receive it and to give it. What I learned is that, sadly, you might have become a phenomenon but it could still happen. It might happen in the best families as well.

Maybe what really matters is to enjoy your life, every instant. On this *the Maestro* is a leader, that's why I'm telling his story.

After the Scenography exam with him I still had to get rid of a bit of junk - sorry, exams - before focusing on the thesis, and of course he would have been the only person in the world who could have been my supervisor. So I wrote to him an e-mail, which he replied to:

«Call me after midnight and we may arrange that...».

You can figure how he was, *the Maestro*. All the others set a certain time for the phone-calls, like in the morning or after lunch, but he wants to be called after midnight. Terrific.

At half past midnight I called him on his landline and he says to me: «Very well, I'll see you tomorrow at 10 am...» that kind of phone-calls take-it-or-leave-it that I adore. The next morning at 10 I'm in front of his door and here it starts the interesting part. You know when you're walking on thin ice but nobody told you it was thin? That's exactly the kind of ventures *the Maestro* loves, in his sophisticated and classy way of putting you to the test, to see if you really mean it.

The entrance to his manor house in front of the mount Civetta is in fact a mystery. There's a grey wall with a dark green front door with a peephole in the middle where *the Maestro* quietly watches the show and a light wooden knob at the top on the right. No bell, no nameplate, nothing at all. Most of all no instructions. When in front of his door, if you don't quickly understand that that knob is the only way to draw his attention then you will stay out, because if you knock or you start calling his name he will never open. You lost him, forever, so you didn't really mean it.

I can tell you about it because I solved the green door puzzle. The magic experience of pulling that knob makes you feel challenged and ridiculous at the same time with that arm lifted, as if you were saying hello to someone from afar with the your armpit uncovered and you never know what it might happen pulling it. Maybe a trapdoor opens and swallows you, some bikers come to beat the hell out of you, some maleficent witch kidnaps you or Harry Potter comes to open the door.

After a few endless seconds a thousand bells start ringing inside announcing the guest up and down the stairs. Magic. To get in you have to lower you head, if you're not a garden gnome. On your left there's a wooden stair which goes up to the library and a landing that gets you in kitchen. A kitchen he had built all by himself with customized furniture and the strangest objects, that you can stare for hours like enchanted.

Going to his place is like going into a dream.

Everyday he would let me find different books in some strategic spots, without saying anything, so that I could snoop on the sly when he would leave on purpose. Inside of each one I could find a message in a bottle for me. It was his way of educating me, with no display or declaration.

Initially I was supposed to write a thesis about The Simpsons, but then *the Maestro* stopped me because he couldn't see any relation to me and he hated those works that you just have to fill out and don't add anything new to your life. He wanted more. It was the end.

I went back home desperate. Inside me a void. I thought I had made it and instead I found myself with empty hands, disappointed and bitter. I was about to give up, of throwing in the towel: him or nothing. I had no idea about what to do, I only knew that I was more into the journey than into the destination. I had the feeling that my life had to pass through it. I still dreamt of those moments when he would leave his books around the house for me and we would stand watching the mount Civetta from his terrace listening to Wagner.

He used to talk and I used to listen.

The morning after, a mysterious force wakes me up from that nightmare and urges me to get in the car as if in trance to go back to him. Like *the Maestro* back in the day, I used to think that *the task had been cancelled in the end but someway the show had already been announced.* I discover only now, reading again his preface, another message in the bottle for me.

That morning when I left home I had nothing in my mind that could have changed his mind but my *improntitude*. There was just me: defenceless, starving, desperate.

«Ale, what are we going to do now? I don't know we will manage something».

War according to Sun Tzu, this has got to do with death and with throwing the troops into the fray because men are moving stones only if they stand on the top of a cliff!

Luckily, during the ascension I also come up with an idea, like a rabbit out of a hat: telling my story in the Centro Interessi, the youngster's centre in Belluno, which I helped managing. I used to stage settings for the young kids and I could have talked about this, about how the environment influences our behaviour. I could have brought my experience of my life in a youngster's centre, as an actor and as audience. The more I got closer the more I realized. I was punching my Fiat 500's steering wheel and shout to myself enthusiastically: «This is a good idea! Believe in it! *Here we go!*». The more I drove and the more I grew confident about my idea.

But I needed him to open the door anyway.

The day before it had been a goodbye, among intelligent people there's no need to add anything else: his had been a definitive no.

Still, I had arrived by then. *Another version of a similar strategy were Cortés' ships, those ships he burnt because nobody would even think that they could arrive in Spain... and that's how they conquered Mexico!*

I burnt my ships pulling once again that magic wooden knob. Luckily my *improntitude* had been his as well. To him it was to receive a grant, to me a thesis. For the both of us it was about life.

He looked at me from the peephole, maybe thinking about his story while the bells announced me in the whole house as a wanderer at a castle's door. After endless seconds when the only thing you can do is praying and stay put, sure that in the end you're a good guy, he opened the door and without saying anything he made me realize that he had understood.

That door left me with no more fears.

I told him everything about it like a flood, sure that I would have got straight to the point. It would have been titled "**456 days at the Youngster's Centre** - a video deposition of my life inside a youngster's centre: set design as ground".

At lunch on that day he made me sandwiches. To celebrate he made three, but he cooked only two of them. We enjoyed them with several sauces on the little table in the living room next to the farmhouse kitchen.

Another human being would have made four sandwiches, because there was plenty of cheese, ham and bread. Another human being, if he chose to make three he would have cooked all of them together. Not *the Maestro*, he was waiting for the right moment to ask me:

«Shall we split another one?»

Small gestures of infinite class, like the way he split it in front of me as if it were a particle of our alliance.

The grandeur of a life is in such moments, in the pleasure of the *how* the *what* transcends.

In that year we had been living together he introduced me to Aristotle, Nietzsche, Sun Tzu at a level that I could have never even thought about. He explained to me the statute of the architecture: *a steady place, that opens and closes, representative of a world.*

After 456 amazing days my graduation day arrived and also on that occasion *the Maestro* proved himself as coming from another world.

«It's been a couple of months that I talk about you vaguely and mysteriously to the Commission. They can't wait to meet you, ha ha ha, we got them. I had your turn at around half past midday, so they have the time to get bored and then it'll be our turn» he said to me enthusiast as I arrived at the university. I was perfectly at ease and smiling, I already knew I won a *treasure* that was not the graduation.

After the proclamation, *the Maestro* took me aside to tell me about the conclave's backstage:

«The commission was enthusiast about you, they proposed the full mark, but I said that 108 was fine for you. After all we started for another reason, didn't we?» unravelling the enchantment of that journey together where he had been my father, my guide, my educator and mentor, trusting me and teaching me to live following his example. *A lot of stuff.*

«Moreover I graduated with 108 in philosophy, I couldn't let you outdo me...» he said to me winking and hugging me. Fantastic! *Number 1.*

Renato Padoan taught me how to say *yes*, to enjoy the *small things* and to keep *my door opened*, as he did with me, saving me in very way a person can be saved.

This is what I *hope* I have learned from *the Maestro*, my *lucky star* that nobody can outdo.

SECTION II
SELECTION CRITERIA

Ambarabacci ci coco tre civette sul comò...

LE CONTE

STAFF BUILDING

14. SELECTION

> *In the quest for life's harmony we must not forget that in the ordeal of our existence we're both actors and audience.*
> NIELS BOHR

Everyone knows that there's a wide literature about how to select people and that is why I aim to introduce my very personal criteria. A bit naïf if you want, but I hope they may give you some interesting cues about how to select your *Right people*.

As a premise, let me remind you that in the career's world an interview is not (or it should never be) an exam: the collaborator introduces himself to the firm and the firm introduces itself to the collaborator. Anyway, each one "wins" something, as information. And the information in the human resources are definitely gold nuggets, because using them in the right way you can reach your goal. Look at WikiLeaks.

In the staff building this principle of reciprocity still applies, because the opportunities always come from both sides.

In the selection my keywords are results, values, cultural context, skills, aesthetic judgment, big brother, sixth sense.

RESULTS

First of all: start from the end and look at the results that the person has reached in his/her life.

Gaining a trophy is always good, no matter what kind and what category has been reached and what level of responsibility that person had in that project. Just like reaching the budget in a firm's life.

In every sport you can find some excellent athletes, coaches and managers who have never lifted a trophy, that is to say they have never tasted the kinesic pleasure of having in their hands the physical and symbolic fruit of their work.

And then there are the *lucky ones*, athletes, coaches and managers, who have a sort of magnet for success and great talent of knowing how to make their tasks, their passion and their abilities become something important, meaningful and for everyone to see. You have to look for these people. Of course.

Then you also have to eat healthy food and exercise.

In the business and in the sport world the results always are the fruit of an excellent and never accidental work, where many individualities have cooperated. Those individualities have demonstrated with the facts that they knew how to build something tangible all together. And this is already a skill: it's the ability of knowing how to work as a team to get to a common goal or as *the Specialist* would say: an only goal. *A lot of stuff.*

Then consider that only by exposing to winning model you can determine a deep change in your way of living, thinking and working in a staff and in a specific project. That becomes a true investment because people are able to grow more quickly (and better) when inside a working team there are human beings who already know how to win.

The change Ibra-Eto' with the Barcelona allowed the Inter team to win at the Champions League after 46 years. President Moratti brought home a champion who had already won two, scoring a goal in both the finals and letting go a phenomenon who had never won one, always playing not at the best of his fame in the most important matches of the Champions League. The same great Inter's captain, Javier Zanetti, during an interview after the winning match in Madrid in 2010, told how important for the team had been looking at the peacefulness of Eto' before going on the field at the Santiago Bernabeu: they were sure that with him they would have made it. "These things always come in threes", this was the mantra they kept on repeating till they grew confident, turning it into reality. Self-realizing prophecy.

What you have to remember is that reaching a great goal together creates an *emotional patrimony* that might become a leading star towards every success. Just like I was telling about the *Czar*, the first great finish line I have accomplished as a member of a staff in the sport field has been that incredible recover that got us the promotion to league A1: an experience that has deeply changed my way of perceiving the staff and the job of coach, creating the premises to become a Coach.

In that project I was just a volleyball coach assistant with only a few responsibilities, but with such a level of incredible emotional and professional participation, because I always felt important and inside the project. Thanks to me and to Caprara.

The team participated in the Championship of volleyball league A2 with the aim of winning, but instead of being in the chart's first places it was in demotion area. Injures, bad luck, bad choices, they have all undermined the group's confidence that they could have suddenly come back to A1.

In December the society changes the coach and starts an incredible recover that brings the team to the play-off promotion on the last day, apparently by the so called skin of their teeth.

I remember the excitement of that day because we were coming back from an away game on the bus and we were waiting for the other teams' results to find out whether our recover had happened.

There was an incredible atmosphere. Suddenly the news that we were waiting for arrives and turns everything in a thunder and in a terrific party among us, with true emotion and crave of making it together. *All together at the same time* we promised each other of getting till the end and conclude our work.

During the play-offs I remember the emotions and participation of the audience and of the city, all united to support us until the end to crown one of the most sensational sport ventures of the Italian volleyball, if not of the sport in general.

The play-off games were the fruit of such exceptional confidence and communion. A sportive triumph came out of it, because we won home and away the semi-finals and the finals.

This success generated in me and in all of us a powerful well-being that lasted for weeks and that it reinvented itself as we were approached in the streets from enthusiast people or when we would meet in the gym and around. It was always a feast.

After many years the link between us still remains the same and every time we get to meet it seems like it was yesterday: we smile with no reason, high on Beta endorphins and dopamine.

For all these reasons, the people who were able to participate with the facts in the achievement of a great result, no matter what role they had inside that project, they bring along a patrimony of emotions and of skills that can represent an added value for the building of a successful staff, simply because they want to live them again. And then again, and again, and again.

That magic sensation is an irresistible drug that makes you a better person. If you tried it only once in your life you cannot live without it and you do your best to get another shot. To me, luckily, it happened many times and I have become an emotional addicted to the victory.

VALUES

Second thing: ask about values.

You train for skills and you hire/fire for values. This is the rule you always have to keep in your mind, because it's easy teaching something to one who has got the right attitude and shares your value system, instead of the opposite. Changing the attitude and the range of values is possible, but it takes longer, it takes more commitment and more proficiency. Call me if you need, it will be such an honour and a pleasure being your Coach. But in the meantime, I suggest to start from a solid and shared base of values, that is the driving force. You have to know very well what moves a person *towards* what he/she wants (what's important for you in your life?) and what moves a person *away from* what he/she doesn't want (what would you like to avoid in your life?). The classic NPL meta-programming *towards-away from*.

In a few words, the basic question is:

why are you here?

Then I suggest to go deeper starting from what the person has answered and most of all *how* he/she answered. Like Peter Drucker says, "the most important thing in the communication is listening to what is untold". You have to know how to read between the lines and find out what has *marked* his/her communication on a para-verbal and non-verbal level. If during the conversation they say «...I am a *honest* person» and while saying this they have the same nervous tics of detective Clousneau, then you better be suspicious.

Be careful who you let in your house, because the "reputational risk" is always yours. You're responsible for what you do and for what your staff members do. If someone messes up, you're responsible, and by that I mean that you will personally pay the consequences, one way or another. That's why it's important to chose the *Right men*, shall they be male or female.

CULTURAL CONTEXT

Third thing: get to know the person's cultural context.

This information allows you to find out what influences, personalities and environment have formed and produces the person you're facing, according to what you're looking for in your staff. To better explain, let me do an example from the music and cinema world, since we have to learn from the best.

DJ Francesco, one of the Italian hosts of the TV show The X Factor, is Roby Facchinetti's son, one of the 4 members of an historical Italian band: the Pooh. Francesco was born with the music flowing in his blood and since he was 2 he would follow his father in the concerts, experiencing the rehearsals and the show in different parts of the world where the Pooh would tour. Also thanks to these opportunities and to his cultural context he has been experiencing since he was born, he developed his artistic career in the music world.

Like *the Maestro* Renato Padoan says, "remember, no one is born under a cabbage" and you can apply this to everyone.

DJ Francesco wasn't born under a cabbage, he breathed music since he was born and today he has become one of the best Italian hosts, with his style, his values and his contagious passion for good music, so to launch his slogan on the TV: "let's support and buy the good music!".

With a nice soundtrack let's move to the cinema.

Tinto Brass, who's become the filmmaker of the Italian erotic comedy thanks to the good receptions of "La Chiave" in 1983, a film based on the novel of the Japanese writer Tanizaki Jun'ichiroo and starring the beautiful Stefania Sandrelli, he was not born under a cabbage, but in a certain historical, family and cultural context.

Painter Italico Brass' nephew, Tinto moves to Venice when he is very young, he graduates in Law in Padua and mostly he grows passionate about cinema, so much that he moves to Paris, in the Fifties. Here, for two years, he becomes the Cinémathèque's archivist, the cradle of the Nouvelle Vague.

In this cult place, where the Nouvelle Vague filmmakers used to meet, like François Truffaut, Jean-Luc Godard, Jacques Rivette, Claude Chabrol, Eric Rohmer, those "cursed films" were shown, cursed because they used to deprecate every rule and because they "tripped the dogma", literally becoming invisible, according to Jean Cocteau's definition.

Most of all they were films of great European filmmakers widely unappreciated back in the day, like Jean Renoir, Roberto Rossellini, Jacques Becker, and of post-WWII American directors like Alfred Hitchcock and Howard Hawks.

When he goes back to Italy, Tinto Brass continues his artistic education becoming the director's assistant of Alberto Cavalcanti and the photography's assistant to a great maestro like Roberto Rossellini. Such a nice way to learn from the best.

Nowadays we might appreciate or not the erotic-transgress genre of Tinto Brass, this is a matter of taste, but we cannot deny that he built himself or, as he would say, "worked his ass off!". And, talking about "asses", no one has ever doubted his magnificent aesthetic sense when it comes to the actress' choice. *A lot of stuff*. Thank you Tinto!

SKILLS

Forth thing: look for specific skills.

It all depends on the skill you need for the job opening and from this you start, considering that, in some jobs, knowing how to be, the emotional intelligence and the relational capacities might be dominant compared to all the rest.

The future member of your staff has to know how to do something very well, much better than you. He/she needs to have an excellence around whom he/she can build all the rest.

Personally I'm wary of the mister know-it-all, of those who are able to do everything. I prefer focused people, someone who can perfectly make a pan's handle, who have had lots of experiences in a specific role, who knows how to do something specific that *the whole team of evolved people* can take advantage of and trust when they come to terms.

In the building of capacities, in fact, you always start from a natural inclination, from what you can do very well, with the aim of making yourself the best at that. Then, around this utter skill, you can build all the rest starting right from the trust and the climates related to this excellence.

In the golden era of the male volleyball national team, coached at that time by Julio Velasco, a guy who "couldn't" do the bagher arrived in the team, and that is a basic skill for a game's building. It was as if he had learned how to run without learning how to walk first.

What had happened? This guy had been selected by Velasco for the attack and, in fact, his coach at the club's team, Marco Paolini, one of the best coaches for youngster in the whole world, had pointed right at this young striker's qualities, working on them so to make him stand out and get noticed by the Italian scout. To make it he had certainly "neglected" all the rest.

Once he got in the national team, that guy learned even how to walk with the same confidence he had when running, so he became good at making the bagher to an appropriate level for the Italian national team. But if he didn't focus all of his efforts during the training on the development of a specific talent, all of this would have never happened.

AESTHETIC JUDGMENT

Fifth thing: trust your aesthetic judgment.

On a summer day of 1999, while I stood on the *Maestro*'s terrace in front of the mount Civetta, or, how he would call it, "in front of God", we ended talking about the selection processes of the "head hunters" and Padoan expressed his persuasion that the best possible criteria is always the aesthetic judgment: «In the end it's all there!» he used to say.

This statement impressed me and I started looking at the people, their faces, their attitude and their behaviour, because there's a strong link between physical and behavioural features.

In fact, there's a pseudo-scientific discipline, the physiognomy, which claims of assessing psychological and moral features from the physical features, especially from the face features and expressions. This term comes from the words *nature* 'physis' and *knowledge* 'gnosis'.

According to this discipline, all the human knowledge rests on the concept which *the Maestro* referred to, that is "on the assessment through the senses and the morpho-genetic observation of the nature, of the becoming-in-action rules which the man as conscious part of the nature is in".

To put it in a simple way let's think about Hollywood. The roles are assigned to the actors according to their face and body. Woody Allen cannot star as a superhero stud or else that film becomes a parody. Doctor Hannibal the Cannibal Lecter has Anthony Hopkins's face, not Harrison Ford's. There are actors born to star as the good ones, others to star as the ugly ones and others to star as the evil ones, like Sergio Leone teaches in his spaghetti-western "The Good, the Bad and the Ugly".

Then there's who can only star as himself, like Tom Cruise.

William Shakespeare was a fine drawer of marvellous characters giving them extraordinary abilities. Othello and Iago are shapes, that in the interpretation of Orson Welles and Micheàl MacLiammoir are dragged to the limit of their essence. Between them, first of all, there's a difference of shape that applies then to the substance, the character, the moral, like the one between Scar and King Lear. Compared to the good ones, the evil ones are more shut in their posture, they release a dark light, they breathe shortly. They have a different colour. That is why they can become scary masks like Joker or Dart Fener.

Human beings are shapes that we have to understand.

BIG BROTHER

Sixth point: sneak on them through the peephole.

As the father of the quantum physics, Niels Bohr, Nobel Prize in 1922, taught us, "in the quest of the life's harmony we must not forget that in the ordeal of our existence we're both actors and audience". Hence, dear Big Brother's fans, here's an extraordinary resource to investigate the person's level of coherence, especially with the ideas he/she expresses about him/herself.

If you have the (legal) chance of observing on the sly the people you would like to select in their backstage, that is before getting in touch with you, this is one of the best ways of collecting quality information about who they really are. About this, it doesn't really matter listening to what they say, you don't need spy-microphones, what's more important is to observe "from the peephole" what they do, because when they will get in touch with you they will stand in top shape, that is they will start playing the part they have been preparing at home. In my experience, this is a method used by the *head hunters, the managers* and *the moms* in the whole world.

- The really good *head hunters* don't care about what but they care about *how*, drawing much importance to what is happening before and after the interview. Their office is strategically located so that they can see who comes and who goes, finding out through the hidden cameras or through the window the unaware candidate's behaviour. They're some damn bastards and they often love to trick you as well in order to find out the motivation's level of the appliers, calling in unusual hours of the day or setting meetings without notice or suddenly cancelling them. All to discover how the person reacts and if they may introduce him/her to who has the job opening. Once passed the exam - so once found the right person - they skilfully support the candidate because they earn money if the commissioner hires him/her. So nothing they do is accidental. Asking yourself: "how did the interview go?" is a misleading and reductive analysis. To make yourself better ask yourself other questions, like: «how did the pre and post-interview go? Was I already smiling when I left home? Was I myself all day long?».

- From the commissioner's side, all the *entrepreneurs* of a certain level that I know tend to observe the behaviour of their potential collaborators when they think to be unseen. *The Secret Agent*, for example, involves other reliable staff members to know exactly at what time the candidate has arrived at the meeting, the way he/she greeted, how he/she sat down, how they walked through the doorsteps, how he/she breathed and how he/she waited before getting in his office. Obviously who arrives late is already doomed, and that is he/she has no chances of being hired. Then again, if he/she doesn't behave or he/she's disrespectful, he/she's out.

- *Good manners first.* Never be too friendly or take liberties. Never do it, even if you become very intimate with your boss, not even if you're BFFs. What you do on your first day, do it on your last as well. Always ask permission before getting in, particularly when the door is opened.

Roberto Oliva often has other managers too attending the interview so he can use them as a back-up, so that he can create a more complex environment for the candidate and he can gather feedbacks on the perspective collaborator from all the attendants. The mistake lies on time and money, so you better invest energies and skills to make the best decision for your firm.

- All the *mothers* in the world watch their sons sleeping. To them it's a real addiction. With any excuse possible they get in their room, they make sure that their sons are sleeping comfortably and they cuddle them. It's something *they cannot help and never will*, not even when they're 70. They dream of watching their sons and nephews sleeping together in the same bed, so they can watch them all. Pure ecstasy! In that event, like it happens to my mother with me and my son, they get in their room at least once per night, they set the alarm clock at five in the morning and get in in the dark, with a torch or with the light from their mobile. This might cause you a stroke! Finding a witch in a night gown with rollers on her head pointing a torch against you while you're sleeping is such a scary and incomprehensible experience, but that's how moms are. This energetic emotional shot is essential to their survival, especially when their kids, when they're up, are a pain. "Look what an angel...So lovely when he sleeps...Isn't it a real gem?". That's what all mothers think while they watch their sons sleeping and in a second they forgive them for all the mess they have made while they were up.

"Looking at him like this you would never think that he burnt the house...".

I'm confident about the fact that "Michael Jordan is Michael Jordan", even when he sits on his toilette, I mean he doesn't change in his posture and in his behaviour when he's in his private space. MJ never ceases to be what he is when no one's looking at him! He remains Michael Jordan.

Concerning this, I remember a friend of mine's story, who, in Chicago, during the Bulls' magic years, has been lucky enough to meet the terrific MJ in a club. Here's what he wrote to me in an e-mail telling me about that fantastic experience.

E-MAIL FROM ALE'S FRIEND

OBJECT: God exists

Ale, that's how it all started! Suddenly the music stops and an amplified voice says: Ladies and Gentlemen, with an immense pleasure we announce you that tonight his majesty… his airiness… Michael Jordan is with us. Let's welcome him with a big applause. Yessss!
We were thrilled. Can you believe that? MJ flash and bones was there, flash and airiness. After a few endless seconds, from a small door he appears, "history's greatest basketball player" like Federico Buffa would say, and the crowd opens like waters in front of Moses. In fact the MJ's M stands for Moses.
The best part, man, was his pace, slow and awe-inspiring. It took so long for him to get to his table, he looked even bigger and taller than how he actually is. He was huge and cool.
He expressed such a self-confidence that we were left speechless and we worshipped him and let him pass by like the Messiah.
Guess what I did the day after? I went to a mall to buy his shoes… the great MosesJordanAir!!!!

What an enthusiasm! I think about the emotions this friend of mine must have experienced on that night and other similar examples come to my mind.

Everything is possible, but I can hardly think that his majesty Roger Federer would let himself go to bad manners like John McEnroe in the privacy of his house. Peter Sampras, on the day Roger won his fifteenth Slam's cup surpassing him in the all time's chart, called him "a classy guy in and out of the court". I can hardly figure him chasing his dedicated wife Mirka like Jack Nicholson would do in "Shining", shaking his racket like a lumberjack's axe to kill her. And all because she used a Gillette razor to shave her legs.

«Mirka...I'm home darling. I found my used razor on the floor...Come on, where are you hiding? (Knock knock) Crusade Red Hood, Crusade Red Hood, come on... open the door! Come on, open the door, didn't you hear my knock knock?.. You want me to do an ACE!!! Then I have to open the door by myself .. (and down with his racket while Mirka screams hysterically panicked: Rogerrrr, nooooo! I had to go out with my friends and I needed to shave my legs... Pleaseeee... I'll buy you a new one!)».

I'm sure that a peaceful person will always be confident and happy, at home or out, and that, however, he/she is not that different in public or in private. So if someone is with you, while he thinks him/herself unseen, he/she might be cheating. And in that event you're allowed to demolish the door and say:

«I'm the big bad wolf!».

SIXTH SENSE

Sixth: use your sixth sense, trust your instincts.

We humans are chemicals in movement, we're energy, thoughts and emotions. What has happened is that "we have mistakenly given more importance to our cortex that to our spinal cord", Niels Bohr wrote in a beautiful letter to Albert Einstein.

The meaning of this message is: trust your feelings. Always. If you cannot stand a person on your first impression, don't bring him/her in your staff. Let him/her go, because you already know what you need to know. There's no need of finding out superficially what has already been shown in depth. That result is all you need in order to decide, so: cut it out.

We human beings always are *all together at the same time*: there are things you cannot understand with your logic and things you cannot see with your eyes.

SECTION III

MY WAY

*I've lived a life that's full.
I've traveled each and ev'ry highway;
But more, much more than this,
I did it my way.*

FRANK SINATRA

15. BELIEVE

> *Take the first step in faith.*
> *You don't have to see the whole staircase,*
> *just take the first step.*
> MARTIN LUTHER KING

I think *fooling around* is an essential moment in a person's life.

Yes, that's how I start this chapter, with this belief within me: *fooling around* is an art, because when you do it in the proper way it makes you recover your energies and may help opening new essential worlds for your existence and for a full self-fulfilment of yourself. Kids are great at this because they were born to fool around/play. Their life is all a game, like a game should be all the sport, my great passion.

With the amazing athletes I've had the chance to work with, about whom I will tell the story in **Five circles** *champions' stories*, I value and we value consciously fooling around as well, and by that I mean making room for a useful physic and mental regeneration in order to have the best performance at the competition. Moments that are never accidental but always carefully selected.

Everyone knows that in the high level sport having a good rest is as important as having a good training, but only a few invest in ideas, time and energy for the rest/fooling around. For this reason, in the building of my mental training program *I always start from the end*, and that is from the relax moments. We set those first and then the rest. Initially the athletes take me for a fool, because they're used to do the opposite, that is only thinking about when they "have to" train. This habit is so established in them that they often forget to value the rest of the time as well. As if it weren't as important.

Let me better explain. Every trainer in the world, in every sport of the world, builds his relationship with the athletes starting from what they need in order to express the best performance level in the competition. Someone thinks exclusively about being exceptional at that, in their core business, that is in the moment when they work with the players or when they have to guide them to the competition.

So, starting from the competition's calendar, the chief trainer builds up a work program where he highlights the moments of physical, coaching and tactic training, leaving empty spaces where the athletes "don't work with them". They often don't even want to care about the times when the athletes rest, hence "do not work". It's not in the contract. But what's the use of a fantastic training when a player doesn't participate at his best because he gets there drunk or doesn't even gets there? This is the reason why I care about the empty spaces as well.

"I only think about the training. The sport society has to tell to the athletes they have to drink less alcohol or they have to sleep at night. That's not my job!" said a lousy league A trainer whining (in a late interview) about the society which he had worked for and had exonerated him after only three championship's days. Who knows why such an unfair thing had happened... Nevertheless on the soccer field they would say that he was such a good trainer. Well, I think that man is a bit backward-looking and he is not a great leader, like the results show. Really good trainers, not only build up a work program in order to "force" their athletes to lead a healthy life, with healthy food and a proper rest, but they also care about them as people.

This is what makes it different, what makes the *number 1s* different from the wannabes. The *number 1s* also take responsibilities for the relationship and they really care about their players, because they are aware of the fact that human beings follow you when they respect you and trust you. So if you respect them and if you trust them. People listen to what you have to say if you have shown a real interest in them first, or else you waste your time. To put it as John Maxwell, leadership's world guru, "people don't care about what you know until they know how you care about them. You need to touch their heart before asking for help". The great leaders are extraordinary at this and they know how to overcome the stereotypes and get under your skin, or else you couldn't explain the difference in motivation and performance between same players with different Head Coaches.

Working with people is an art that's based on believing.

As a Mental Coach I care about the empty spaces because they determine the full spaces.

What do you do to regenerate yourself?
Where are you now?
Where do you feel at home?

What I learned is that:

athletes train better when you value properly the rest time;
during the competition their performance improves when they learn how to better live the time before and after the competition;
the best performance is always related to the fun;
you have to believe in order to see.

Human beings always bring along all themselves, never leave a part at home. To learn how to focus some energies in some moments they needs to look for those meditative states when they recover them, when they recover their forces, they clear their mind and have real fun. Just like the creative talents need idleness, the athletes need to *fool around* and to *believe*. Through certain meditative states the brain starts waves of regeneration, the same Alpha waves in which some children are in until 5, like Obelix in the magic potion. Such moments are essential in order to grow and express yourself at the best. Like it is essential the act of believing. The secret lies in giving importance to life as a whole, not just the agonistic one. That is why I choose the *fooling around* as a moment of fundamental regeneration.

"Very well. I really want to enjoy my day off in the crowd, wandering in the Philosophy festival's pavilions, only led by the stands' colours, by the music of the streets artists and by the perfume of Borlengos". With this statement of purpose, written the week before that Saturday September 18th 2010 on my agenda, I was peacefully fooling around in Sassuolo, when a charmer's soft voice caught me for its loveliness. Charmed by that quiet, confident and warming voice I get closer to that crowd that filled half the square only to listen to him. From a poster I learn it's a priest called Enzo Bianchi, who, judging from the interest he aroused in the crowd, had to be someone cool.

Getting closer to him was impossible, but like the good old God says, "the last will be first" and they will be able to watch the show on a maxi-screen. So I get closer in order to see him: white hair, white beard, white eyebrows, white pubes. I didn't see them, I'm just assuming. Maybe he was shaved, with his gland pierced and a small butterfly tattooed on his groin... Do you ever try to imagine what's a person like down there? I like doing it from time to time because it's also a Coaching technique called scramble.

It's cool, you try to change your impression of a person or of a situation and to laugh about it in order to change the emotion that you linked to it. If you laugh off something/someone bad isn't bad anymore. That time your father or your mother hit you will still be there, but by changing the codes that your brain has been producing in that moment you also change the way you live your present. So you feel better, you can give to it a meaning that is more apt to the way you are now and the way you want to be tomorrow.

Thinking about that "enormous maleficent dwarf", a professor who gave me bad grades for two years in high school, while she runs screaming because a 8 feet tall cross-dresser in pink high heels and garters is chasing her, well this doesn't give me good grades but it still makes me feel better. I start giggling for no reason and life starts smiling as well.

That Saturday's smile was the one of the founder and prior of Bose's monastic community, who, with his deep voice tells about his experience of a man and an expert of mystique and spirituality. Between a sip of citron juice and a mouthful of Borlengo I learn that "the word praying comes from precarious. Faith is never an acquired space: it stands in the space of belief. Faith and disbelief coexist in the believer since the doubt is part of the believing. Every day faith renovate itself and in it we are always pilgrims, never residents. Living is a job as believing is a job too".

I start getting emotional because the old wise man with the piercing and the tattoo is talking about me, of my job as a Coach.

"Next to the reason and to the language there's the faith. Humanity cannot be without faith. We were born incomplete and we need someone we may trust and who relies on us at the same time".

Wow, *a lot of stuff* the small priest with white hair and gnome beard...

"The child believes in his mother and believes in life. We need to believe in someone in order to grow. It's impossible to grow up without trust. The child needs someone to believe in him and someone to rely on, or else he will feel threatened in believing in himself or in having a good life".

So much truth in these words...

"In Hebrew the verb 'to believe' is 'to adhere'. Believing is a human operation that satisfies the crave to love and to being loved. I think that a child grows up as long as someone believes in him".

I'm ecstatic and I start thanking my *fooling around culture* that brought me to him, because nothing ever happens accidentally.

After the conference, walking towards home I start thanking God and thinking about people I love. Step by step I regenerate myself and the Commencement Address by Steve Jobs in Stanford in 2005 comes in my mind, when he said that you can only connect the dots afterwards, now follow your heart. You have to be confident that those spots will connect in the future. *You have to believe in something, anything.*

What matters is the act of believing.

As Martin Luther King used to say, you have to make the first step and be confident. Trust yourself, your sensations, your companions, your team, your staff. You don't need to know everything, you only need to believe in it.

16. STATE

> *Shit state shit decision.*
> ANTHONY ROBBINS

This is going to be a shit chapter. Shit state shit decision. It doesn't take a guru to know it, but we often forget about it when we have to make strategic decision of a vital importance. With brown results.

Like my friend Roberto Oliva says to his collaborators: "If you go to a client in a bad shape you will always result as shit. Maybe fun, but shit anyway. Pull yourself together first of all! Arriving late but in a good shape is better than arriving on time but out of shape. So arrive early and in a good shape!".

Being in a good shape is a fundamental choice, like following a woman who walks in the rain. The way she opens her umbrella, which street she chooses, the way she looks for the keys in her purse, the way she moves her legs step by step, you can understand how good it must be making love with her. Does she splash in every puddle? She's adorable. Does she look for the car keys a mile before getting there? She's got a sense of humour of her own. Does she put her umbrella on the backseat before getting in the car? She's stylish.

Instead, if you're not smart enough and you choose to stand under her umbrella only to better smell her perfume, than you will lose the poetry that only a higher being like a woman on a rainy day can create.

Out of shape you will never notice certain things, because you don't have to smell her like a anteater with its nose in the cocaine to understand if she suits you chemically, you only have to look at how she moves her arms and how she smiles. If you're left charmed and you would spend everyday looking at her without the need of eating, drinking, sleeping and executing some other vital functions, then you already know what you need to know. The unconscious is never wrong.

Being in a *state of grace* helps you noticing details, reading between the lines and listening to your feelings.

One of life's biggest satisfactions is to find that my child always draws me *smiling*. In the car, on a horse, on the mountain, on the bike, while I pee. In my workshop of adult-child communication **For our kids** - *how to improve our communication to improve their life*, we work hard on how to put children, teenagers and young people in the right condition to study, eat, sleep, pick their nose, socialize. I think this is a parent's biggest responsibility: experiencing the desired condition first and building the right environment so that it all comes easily *for our kids*.

Fighting in the bedroom where the kids are sleeping or grounding them on their bed is a great way to give them sleepless nights. Emotions set in the memory of the places where they are experienced. Talking about the rope of the hanged suicide victim where it happened is not just rude, but it also transfers that pain in the place where you talk about it. Next time, unconsciously, that sad memory will come up by just getting in that room.

Jumping naked in the bed singing loud "I'm not scared" with your kids, instead, will give a much better sleep, even though you will have to get the broken bed changed quite often. Generally, you better keep the relational junk out of your home and out of your mind, because what you ingest will come out sooner or later. In the programming language it's called GIGO, garbage in garbage out, so if you fill your head up with bullshit you will have a shitty life. I told you it was going to be a shitty chapter!

An effective strategy consists in jumping, making funny faces at the mirror, laughing out loud before defining your goals. You need to look at the future with the right state in the present. Before a goal setting you need to be in a good shape and to ask yourself some good questions, so to vacate the field from your own limits. We learn from *the Marine* Piero Monestier that limits are something you build from the inside. The worst obstacles are those you have created in your mind.

I'm not tall/thin/smart/handsome/rich enough to... fill in, dear reader, I know that sometimes you do that.

I have too much cellulite/ halitosis/ flatulence/ bad luck to... fill in, dear reader, I know that you thought about this at least once in your life.
What you're about to read are some of the questions I usually make before defining the goals. When you have time to do it, pull yourself together and start answering, you'll realize some interesting things.

What does really matter for you in your life?
What have you been mostly dedicated to so far?
You'll die in six months. The good news is that you'll be very healthy and you'll have the energy to do what you want but only for six months. What are you going to do straight away?
You've just won 10.000.000 Euros no taxes, what are you going to do first?
What would you do if you were to do something that would always result successful?

What would you want for yourself if you had no limits in time, money, skills, resources?
What is something that you've never done because scared of being mistaken that you would do?
What is something that you've never done for lack of a resource like money that you would do?
What do you really like?

Whatever you answered here's another question for you:

why waiting?

Do it right now! That's it. Just do it.

17. GOAL

> *"Would you tell me, please, which way I ought to go from here?"*
> *"That depends a good deal on where you want to get to,"*
> *said the Cat.*
> *"I don't much care where...," said Alice.*
> *"Then it doesn't matter which way you go," said the Cat.*
> LEWIS CARROL, Alice in Wonderland

I'm not going to tell you how important it is to follow a goal in your life, since *no ship leaves the harbour without a destination to reach*. And if you wish to travel, you better know where you want to go, aware that what you're going to learn in the journey will be a treasure itself.

Having a goal is important because:
- it gives you a mental focus and starts your R.A.S. (brain's reticular activation system, our search engine);
- it increases your motivation to act (we're fully loaded with energy);
- it takes advantage of your creative imagination's power (we're able to find solutions);
- it represents a constant referee (it's our leading star);
- it helps keeping focused (we eliminate useless distractions);
- it allows to supervise our work (we always know where we got and what we still have to do).

Then, how I learned from my friend Martina Gennari from Meemu, a top Italian advertising, graphic design, events agency, whom I had the great pleasure to work with, "keeping focused on your goal makes you do better all the rest as well, because it's a matter of method". So, just like in the sports an intravenous injection is doping (doesn't matter what you inject in your blood, it's the method that's considered illegal), in the Coaching *the goal is the method*. Having a goal helps you to live better because "you're responsible for what you do and you give a meaning to your life". Moreover, the more you train your brain the more you get faster, effective and responsible, that is capable to react in other situations as well.

So, what do you want? *Yes, what do you want?*

Answer me to answer yourself, because this is the most important question I can make right now. Please, stop, pull yourself together and answer. And *write down* your answer, do it for yourself. Do it now. Write down whatever you wish. With the e-books you can create a note by selecting some words

MY GOAL

Written?

Very well. Congratulations! Now let's work on it.

In the definition of goal you always have to start from the end, from the result you intend to accomplish. You have to express with words what you want, not what you don't want or what you want to avoid. So, everything in a positive perspective, that is in a linguistic form without "not". If in your sentence there are some "not" get rid of them and *turn everything into positive*. For example, I don't want to be scared turns into I want to be brave; I don't want to be sick turns into I want to be healthy and happy. Many people think that positive thinking means having good intentions in life, being optimistic, smiling. That is utterly wrong. *Positive thinking means simply creating sentences without 'not'*. And, at the same time, showing good intentions, being optimistic and smiling at your life. You have to feel excited while you see, hear and feel yourself approaching to the goal. You have to enjoy. The more you enjoy yourself the more you create in your brain that nervous trace that will lead you where you wish. The more you enjoy yourself the more you create that Grand Canyon of amazing emotions that will lead you to your goal. *The more you enjoy yourself the better*, however that may be.

Let me better explain myself with some examples. Working with sports I've often heard statements like "You cannot do wrong!". This is not positive thinking, it doesn't take a genius to see, but maybe it takes an in-depth to better understand what are the short and long term consequences of such a statement. Such an expression is in fact a communicative suicide, a *hidden command* that very likely determines a mistake. If I say "Be advised, do not think about the green elephant with the pink polish-nail..." the brain has to build this sentence in order to understand it, so it has to figure the green elephant with the pink polish-nail and then erase it. So, whether you want it or not, a green elephant with pink polish-nail will turn in your head. Basically, you draw attention on what's after "not", so we have to be aware of what remains in our brain when we talk.

In the soccer example "Do not miss the penalty kick", we express a good intention in a very bad form, because to understand the meaning our brain already absorbed unconsciously the images related to missed penalty kicks and with them, what's even worse, the negative feelings related to them. That's a mess. The negative thinking changes your mood and in the wrong mood you hardly do things right. It's a law of nature. That's how we human beings work. *Shit state shit decision.* Like my surgeon granddad Alessandro used to say in one of his famous sentences, "when you enter from the back you'll always find shit".

So, it would be like going on the soccer field with a vivid memory of the penalty kicks we missed in the past and that made us suffer so bad. It would be like going on the field with Roberto Baggio's mood after he shot that ball out at the world cup's finals against Brazil during USA 1994 or John Terry's mood when he slipped on his foot dislocating his ankle and kicking out the crucial score during the Champions League's finals in 2008 in Moscow. Something you have to strongly avoid.

You better walk on the soccer field with a great game's mood in your head and in your body.

"Goal!", this is a positive thinking and a good command to say to yourself before kicking. All the rest can be left to the unconscious that will find the solution to deliver the ball in the net, no matter how good proves the goalkeeper, how high is the stake or Belen Rodriguez in the gallery who supports you showing off her little butterfly, or Brad Pitt shirtless in the gallery with a banner saying "I love you" (for those with different orientation).

Very well. Once you have defined what you want, express it in terms of results. Getting to gain more money is not a well formed goal and so is losing weight. How much money do you want to gain? I want the exact number! What is your ideal weight? I want the exact weight.

Then again, everyone knows that the goal has to be challenging, specific, measurable and absolutely under your control. If I wish to be invited by the President of the Republic at dinner at the Quirinale, I'm setting a goal for him, not for me. So I have to do something that relies completely on me.

Who does your goal depend on?

If it depends even just 0,1% on somebody else change it straight away, or transform like I do, putting in the magic words *"do all my best to"* before what I want. I want *to do all my best to* win the Strawberry Cup... I want to *do all my best to* date Belen... Or Brad... Or whoever you wish.

One day a girl, during a *course about goals*, asked me if it was right to have as a goal the relationship with a guy and asked me how to win his love. Well, «If you like him, do whatever you can to build a goal which achievement depends on you and not on him. You can do all you can to be yourself and to let him know you and who you are. Then it'll be up to the both of you to choose. Time will tell. Break a leg. Then, teaching to a woman how to seduce is like teaching to a cat how to climb» I answered while she was fluttering her eyelashes. Meow.

Anyway, it's not that easy building a *well formed goal*, because many athletes come to me because they want to win this or that competition. In those occasions I reply: «Hey you, do you know anyone who wants to lose?». A bit rude still effective. I mean, apart from those involved in the soccer-betting scandal, all the others usually dream of arriving 1st, so we're talking triviality.

Victory is never under our absolute control.

Everyone or almost everyone takes off willing to win, but then there's the opponent, the referee and an infinity of variables you have to cope with. The very word says it: the result is the result of the "summation" of the physical, training, tactical, mental preparation. And even if you give all yourself, sometimes it's not enough to win. There may be someone better than you on that day. In this event, if you've a built in the proper way your goal you'll manage to keep up and do your best until the end anyway. You'll feel bad but you won't feel depressed. Mental breakdown are born, in fact, out of confusion between an expectation and a goal. Like being on the wrong end of the stick.

Like Matteo Manassero - a great golf and mental maturity champion - says, what matters is focusing on the movement and on the spot you want to kick the ball. That's the only thing you're in control of, then "it's about trusting what the ball will do". Like saying "I trust what's going to happen but I focus on what comes before, on what really depends on me".

The goal is mine, it lies on a precise spot inside me and fighting for it makes me feel good. Expectations are some imaginary buildings that are inevitably compared to the reality and never corresponding. Mathematic. And out of this very mis-matching is born disappointment, because like Richard Bandler says, "disappointment requires preparation". You don't get disappointed if you don't do something first in order to be disappointed then. So you better build some well formed goals, you'll live better and people around you will live better too. Dealing with a sad, disappointed and angry athlete is a pain in the ass. Excuse me if I might sound rude but that's how it is. Meow.

It's time to get some cat food for our pussycat. What's written on the top? Besides the brand, somewhere up or down you'll find the *expiry date*. I say it again, date, not expiry span, like "best consumed by the end of the year, month, week…" In the end you need a date, or else the goal will move forwards as time passes by and you'll rot. As human beings we need a benchmark, so that our unconscious mind works to reach it even when we're doing something else. Because that's how it works and that's what we need.

To sum up, a *well formed goal* is:

- positive built;
- expressed in terms of results;
- specific, measurable, doable, motivating;
- dependent only on me;
- with an expiry date;
- written down.

I purr. Meow. Grrrr.

As for the staff, you can apply the same rules, because there are no motivated or demotivated people but only motivating or demotivating goals. So, what goals do you have for your *team of evolved people*? What do you really want? How will you realize that you achieved it? Make a note with words, if you want

MY STAFF'S GOAL:

Once you've established the well formed goal for you and your staff, now you only have to turn it into a question to build the action plan. The method is very simple, it's called brainstorming. Sit down comfortably and symmetrically, all you have to do is writing:

How can I do all I can to (add the well formed goal) *in a simple, easy and funny way* (add the way, that is how I want to achieve it) *by* (add the date)?

You need to give at least 20 answers to this question. Even though, personally, I say to my clients: «If you don't find at least 100 ways to achieve it, it means that it's not such a big goal for you or that you don't really care about achieving it». About the *goal brainstorming* I'm a fanatic like I am about the *feedback*. This is important. To get results you need to work hard and not just have fun. Besides the taxes in Italy, nothing comes out of nothing in the world.

Talking about it, I owe one of my best memories related to my activity as a trainer of goal setting in the sport to a beautiful very young athlete of Alex Senoner, another *number 1* and Golf Coach of the Italian Female National team, who I met at the San Domenico Golf. Alex invited me to teach a class to her guys of Golf Vicenza and among them there was her. After one month from the event, the great Alex texted me: "Angelica has won the Little lion today, important competition in Venice. She had written 100 things to do in order to win it!!!".

Meow bye woof woof.

18. MOMENTUM

> *Did your parents have any children that lived?*
> SERGENTE HARTMAN, Full Metal Jacket

Everyone knows that, to form a successful staff, it takes clear ideas, time and lots of energy to invest. But only a few know how to and most of all how to start and from where.

The first day together is fundamental. Once chosen the *Right Men* it's a matter of putting them together in order to make them a *team of evolved people*: out of your staff!

Well done, ready set go!

First of all you have to set the *X hour*, that is the beginning of your life together for something bigger than you, the reason why the staff has been formed, the dream that becomes a common goal. The *right men* are in fact together for a purpose, for a mission, for a vision and, if you've done things correctly, each one of them is already aware of it before starting to work together. Everyone will wait for the *X hour* with curiosity, impatience and emotion. For this reason I suggest you to be inventive about the *time* and the *place* of the first meeting, since you're lucky to have them all together. *Pick a symbolic, unusual and someway special environment*. Pick a supplo and special time, one they will retain. Nothing has to be accidental or, even worse, usual.

Let me better explain. All human beings who will become your *team of evolved people* will arrive at the *X hour* with their means, their clothes, their stories, their memories, their experiences, their habits, their beliefs, their identity, their life. The first day is useful to erase all of this. Yes, you got me right, I wrote erase all of this. The first message to convey strongly and clearly - unmistakably I would say - at the *X hour* is that here you start something new *all together at the same time*.

The past stays in the past. «Last year you won a price? Good, I'm glad for you, but if you're here to live of memories this is not the place to be. Last year you arrived last? Doesn't matter, now you have the chance to show what you're made of. Only the present counts, because our future depends on what we do in our present. We're here for this reason now. Our goal is... because...» and you can start explaining again and to everybody the *affirmation of leadership* that keeps the staff together.

Purpose, mission, vision and goals.

You must be asking yourself: «What? No cuddles and cupcakes on the first day? Doesn't it make them comfortable? Shouldn't we start little by little loving each other?».

Sure, if you want to go fast straight to the failure this might be a good system. Personally I prefer another one that according to my experience works better. It takes *rhythm, firmness* and *momentum*. You have to pull your heart out of your chest, throw it beyond the obstacle and then go and take it back. You have to set the example straight away and you have to show *the side to everyone in the right way*. If you leave people in their old environment you're doomed. To make room for the new you need to throw away the old. On the first day you have to take everyone out of their comfort zone without giving them the time to realize what's happening.

You have to gather momentum!

If you think about it, the process of building a new identity and a team spirit goes through the demolishing of the past, initially. You need to make room. Whether you want to become a fireman or a Marine like Piero Monestier, the treatment remains the same. On your first day of training you'll find a fool who will treat you very badly asking you where you come from. No matter what you'll answer, in that place they will all be bulls or puffs. You can bet on it! "I cannot see your horns, so you must be a puff!", like in An Officer and a Gentleman. And you cannot even reply or it would male things worse. Then they'll cut your hair, they'll give you a uniform you'll have to honour and love, they'll make you such nonsense things (loyalty is born out of it), they put you straight in line ("I cannot believe my eyes, where have you been so far? An orgy?"), they'll make you run and sing ("Surrender is not in our belief", so your brain will not think and in the meantime they install in you the mind they wish), they teach you a job (you'll acquire new skills), they'll train you to overcome obstacles (you'll be persuaded that you can make it), they'll convey values, you'll form in you a new identity and you'll experience the Corps Spirit you belong to.

In a month or two you'll be guilty or you'll contribute to some haze, like the ones you've been subjected to when you arrived, and that's the end of the game: *you are* a fireman or a *Marine* if you wish. And that crazy Sergeant will do his best, until the very last day, to put you to the test, to expose your limits, to make you give up. That fool keeps his selective promise "I count on losing half of you before the end". And this is another basic rule to form a team. If no one leaves, it means that you're going too slow to win or you're not building a team. People get together in difficulties and in passion, which comes from the pain and the sacrifice as well.

In the staff building the principle is the same. I'm not saying to welcome your *Right Men* like Sergeant Hartman from Full Metal Jacket would, screaming: "I will PT you all until you fucking die! I'll PT you until your assholes are sucking buttermilk". Ha ha ha, terrific! Or, asking to a private "How tall are you, private?", and he goes "Sir, five-foot-nine, sir" and you "I didn't know they stacked shit that high!" because you might end up alone, or even worse, killed by some "fat body".

What I'm telling you is to believe in the creative process by going yourself first, keeping an incredible pace, having them doing things they've never done before, having them playing together, putting them to the test, having them dancing and singing. I'm telling you to make a *big planned mess*. I'm asking you to assume in the communication what will be, like Gunny: "Today, you people are no longer maggots! Today, you are MARINES! I got your name I got your ass you will not laugh you will not lie you will learn by the number I will teach you now get up on your feet you had best unfuck your self or I will unscrew your head and shit down your neck".

I'm telling you to have fun, leave your mark and gather the momentum.

One of the best compliments I received after a team building was the one from "Ciro Esposito", nom de guerre of one of the great guys from the "Glass Style and Design" course in Certottica, who I've had the honour to initiate as a teacher, who told me:

«Coach, you didn't give us the time to hate each other and we've found ourselves being a team».

Fantastic! Thank you guys, the world needs your energy.

19. PRE-BONUS

> *Is there someone who wants to feel amazing*
> *for the rest of his/her life?*
> RICHARD BANDLER

The first commandment is always the same: start from the end and then go back. Go till the end and then start with two questions:

What feelings do I want to keep in my life?
What feelings do I want the others to have together with me?

Fear, disgust, rage, sadness, hatred? Or confidence, trust, peacefulness, participation, involvement, fun, wellness, love?

We learn by Woody Allen that:

"In my next life I want to live my life backwards. You start out dead and get that out of the way. Then you wake up in an old people's home feeling better every day. You get kicked out for being too healthy, go collect your pension, and then when you start work, you get a gold watch and a party on your first day. You work for 40 years until you're young enough to enjoy your retirement. You party, drink alcohol, and are generally promiscuous, then you are ready for high school. You then go to primary school, you become a kid, you play. You have no responsibilities, you become a baby until you are born. And then you spend your last 9 months floating in luxurious spa-like conditions with central heating and room service on tap, larger quarters every day and then Voila! You finish off as an orgasm!".

Genius! So, why waiting until tomorrow to reward with a *pre-bonus* your staff members to reach the results you wish? Do it right now, before they start working for you and with you. If you chose them then you better start showing you trust them with some facts.

How would you feel if on your first day at work you received a golden watch as a reward? Quite an interesting way to create an extremely strong positive association with the activity that will take a big part of your life, isn't it?

The secret of success is assuming things by creating the conditions so that things will really happen. Success, if you think about it, is making things happen, it comes from *succeed*.

How would you feel if your boss during your first meeting gave you a 20.000 Euros check and told you: «This is just a sample of what you'll get when we will accomplish the result». What would you do? I would dance on hot stones and would throw a bunga-bunga party, like Silvio Berlusconi teaches.

Think about it. How would you feel then? How motivated would you be? What would you give for your boss? What would you do to achieve that goal? How much determination will you use to stay inside such an environment?

It's a bit like at the restaurant: someone doesn't tip, someone only tips afterwards and someone tips beforehand. I always prefer who tips beforehand... (in every sense). In your opinion who will be treated better? How will you be welcomed next time in that restaurant? Which atmosphere will you find and most of all what impression of you will the other attendants have?

Basically, no matter how much, what's important is that you anticipate the sensations that come from the success you want to achieve. Such sensations will be the *nourishment* of all your future actions triggering a virtuous circle of wellness, commitment, longing to win. And big big enjoyment.

The more you enjoy yourself, the better.

STAFF BUILDING

20. EQUIPMENT

> *I've got three young kids: when I hope for them something really big,*
> *I wish them this:*
> *that their passion may become their life.*
> ALESSANDRO DEL PIERO

One day, a few years ago, while I was reading "Sport Week", I was impressed by the article dedicated to the official photographer of the Juventus Football Club.

This professional, since many years, has the privilege to take pictures of Juventus players when they wear for the first time their new jersey and he has collected an illuminating series of stories about it.

Working for the Juventus for many years, he has seen generations of soccer players passing by, from great champions to those who revealed themselves like walk-ons and they have been quickly given away somewhere else.

The interesting story for us is about Alessandro Del Piero and his attitude towards the uniform, an attitude that has to be considered like a *must*.

When he got to the Juventus acquired from the Padua for 5 billions Lire in 1993, Alessandro was a promising young kid with a great talent and clear ideas about who he wanted to become.

We might say that Del Piero already had the picture in his mind from the beginning, and starting from his final goal he has built his career in the Juventus from the very first day.

In such a lovely way the photographer tells that there are players who wear the Juventus jersey as if it were a simple T-shirt and after the picture they throw it on the chair as if it were a piece of cloth and then leave.

These ones will leave, in all senses. Usually these players don't go very far because they prove they haven't realized where they are and what is the way and the mentality to embrace in order to be successful in a great club.

What really stroke the photographer was the attitude of young Del Piero who, differently from the others, treated the Juventus jersey as a real cult-worthy object, as the beginning of his dream.

"His eyes sparkled and he started looking at it, to caress it, to holding it tight to his chest. After the picture he folded it up and put it carefully on a table. Inside me I said: this guy will go a long way" the photographer tells.

Said and done. This guy has simply become the Captain, the flag and the history of the Juventus keeping on showing the same love for the jersey since his first day.

The jersey in fact is a symbol, a word that comes from Greek and means literally "putting together".

For this reason it's essential to draw the uttermost importance on the creation of uniforms and when you deliver them to your staff and your team members, so to turn this moment into a real fidelity event.

Uniform creation is an artistic project that has as a goal the merging of past and future in the current interpretation of the values and the affirmation of leadership (mission, vision, goal) of the entity that the uniform wants to represent.

Such artistic creation has to be followed and matched with good care and emotional participation until its realization, aware that what is environment, like a simple jersey, is neurology 24/7, despite our will.

Wearing an uniform that is uncomfortable or ugly or unapt to the function it has been created for is like constantly living with a pebble in your shoe.

The look from outside of a uniform that is uncomfortable, ugly, unapt or, even worse, badly worn, arouses a negative perception as if it were the betrayal of what it represents. This bad feeling may determine an immediate loss of value and trust in your team with an awful impact on the achievement of the fixed goals.

Sometimes people forget that trust relies on the face and on a process that, however it develops, also depends on what you see and on what makes an impression. Like in a picture.

Just because we all know that an image is more worth it than a thousand words, when the uniforms have been created, you need to build an event around their delivery, privately and publicly.

Some consider this great opportunity as a predictable duty to leave to the warehousemen or to the logistic people, without giving the slightest ritual, this way losing a great occasion to take advantage of the sensations and the emotions of this magic moment in view of the result.

In my experience, the delivery of the uniforms is a strategic moment in the *team of evolved people* building and that is why it must not be left unexploited.

First thing, it's important that you create the right environment, an anticipation that is deep in meaning and an amazing sensation to link to the uniform, to who is going to wear it and to the project that we are going to share. This event is symbolic and as such it has to be built with clever verbal, para-verbal and non-verbal communication, by picking the *right jersey* for this initiation ceremony.

Only afterwards the staff or team members will be able to go and take the rest of the equipment somewhere, following a ritual this time too, linked to the ceremony.

Another usual bad mistake you have to avoid consists in the diversity in treatment provided to different staff or team members in relation to the importance of their contract.

To build a successful staff you need to make sure that every collaborator, no matter his/her role and his/her wage, might have the same possibilities of feeling his/her uniform and experience it with great pride, feeling as a fundamental part of the project.

The commandment is always the same: start from the end to appraise each resource providing them with the best treatment ever.

No one better than the champion Alessandro Del Piero can have the last word on this story. With the Juventus 18 awards, 4 times top-goalscorer in league A, 289 goals, 704 participations, 48.365 playing minutes. On his last day as Juventus captain on his official website appears a championship and inside it "09/12/1993 - 05/20/2012; One Love; and his stylized face becomes a logo".

One logo, one thought, that I dedicate to you with my heart.

ALESSANDRO DEL PIERO'S LETTER

"It ends here, my contract with the Juventus expires today. It's no news, though knowing that it's 'official' impresses me anyway. To me it's not a sad moment, no regrets nor homesickness. Not anymore. Because in these days I've had the chance to rethink about all that has happened during my last season in this team, then from there going back, and revive the best dream I could have ever dreamt of. All the memories, all the joys, all the triumphs and - frankly - some bitterness too... today all these images are in front of me and at a certain point they blur and they fade in that beautiful embrace of my last match in Turin. That's the picture that says it all, the still that I always want to bring with me, the picture of May 13th stays in my heart. Unforgettable. Some time ago, before leaving for the holidays, I emptied my lock in Vinovo and, while I was leaving, I stopped where for many months you have been waiting for me to take a picture, to have an autograph, to say hello... in the snow, in the ice, in the rain, in the sun. But this time I did want to say bye and thank you, as you did with me. Players come and go, the Juventus remains. My companions remain, to whom I wish all the best: I will always root for them. Most of all you supporters remain, you are the Juventus. That jersey that I loved and will always love remains, that t-shirt I craved and respected, no waiving and no discounts. I'm glad that others after me will wear it, especially the number '10' which, since they put names on the jersey, has always had mine. I'm glad for who's going to wear it next year, I'm glad that somewhere - in Italy or in the world - someone is dreaming of wearing it. And I'd be proud that this guy wished to retrace my story, like I did with other champions, other examples, other legends. From tomorrow I will not be a Juventus player, but I will always be one of you. Now another venture starts. And I'm excited like 19 summers ago. Good bye, guys. Thanks for everything".

Alessandro

21. ANCHORS

> *We're animals sensitive to odours,*
> *we're human beings*
> *looking for love.*
> GIORGIA, Tu mi porti su

Enjoy, in advance!

This chapter is about underwear and will be slightly edgy. If you don't think you'll be able to stomach it, I suggest you move onto the next chapter. I won't be upset, nor take it personally, promise! That's not my style. Skip forward, if you like, but if you really decide to read it, you can't say I didn't warn you.

This is a novel from a male perspective, but I am sure women will not be taken in by appearances and understand the sense of what I have in here (in my underpants), as Laura Pausini sings. For us men, instead, it will be like playing home and going back to the roots.

Let's start by some outing...
There was a time in my life, while playing volleyball in Belluno, when for comradeship and typically male ignorance, I superstitiously wore my "winning underpants", the ones that made me triumph on the court. It was not about the model but about the underpants themselves, that I never took to the laundry not to run the risk to lose that halo of magic. As you can understand, achieving a winning series had a very high price to pay, because at the seventh win in a row my underpants played by themselves, setting and smashing the ball. Once I also heard them call the plays and high-five with my other mates' underpants, as they were also involved in this funny habit.

The ritual we followed went like this: once the match was over, sweating and smelling like gladiators in an arena at the end of a fight, before having a shower we would put away "the nuclear underweapons" in little plastic sealed bags, to take them back out the next week, short before getting in the court while shouting "never change winning underpants". I can understand it if you feel disgusted, but let he who is without sin, CAST the FIRST UNDERPANTS.

In this tribal ritual anything could happen and you can understand why. In the locker room, a sacred place for athletes, *I've seen things you people wouldn't believe...*

I have seen a mate, at the end of a match, sniff his underpants at the top of his lungs yelling: «This is the smell of success!» and then naked pursue us to let us sniff them too. Ideal profile of the door-to-door salesman.

I saw another evil genius talking to his family jewels before the game, trying to convince them desperately to accept close contact for the sixth time with the same filthy underpants. «C'mon Guys, please, don't be such bollocks just now! (Guys were his "bollocks", which he was talking to, looking them right in the eyes). Prick, c'mon, we're playing the championship! (Prick was not a vulgar verbal tic, but his "thing", which he was flapping around in the act of persuasion to enter the filthy underpants). C'mon Guys, Prick! (talking exasperatedly to the entire package), I assure you that there's no danger of infections or diseases. In just a couple of hours it will all end, we'll score 3:0 quickly with these nerds, then we'll take a shower together (as if usually he detached them to wash them separately) and tonight I'll take you to our girlfriend to have fun! Ok? (waiting for an answer from his lower parts, which was never to come). Prick, guys, what a thing! (this time looking at us, all smoked up. Nice! What a consideration! He referred to us as his reproductive system)». Today, for the record, he is a successful lawyer. I dare not imagine how he enters the courtroom.

Then I saw another crazy idiot arrive to the locker room in desperation, saying «Guys, tonight we have to lose or I'll be looking at divorce» - and us: «Why?» - and he: «My wife got pissed off because of the whole underpants story» - and us: «You didn't have to tell her, right? It was our secret, you idiot!» – and he: «I didn't tell her, she found them by herself when she smelled something stinking...» – and us: «Well, where did you put them?» – and he: «In the living room, behind the CDs... (what an idiot!) Yesterday evening, while we were watching TV on the couch, she said to me: *Honey, can you smell that? There has to be a dead rat here somewhere...*» – and us «There's a dead rat in your brains, there is!» – and all together we began to scan «I-DI-OT! Fortunately you play on the other side, you just have to shoot heavily, without thinking! You stupid idiot!» Ha-ha-ha. What laughs in the locker room!

Then, when I entered Gianni Caprara's staff, I discovered that the whole world is a village, or better still, an underwear. This lovely northern superstition was practiced also in Southern Italy by that ignoramus Carmelo Borruto, Gianni's legendary "calafrican" scout-man, who kept for months the "winning underpants", waiting to take them off in a knock-out game which would be suitable for the title. On one occasion I was sitting next to him and I assure you that the atmosphere was terribly heavy. No air! Other than dead rats!

With Sirio Pallavolo Perugia as well, we enjoyed the "Underpants Games", exhibiting our underwear to female players in a memorable show during the technical meeting before the semi-final of the Champions League. Good times. Maybe that's why none of us from the staff finished the season... In fact, it was all studied (as always when working with Caprara) to give *balance* to the team, releasing nervous tension. If there is too much of it, you play badly, if too little, you play badly. The right tension is needed, and search for it is not for everyone. The task of the *team of evolved people* is to give emotional balance to the team. Even with underpants. That year we won nothing, but we tried them all and we had a lot of fun. It was an unforgettable year.

Regarding memorable experiences and anchors, the story of "Wild Pant" I'm going to tell you now, is sensational. The protagonist is a very sensual woman, later nicknamed "Wild Pant" for the merit acquired in the field, pardon in the bed. This lovely woman knew a lot about how to make her man go crazy. Not knowing how to read or write, this innocent creature of the opposite sex who wouldn't certainly have eaten the apple instead of Eve, used to hide the perfumed underwear she was wearing while making love with her male, in the pockets of his clothes or in the briefcase or in the dashboard of this guy's car. Being him a representative of trade and not seeing him for days, she wanted to make sure that he always thought of her in every single moment. A fully achieved result: he resigned after a month of such treatment, and they got married in Las Vegas next month.

What "Wild Pant" knew was the power of anchors, or what blocks or recalls the boat (or the lover) in a certain condition. In my work an *anchor* is defined as a *neuro-association acquired stimulus-response*. Pavlov's dogs, when they heard the bells, began to slaver even when there wasn't food. The former trade manager, when he saw and felt the smell of the pants of his lover, turned the car and went back to her, absorbed in those sublime moments of pleasure.

"Wild Pant" also knew that smells go directly to the *reptilian brain* and therefore are powerful. She didn't need to read "In Search of Lost Time" of Proust to know the history of the Madeleine, whose scent brought *involuntarily* the protagonist back in time. In Japan, in the nearby to the distributor of used condoms (joke), there are the distributors of pants worn by young girls in the days of ovulation (now I'm serious). It seems the old men of the Rising Sun go mad for these fetish ladies wear and that this business is flourishing. The thing to remember about the *anchors* by the way, is that is that they are *unconsciously* created and established, against my will or that of someone else's, with my awareness or that of someone else's.

In fact, the brain has a code for everything, to recognise/re-experience pleasure and to recognize/avoid pain. This is the reason why our favourite T-shirt brings back the feelings we experienced wearing it, our favourite song reminds us of that magical romantic moment of our sentimental life and certain scents bring back our youth. All of this cannot be helped because it is a conditioned reflex at a deep level, as "Wild Pant" teaches.

Now, when you see, sniff, wear your "Wild Pants" please don't think of me whilst laughing!

262 STAFF BUILDING

22. ALARM CLOCK

> *What really matters is your heart and your brain.*
> *Your ass will fall apart sooner or later.*
> EMMA

Everyone knows that in order to succeed, and by that I mean being able to make things happen, one of the most important secrets is to *live in the present.*

All the great champions in the sport have the talent to focus only on what they're doing, trying not to think about the consequences of a victory or of a failure.

What makes the great champion Valentino Rossi different from the others, for example, besides his talent of pushing his motorbike to the limit during the competition, is his ability to live in the present. His strategy is pretty simple and you can sum it up like this: when I get my motorbike ready I make my motorbike ready, when I do my last curve I do my last curve, when I celebrate I celebrate.

Developing this habit of being there to fully live what you're living is the real plus and it's something that you need to build as soon as possible. Sometimes it happens that, no matter your commitment or your will, sometimes life hits us on the head and we find ourselves involved in some painful situations that we're forced to accept because they're part of our life, like being old, being sick or dying.

Joy and pain together is what makes life beautiful, just like its predictability and the sense of wonder that children experience. The better we become at enjoying our present and to cope with disappointments, failures and losses, the better we will feel and play the best game possible with what we have to offer.

If at work we have a hard time and we bring such hard time at home, then we have two hard times, one at work and one at home. If one day is made of 24 hours and we spend all of them being sad, we won't have much time to be happy.

In some cultures, like the Italian one - especially in the South , if a woman is made a widow, they usually proclaim explicitly a mourning time. During this time the widow, out of respect for who's not anymore and out of her own reputation, will stay at home, will wear black dresses, she will focus exclusively on her family and the religious cult of her deceased husband and she will avoid inconvenient behaviours. After this term, the widow will be able to start to get a new life in the same community she belongs to. If you think about it, it's genius.

Let's go beyond the mourning and let's embrace the bigger picture: there's nothing worse than longing to be happy when you're sad. It really doesn't work. It's much better deciding consciously to be really sad for a definite time and then setting an alarm clock, something that will remind unequivocally to our brain that something is over and something else is about to start.

That's what Emma did. After a moment of immense pain she turned the loss of her boyfriend (stolen by Belen Rodriguez) into a switch-point in her career. I agree on everything she said, but I'll give Belen this: until it won't fall apart, her ass is *a lot of stuff*.

From love to soccer, if we're nervous for the rest of the day when our team loses maybe we better change team or decide to be really untouchable for 10 minutes, until the alarm clock that we set tells us to stop. Maybe we could set some regenerating music as ring-tone and we may share with all the others our *alarm clock's strategy*, so we avoid them making fun of us.

To make the *alarm clock method* work better, the trick is to chose an unusual, special and extraordinary signal, that is something different from the one our brain considers ordinary.

Let me put this simply. If we usually open and close a door when we go from one room to another, opening and closing the door won't be an appropriate signal to convey to our neurology that we want to get rid of a certain state of mind in the first room and experience a different one in the second. That's why we should do something different, maybe opening and closing twice the door and in a certain way, so to convey the end of something and the beginning of another.

With your flowers at my door
With your face
I'm pretty sure you cheated on me
Or you'll do it tomorrow

Because I know that the poetry
You don't read it and you don't write it
Nevertheless the tenderness
You don't want it,
You don't give it!

Drin Drin Drin
like an alarm in my head
Drin Drin Drin
I don't know whether to love you or to throw you away.

RAFFAELLA CARRA, Drin Drin

23. SCHEME'S INTERRUPTION

> *The way of thinking that creates a problem cannot solve it.*
> ALBERT EINSTEIN

Scheme's interruptions are one of the funniest part of my work as a Coach and I'm sure that they will become one of the funniest part of yours too. Personally I use them each time I need to interrupt something that doesn't work to turn it into something that really works.

With great simplicity we may consider scheme's interruptions as what separates the kid from the dirty water, to avoid throwing them both away if we have little time and we're in a complex situation. Scheme's interruptions, and by scheme I mean something that repeats itself as it is, are an effective *tool*, because you can use it whenever you need a change of directions or state of mind.

This change might be small or big, but the principle is the same: to go from "negative" to "positive" you need an intermediate passage, a return (of a certain kind) to the "neutral".

Scheme's interruptions are useful to quickly clear, purify and renovate a person's neurology, preparing it to go towards a new direction in a new and better state of mind. In fact, many people tend to forget this intermediate passage and pretend to change a person's or a team's direction or state of mind without a certain solution of continuity.

If you don't care about a passage in the neutral, you waste your time.

For example, taking for granted the principle that when we're very angry we do not make good decisions, if a person gets furious in his body some chemicals start flowing, which were not there before and which change his state of mind from the inside. For awhile.

These chemicals won't go away very soon, they stay in circle and it takes awhile before they naturally flow away. The fact is that in most cases we don't have enough time to wait for it to happen naturally. That is why we need something to accelerate the whole process, we need a *reset* button, which once you push it suddenly allows us to start anew in the right way.

This reset button is the scheme's interruption and when you do it well it has another function too: creating in that person the first big obstacle to the comeback, that is to the negative state.

The destruction of the ships by Hernan Cortés was one of the most sumptuous and effective scheme's interruptions in history and an extraordinary example of an apparently crazy strategy, but actually it was extremely effective, because it aimed to eliminate the option of the comeback.

Once they landed in Mexico in 1519 the Spanish soldiers were tired, starving and scared, because they didn't know what to expect: basically they longed to go back home. "Why the hell did I do this for? Why am I here with this imbecile? I just want to go back home!", this must have been everyone's mantra.

As that imbecile, Cortés, had sensed, these were not the best psychological conditions for the conquest of an empire. He needed a twist, which he created in a wonderful way. He let everything and everyone disembark and then he burnt the ships, yes he burnt his ships, giving a double signal: you won't go back (to his men) and whatever you do we're here to stay (to Montezuma).

Guess how they felt, those poor soldiers when they saw the fire and the flames destroying the only means they had to go back home...

The result was incredible: in the blink of an eye Cortés' troops wreaked the Aztecs gaining the right to finally go back home victorious, with new ships. In this story it doesn't matter that Cortés represented the image of the divinity for the locals and that, as a consequence, when they saw him they gave up almost with no restraints at all thinking that it was their god who got down on earth. That imbecile, Cortés, and his soldiers learned this only afterwards, because when they landed they pooped their pants too.

Now, what really matters to me is to convey the power of all this, because you will hardly have ships to burn. So you'll have to make up some other ideas to blow away, together with the scheme, the states of mind that are not effective and the mental obstacles that prevent the realization of a project.

Human beings tend to experience a sense of confidence when they repeat their behaviours turning them into habits. Of course you have good and bad habits. It goes without saying that you need to interrupt the bad habits, building a new direction for our thoughts and for our neuronal paths through the positive emotions that we're longing to experience. Away with the old and welcome the new. About the good habits, instead, you have to experience them always in a different way or, however, always consciously, or else you'll get tired even of eating gourmet and of making love with Marilyn Monroe.

When you change a habit it's like throwing away the old glasses that you used to wear to look at the world. If you're used to look through orange spectacles, then your world will be orange and maybe you'll have an orange juice, you'll go to bed with the jersey from the Dutch Cruyff. This might be a good and/or a bad thing. It may save you and/or it may condemn you, preventing your from opening you *heart and soul* to the new.

Like *the Marine* says: «Every success has a price to pay and every failure has something positive». The great skill is to recognize what's good and what's bad without being a victim of your own dullness and mental obstacles.

Interrupting a scheme that is not so effective is good to empty the basket in a safe way making room for new Apps that are funny and most of all useful to your current life. What has been a resource in the past it's not said that it is in the present.

"We've always done it like this" is the best way to bring books to the court.

EXAMPLES OF SCHEME'S INTERRUPTIONS

In early 2012 I was working with the Italian Female National Golf team in San Domenico Golf in the Puglia region. Wonderful place. One day we were at the hole number 9 and I was lying on the grass pretending of being absorbed in my thoughts, the female training staff was discussing about how to help an athlete who looked always sad, sombre and demotivated. Like sharks, they were approaching me, turning around me. I could even hear the soundtrack from "Jaws" behind their conversation and I was taking notes on my iPhone 4s because they would have soon attacked. At a certain point they're on me: «Coach, what do we do with this girl?» the chief trainer asks.

To draw attention and to take more time before answering, I keep lying, keeping my cool. After one second the director Anna Roscio hits me with her gaze, like saying "get up and do your job! What do you think we pay you for?". Unforgettable, great Anna!

«Well» I say smiling, still lying for a few moments. When no one can take my attitude any longer I get up and finish my sentence, because I'm in danger of being beaten the shit out of me: «If she were a client of mine, the first thing I would do is to break, forever, that broken record running in her head!» and while I start talking I put up another show. After each sentence I take my clothes off. It was very windy, so everyone is shocked. "This Coach is bonkers…" I can read on their faces. I'm about to be fired, but how can I remind them what's a scheme's interruption if I don't even know how to break a scheme? So I trust my instinct and keep on with my speech along with the strip-tease.

«I take a record in my hands and I break it like this!» throwing on the floor my jacket and jumping on it with my feet. Everyone is outraged. «Of course, make sure beforehand that the girl wants to be helped» I say to the chief trainer. «Tell her: hey (name) I can help you. But do you really want my help? If she says yes it's done, because you're allowed to do to her what you wish. First of all you need to change her physiology! You need to take her by her arms, lift them up, move her, push her, touch her» and while I talk I do all these things to the great boss who's embarrassed at first and then starts laughing. «As the girl starts laughing, like you do, boss, it's working. The old neuronal paths have been overcome and you can build a new one» I say almost bare chest. I wasn't even finished that the great Roberto Zappa, chief trainer of the female national team and smashing golf sportscaster at Sky, starts running while screaming «I'm going! I got it, see you later!». Mad.

Everyone bursts out laughing, but I'm a bit worried. «Boss, hang on, there's a second part: what to do after the scheme's interruption...» I shout at him while he's running away, but he's gone. I see him one hour later in the dining room where I see a wonderful scheme's interruption by the chief trainer in the buffet area, while all the staff and all the girls are speechless. A little more and instead of changing her physiology he would have smashed her straight on the buffet table. As if this were not enough he snatches her full dish willing to pour it down on her. Terrific! Magic moments! Bob Zappa *number 1*!

Another interesting and effective way of drawing the attention is with a question absolutely out of context. This way you take the focus far from the critical situation and with it you change the sensations, the breath and the posture that are linked to it. So everything changes.

The expertise at this is Frank Farrelly, author of the book "The provocative therapy", who with irony, paradox, humour and hardcore provocations used to heal people's minds. Such a genius. Like he used to say, "a small element to prompt a big change". The *provocative therapy* was born in 1963 from a moment of discomfort. Farrelly had arrived to the ninety-first session with a schizophrenic patient who had been hospitalized for a long time, and he had no intention to heal.

Furthermore, the patient was regressing, as you say in psychiatry. Then Farrelly burst: "If you go on like this I'll have to feed you with newborn's food. Then you'll lose control: you'll pee your pants and I'll have to change your diapers. And since you have such a big ass it's going to take double sheets. You'll be in the history of medicine as the first newborn with pubes". The patient blushed at first, then burst into laughing and from that moment he started cooperating. In just six sessions he was released from the hospital.

That's how the "provocative therapy" is born, as a way of letting the patients see their image, their world and the people they care about in a strange, unpredictable, unseen, new way, from which a new possibility of representing themselves and of being is born, for the present and for the future. With the provocative therapy you let the troubled person experiment other parts of him/herself, compared to those he/she usually identify him/herself and which are responsible for the problem.

Farrelly's questions are the very milestone of the scheme's interruptions and my favourite questions are freely inspired by him, my spiritual guide when I need to scramble someone to bring him/her back on the right track.

About this, once I got myself in a real danger. But I had to do something, and like you say in the volleyball, if you have to make a mistake, make it big, it's always worth one point. And that's what I did.

We were in my study in Belluno and I was having a session with a very beautiful, elegant and modest woman.

I couldn't take it anymore listening to her sagging about her problems at work, so I suddenly got up and I asked her the following question:

«Excuse me (name), excuse me if I interrupt you *right now*, but while I was listening to you I was wondering something very important...» I said to her and then a long pause followed, creating such a strong anticipation for what I was about to say.
«Do you get pleasure more from the up or the down part? I mean, the cucumber, the baguette, the rocket, how do you like having it?». The sudden move of the focus; the shock for a question that is so out of context; the violation of a formal code between us; the descriptive and emblematic gesture I used to explain the words cucumber, baguette, rocket; the tone I had used, at first serious and then playful; and the laugh that luckily followed have produced the effect I wanted: this allowed me to direct her towards the solution to her problems.

In a different state you see things differently.

«Well, now we can look ahead! Feel free to laugh out loud... you like cucumber don't you? I'm here for you... I'm here to help you solving your ex problems at work... my cucumber your cucumber!» ha ha ha, how she laughed! She couldn't stop it and from that moment we adjusted the problem in a couple of sessions.

Now, the bolder you are the better it works, but keep in mind that you need a communicative bridge that is always alive with that person and you need to have the quick skill of managing the scheme's interruption you created with the most appropriate state of mind.

If you don't, you might get a comeback scheme's interruption, like 5 fingers on your face, it may be pretty strong too. If they sense what you did as something that is not professional but rude, offensive, senseless and out of place, it's going to be a mess.

Anyway no fears, they'll fire you at most.

24. QUESTIONS

Leave appearances, take senses.
LAURA PAUSINI, Vivimi

On 15th June 2012, the day of my "27th" birthday, I received this message from *my angel* on Earth: «Another year has gone... we met each other eleven years ago and it's almost eleven years since we last met... But the thought is stronger... happy birthday... a great hug. Lift up your heart ».

Eleven years ago I was a kid in his career that he dreamed of becoming the new Julio Velasco. Volleyball was everything to me and so I found myself in Padua to take the license of First Instance. The training ended with a 3-day intensive retreat on the Asiago plateau, which would be followed by the written and oral examinations. I was also with a girl, but things were not going so well, in fact. My focus was all about volleyball.

As a player I was not bad. The nice thing about these coaches courses is that you can know a lot of passionate people like you, staying in the world you love 24 hours a day. You always exude volleyball. I chose Padua because the boss was a great coach, one who had real results and demanded a lot during his course. He rejected 30% of the members and if you missed a few lessons you were out. The right guy for me.

In my town of Belluno we have had for years the league and as a child I grew up in contact with the samples of that time. A unique era, socially and sportingly. No Facebook, no Twitter, no Smartphone. Volleyball was our chance to go out and explore the world. When I became adult, unfortunately, there was only the memory of the glorious decades of Volleyball Belluno of which I was part in the junior team. Those who wanted to form was bound to tour Italy. The beautiful thing was that we, people from Belluno, had something more, a wealth of unique emotions within us: we had volleyball in the blood.

In Asiago we practically lived in an army training camp. The alarm was set at 6:00 am. Then breakfast, classroom theory, physical fitness test, basic lunch. In the afternoon, still theory and then practice until late at night. Beautiful! We had a gym and 4 carts full of balloons at our disposal.

At the end of the first day I began to feel observed. There was a tosser that looked at me with a strange expression. Actually, on second thought, She set next to me twice in the classrooms in Padua and, of all the students of the course, she had tried in vain to talk to me and find out something about me. At that time I was a lone wolf and I paid heed to anyone.

I definitely noticed Her the second day, at lunch. As a good mountain wolf I took a table for 4 people and I occupied the other 3 seats with my jacket, pouch and bag, in order to be sure to eat alone. I was only there for volleyball, no distraction was allowed. But fate had other plans for me. And as often happens, you find your destiny on the road you took to avoid it.

With the class of a goddess, a little mother a little bitch like the Madonna by Edvard Munch, that wonderful creature came towards me through the whole room. She weaved through the tables with the elegance of Debora Compagnoni and she told me: «Alessandro, do you mind if I sit next to you?».

It took a while for me to find the words, since I was enchanted by Her. «No, please be seated. Seriously, I'm glad» I said with a trembling voice starting to chew broth. Then, to give me an attitude and be nice, I added: «I always put things on the chairs right to invite others to sit with me ...» and at that point I made a huge mistake: I looked at her smile.

There are days when the sun rises twice.

I had the pulse to 100,000 beats per minute, and as if that was not enough, after a moment also the boss came to sit with us: «This is free, right?» he said shifting my pouch at the center of the table and he sat down between us humming ".. what fault I have if the heart is a gipsy and it goes...".

Perfect. The boss was trying to be funny singing Nicola di Bari... that's all we needed! My face became a rainbow of colors and my body temperature reached 100 degrees. She was his favorite pupil and he knew she was officially engaged. He didn't know much about me instead, he only knew I came from outside, I was good at playing and I was so stunned I haven't noticed anything. Normal he wanted to see with his own eyes what was going on. A coach loves his athletes and is always ready to protect them and to help them. Just think she was his alter ego on the field.

Yes, I do a little outing which is always good! Until that moment I hadn't noticed her looks, her care, her movements towards me. I hadn't noticed a thing. But from that moment on, I couldn't stop looking at her. Lost, gone, full.

As definition, a setter in volleyball has very beautiful hands, head and personality. She's a woman used to choose and to have the courage of her choices. She's a person who thinks the game early and reads the game between the lines. In short, an explosive cocktail of skills, seduction and charm.

In the afternoon we worked in the gym on the patterns of attack. I was in great shape. I used to play every ball she gave me for how hard I hit it. I sent it at the bottom of the field near the row or in the three meters with the typical male exultation. My testosterone was a bit high, I confess. Ignorance had taken advantage on my clearness.

After the attack it was the game. Everyone in the field, two teams, talent scouts were expected at the match. And the boss, for us not to miss anything, put us together in the team. I was playing opposite Her, as a pure spiker. I think I scored all the possible points. I was simply unstoppable: every ball I touched it turned into a point. There was a special feeling. Every moment, every action, every point, it was an opportunity to exchange magical glances and touches, to the extent of the physical contact allowed by volley.

The phase of the game I loved was the 6th. In the 6th phase, the opposite comes up to the net in the 3rd position and the setter penetrates from behind him, very close. In this way there are three attack solutions from the first line, plus a combination in the second line from the center of the field. I loved how she whispered in my ear the attack combination we would performed and how she passed her hand on my back, making me shiver at the same time. She, black belt of seduction. I, entirely in her hands.

I only prayed not to make rotations. In fact, it emerged that phase of the game was statistically the worst of our team, for some reason… She never gave me the ball, to keep me there and make me go mad. I would have still wrong, and sometimes I even forgot to go to the net to defend, in order to extend that pleasure. For three hours we left the human time and space to enter into Pandora, but without Avatar. We were in the flesh to fly over the field, hand in hand.

It was a great party, even sportingly, because we won all sets. At the end of the match, people came to congratulate me for my performance. It was like being again a little boy. I felt a young cock. After singing and teasing in the shower, we had dinner together. This time the boss had prepared a single table to make the team seat together. I sat far from her not to attract attention (what a dreamer!) but we didn't stop looking to each other. After dinner there was an outing in the country all together. We were the only two who didn't went out. "We didn't feel well", this was the official excuse.

We found ourselves in the hotel garden without knowing what the other would have do. We just hoped. We knew within us. We talked till late at night, telling us our lives and discovering to be both "engaged". The quotation marks refer to me.

Towards 1 am we greeted each other, with a little cleverly hidden inside sadness, whishing each other goodnight. «Ale, get over it. She's happily engaged and so you are, though unhappily. Go to sleep, tomorrow is another day, think about the coaching license. You are just volley-friends» I said to myself.

But fate had another surprise. I walked into the lobby and, avoiding the elevator, I climbed the stairs in the dark. I didn't even turned on the light, I was so absorbed in my thoughts that I wanted to just lie in bed crying and I didn't notice I was followed by Her. There were still a few steps, I had it almost done, I was almost totally safe or damned. Four more steps and I would have closed myself in a world of sad loneliness. But... in the silence of the night, I heard her soft voice behind me ask me that question:

«But... what are *we* starting?».

Well, this is a good question! Now, that's a good question! To answer a question like that you must first accept the assumption contained in it: *us*. So I did, and inevitably (caddi come corpo morto cade - Dante) "I fell as a dead body falls" into her arms.

In every training course they teach that *those who question order*. The questioner keeps for himself the power to gather information, to study and to guide people. Then, when you can assume the same question in the world that will be defined at the time thanks to it, the world we're already thinking about taking it for sure, then you can turn any dream into reality. It's like jumping into another dimension materializing thoughts and desires. An irreversible dimension, from which you will never go back, and that you can only live with a new awareness. Magic of communication. Magic of Her.

In every team you can increase your success transforming in good questions the way you are, your beliefs, your ideas, assuming everything in them. With this method you can meet other people and at the same time guiding them toward what you want, making them fall "as a dead body falls" into your arms.

As time passed I realized that she was *an angel came from Heaven* to save me from an unhappy life full of fears: that question changed my attitude towards life.

Thank you again my angel and *lift up your heart, always.*

SECTION IV

3 EXPERIENCES IN STAFF

What happens in your garden, it happens inside you.

DINO BUZZATI

25. COMPANY: CERTOTTICA

*For Attractive lips, speak words of kindness.
For lovely eyes, seek out the good in people.
For a slim figure, share your food with the hungry.
For beautiful hair,
let a child run their fingers through it once a day.
For poise, walk with the knowledge that you never walk alone.
People, more than things, have to be restored, renewed, revived,
reclaimed, and redeemed. Remember, if you ever need a helping
hand, you will find one at the end of each of your arms.
As you grow older, you will discover that you have two hands,
one for helping yourself and the other for helping others.*
AUDRY HEPBURN

"Salami and chicory for me too, thanks".

It happened to me... to be welcomed as a friend, to receive a sweet invitation to lunch, to browse through the production lines seeing a jewel arising from raw, to nibble a small red apple with white flesh and eat a pizza *all together at the same time.*

*

In Certottica I have always felt at home. I've never had the need to bring with me my favorite cookies or hang my bathrobe in the bathroom, as the legendary Pat Riley made his Los Angeles Lakers players do in a year in which the team was unable to express itself as he wished.

From the first day I've always find freshly baked muffins, of which I felt the scent even before entering, and a blue fresh bathrobe in the toilet, with my name's initials embroidered in yellow. Blue and yellow are the colors of the two cities in which I live: Belluno and Modena.

They all welcomed me as if I've always been one of them, explaining me the house's rules and what could be my contribution to make it even more safe, comfortable and beautiful. I found kindness, manners, respect, determination, competence, leadership, involvement, passion, and I hope I've brought the same.

I learned that with time human beings have a tendency to build priorities based on their own experiences of working and living. There are some most important components because they're first and allow the understanding of what comes next. As a Coach, the *atmosphere* is the first thing I pay attention to when I go into a new environment, because from its quality I infer the quality of the leader. To me "shit environment is equal to shit leader". That's it. The fish always stinks from the head. So when I find an immersive, exciting and challenging environment that exudes pure energy, then I know there's a great leader in action. My desire is to know him and work with him.

It went like this in Certottica with Piero, chat after chat, course after course, muffin after muffin. They tested me and accompanied me, and so I grew. I did all my best, listening and asking everyone for help. This is my way of working in staff.

Over time I realized you need two things in order to grow: *trust* and *help*. To trust others you first need to trust yourself and only asking for help you can receive it. It's impossible to help a person who doesn't want it. The act of asking for help is what opens our senses and our door to another world. It took me a while to understand it, but better late than never.

One of the most complex, challenging and fun experience I lived working within the training staff in Certottica concerns a successful northern-eastern Italian firm, 2MDecori SpA, which designs and manufactures custom metal components for customers all over the world.

At the end of the spring in 2012, *the Marine* tells me that there is a job for me: «but take it easy, boy!». Knowing my *improntitude* is the least to say. So we fix a design meeting of our training session with the head of the company at their home, the industrial area of Segusino in Treviso province. We are three under Piero's supervision: the project tutor Dr Martina Armellin, Dr. Paolo Latini professor of marketing, product placement, creative writing and me Coach Alessandro Vianello, team building and strategic communications.

Martina and I travel together on her mother's new white Fiat 500 and I seem to go back in time when I was touring with the old white Fiat 500 of my mother. The name, the color and the form remain pretty the same; inside and outside everything's changed. With the old 500 in order to downshift you had to do the double, that is, put in neutral, accelerate to keep revved the engine, and then enter the lowest gear. If you passed directly from third to second you caused monstrous scraping and the gear didn't enter. So it was the perfect car to learn to drive or make some poor figures just as monstrous. Small, easy to operate; glued to the road, rear-wheel go cart style drive; you could do whatever you wanted, but you had to know how to change the gear.

My father, former rally driver, had found a way of processing it occasionally inserting some crude mothballs into the air filter's sump. These, being an aromatic hydrocarbon obtained from oil distillation, increased the octane number of the gasoline in the combustion chamber of the engine, giving an extra power. Unfortunately, when we alighted from that fireball, we seemed straight out of those old moth-proofing wardrobes. Smelly but fast, crazy how it run. I remember that on the highway the needle of the speedometer came out of the half-moon to move on the I of OIL just below. The speedometer stopped to 120 Km/h, so we practically did 130 Km/h and we did not need to change gear on an uphill path. Our fun was overcome everyone leaving them breathless with a trail of mothballs. We went as spies.

*Has it ever happened to you to feel like you're somewhere else
with your feet firm on the ground
your soul weightless going
going far and further away
where fantasy
has no longer any limits
you have a new world to create
you are so elsewhere
that you can't even go back
but you don't care
because it's nice staying
at the places and time
in which you had found your wings, dreams and heart
it happened to me
and now I can travel*

NEGRAMARO, *Has it ever happened to you*? (Ti è mai successo?)

It often happened to me to feel like I'm elsewhere. The images of the details remain impressed to me: how a person walks up the stairs, how a person leans his/her hands on the wheel, how a person searches for things in his/her bag, how a person sits, how a person greets.

I think you are in life just as you are on the field.

My uncle drove the car exactly in the same way he prepared the fruit salad: cut into large pieces and often left the peel. He went on. He could do a thousand miles without stopping, without paying attention to the engine speed, the curves, to what it was all about. He went on.

Needless to say during that trip with Martina, five hundred things came to my mind. Every now and then I became myself again and tried to gather as much information as possible about the company where I would worked in order to get prepared to the meeting. But only occasionally.

The nice thing about clowns is that when I'm with them I can just *be.* Sometimes I fall asleep and they let me sleep. No one wants something from me. If you're hungry you eat, if you're tired you sleep, if you are sad you cry. They love me as I am and they accept me in everything. I don't have to prove anything to anyone, can laugh, cry, think, joke, dream, travel elsewhere and come back. They let me be. *Just be.*

When you feel so free to be able to even cry then you're home.

It happened to me one day at Roberto and Paola's house, on their dining table, a sad afternoon when it seemed the world had ended. Paola then wrote to me on Facebook stealing the words of a poet, although I have not figured out which one it really was.

«*The man who suffers should be aware that the affections of the heart are like a cedar's branches; if the tree loses one strong branch it suffers, but it doesn't die. It our all the vitality in the near branch, so it may grow and fill the empty space.* GIBRAN
You don't have to keep your pain all inside, it will be a wound that will make the crust very slowly, that will leave a scar, that maybe can hurt when the weather changes, that will always mark your body… But if you look at it from afar perhaps you will realize there's much more healthy space on your body than that occupied by the wound… Don't be afraid to ask, whatever it is, if we can we will do it with our heart and arms open wide».

Now we are almost there and I come back to myself.

«So tell me, what's the owner's name?» I ask Martina all concerned, because the name reveals one's identity. If you're Maximum Penis or Mr Piss certainly you've had to deal with your parents, I think to myself. Since she had not said anything the whole trip, I was sure of being able to exclude Benedict Head or Fucking Mary. Knowing me, Martina would have told me now to prepare me. I swear, I could never do it.

«Her name's Sabina Minute» Martina answers, fortunately.

The surname Minute explains very well the idea of what they do: beautiful small metal details for spectacles, for automotive components, for furniture and luxury accessories, real jewels. Must then be a woman with counted "Minute", super busy between her company and her family.

However I love her name, Sabina, it makes me start another journey within a journey, because it reminds me of one of the most beautiful love stories I've lived with a girl of Venas di Cadore, named precisely Sabina.

We thought we were soul mates, we lived as happily as the butterflies. I loved the way she approached me while I was washing the dishes. That became a ritual, our ritual: «Stop, I do them!» I screamed at home after dinner peremptory getting up from the table and taking possession of the basin, our first love nest, the place where we declared our speechless love.

.. I take off the watch, put on my orange latex and project the sink: first the dishes and the cutlery, then the glasses and at last the dirtiest pots. I wash the grease off and rinse, but I'm waiting for your eyes. Ploff. There you are. Your glass is in the wrong place in the water, but who cares! My torso is there, chained because of your lips, because of the bites on my shoulder, because of those caresses which everyone pretends not to see between a sip of Pernod and the usual chatter. (I'm waiting for your eyes).

I fell madly in love with her when she emerged from a dip in the sea with her face drawn by a trickle of blood out of her nose.

It was not enough I was wet, re-emerged from a dream, seasoned with sighs of that glimpsed passion. It was epistaxis. Sudden, unexpected to both, with butterfly's symmetry marked the outline of your lips. I wiped it with my fingers, touching you and wounding me. (Epistaxis).

To everyone it was an impossible story. It also became impossible to us when we began to believe it. We parted, in the promise of a return that would never come. I also wrote her some *poems* without ever having the courage to send them to her. It takes a bit of a sense of limits. A few years later, in the middle of the night, I even climbed on the slope behind her house to reach the height of her window, hoping to see her and thinking about the first time we made love on her single bed under a canopy of paper stars stuck to the ceiling. The bedspread was blue and the sheets smelled of white flowers. In the asceticism of my remembrance I fell into a manhole up to the neck, dirtying and wounding myself.

We have arrived. Finally also Paolo from Treviso reaches us, with his vintage motorcycle: a fantastic 1979 black BMW R45 with big skin bags on the sides and sparkling chrome mufflers. When he removes his helmet he's wearing his unmistakable expression of Bollywoodian screenwriter. Legendary!

The place is beautiful. But my opinion doesn't count, because to me all industrial areas are beautiful. I think I'm one of the few people in the world when visiting a historic town begins from the industrial area. My friends call it wild madness. I did it once in Florence, dragging those poor human beings to see industrial sites before Brunelleschi's Dome.

«But do you think we came to Florence to see these sheds? Hey, Coach, but are you crazy? What have you done today?» my stunned friends ask me. I have to invent everything to do it: «Here guys, this is the best way to connect ourselves to Florence's history, that's why we're here. Then you will thank me... In these current industrial sites they have schemed and done, laughed and cried, worked and went on strike, our fellow human beings have schemed and done, laughed and cried, worked and went on strike, 600 years ago during the construction of the Duomo in Florence. The first organized strike in history occurred right in the yard of Brunelleschi, how cool! That's why we're here now, to connect ourselves to the past from the present in order to better understand the future. But do you realize how much life there is here now? Look there, a truck is discharging some material, there are people treating, others are planning. Do you realize how deeply we are seizing the essence of Florence between these hangar?».

«Coach, are you crazy? Take us immediately to the old town! Who is your dealer? We want this stuff, too!» they say in chorus.

In fact, they're not wrong, *a lot of stuff*. So, to be forgiven and not abandoned among those sheds, I promise: «Ok, ok, filthy ignorant crawling worms, tonight fiorentina and Chianti for everyone on me... IGNORANT! In the sense that you ignore the beauty of existing industrial sites!». Ha ha ha, how many laughs with my friends!

Idiotic digressions aside, we're excited to enter the company.

The atmosphere is charged with positive voltage. Here they don't even know what crisis means, thanks to the merits they won on the field with passion, work and intelligence. We are welcomed as the Three Kings, they accompanied us to the meeting room on the first floor. I'm definitely the fourth of the three kings: "Simpletor". The decor is modern and classy, a choice of Sabina that I like more and more without having get to know her yet: a beautiful white table with glass top in the center, elegant white chairs with thin black legs, a large screen on the wall, large glazed white aluminum windows, beautiful light. They make us sit on one side of the table offering us coffee.

You have to be very careful to keep the coffee from the top edge of the plastic cup otherwise you burn your fingers and crash the glass to the ground screaming out loud. It has already happened to me once... This time I avoid poor figures and I ask to put carefully the coffee on the table to sweeten it better. Often, there is not enough space on the cold part of the glass to grasp it immediately and when the secretary launches it like a hot potato with a smile of satisfaction, curious to see how you can handle that, you're in trouble. Drama. Then the plastic straight spoon, which already is an oxymoron, always makes me think of the tongue crushes tool that doctors use to look in your throat, making you feel regularly vomiting attacks. How can they do that? Maybe it is a medicine specialization: clinical vomiting applied.

Luca and Adriana, two department managers, and the general manager Stefano Fontanella, presenting the company with shining eyes, arrive after a few moments. Stefano is the classic person that at five am, if he had not the company's keys, would kick the door open to go to work. Passion for work in a pure state. Wonderful feeling. Last but not least, the owner.

You know, thoughts are as naughty as monkeys, so in a moment I remember my Sabi and I cannot help but look at her mouth, face and everything else. Of course I must have been wearing a blessed expression, the classic expression that you'd like to see photographed at least once in your life to understand how "Simpletor" you are. Power of neuro-associations, I'm fine.

In that state of semi-consciousness I even think of that dear friend of mine that to remember the names of all the people he meets, customizes "Golfera method" in this way: he imagines the males handing him over a wad of money and women doing him a little service, Monica Lewinsky Blowjob-isky under Clinton's desk. I have to admit that it works, I remember a lot of names. So if Im' late in returning your hand, you know I'm picturing in my head all these bullshits. Some printed smiles arise right from this.

Once seated and ready, Sabina begins the meeting by saying that «We would like to improve our internal communication and become a team. We have a lot of work to do and right because we're growing we want to be prepared for the future and for the new markets». Wow, I think to myself, Sabi's *so much stuff*!

«Sure. The *growth* management is a critical step because it is likely to enter into suffering if you do not make things right» Paolo Latini cleverly continues the speech. Paolo is one of the most clever minds I've ever known. I love Paolo. He says of himself to be a pain in the ass and to always do the questions no one wants to answer to, but everyone wants to do. So it's the perfect person to investigate the real needs of a company in an exploratory meeting. And since in Certottica there's the belief that talent also means surrounding yourself with more talented people than you, building the best conditions for them to create and develop something, in this kind of meetings he is the King. And I'm the prince, or as he would say, "the Prince of Andorra", given the number of my friends on Facebook.

«Who will participate to this project?» Paolo asks curiously.

«The four of us plus twelve between workers and employees in strategic positions» the owner replies.
«All together here?» Paolo urges in a firm tone. Here, this is the question I would have done immediately if Paul was not a war thunderbolt.
«Yes!» Sabina answers.
I thought to myself as Asterix does: "These Romans of 2MDecori S.p.A. are crazy!". All together? Master, managers, designers, workers, performers, all in the same arena? Working on communication and team building? Lucky who begins…

«Don't you think the simultaneous presence of people with different roles in the same environment and the possible presence of internal conflicts may affect or limit the effectiveness of this training course?» Paolo continues more and more rapid and insightful. Ih, ih, ih, if there is one person that I would always want by my side to gather information and understand the dynamics of a work group through the right questions, that person is Paolo Latini: a hot knife into a piece of butter.

«Yes» Sabina answers after a long pause, during which she admits on a non-verbal level of not having really thought about it all the way or not at all consider it a problem. «Yes, we know it, but you're here for this, *right*?» she asks as if to say this is a problem I hope you know how to resolve for the best. So, it was the latter. Great Sabi, that's it! I'm beginning to warm up the engine.

«Right!» Paolo underlines rising his voice's volume and echoing the last owner's word: «And right for this, I think, if you agree, to start with 2 sessions on Conflict Management held by my brother Dr. Roberto Latini, and pass then to 3 meetings on Communication and Team Building with Coach Alessandro Vianello and finish with me with the Communicative Approach to New Markets and Growth Management Company».

«Yes, we agree!» Sabina says smiling. Yay! Here we go, everything's going smoothly and smells like the Tuscan cold pressed extra virgin olive oil.

Very well, the operation is successful, the surgeon Dr. Paolo Latini concluded his open-heart surgery. We now need to sew up the patient and that it is up to the expert hands of plastic surgeon Dr. Martina Armellin: «Ok, let's go building a tailored suit for us!» says with a needle and a thread in her hand as if she has to sew a Dolce & Gabbana suit for a fashion show. The dress is ready in a flesh, she disinfects and awakens the patient thanked him for the very nice welcome and good coffee. When we're all close we greet everyone with a warm goodbye.

As soon as we go out, we have a long sigh of relief, we know the best is yet to come having perceived the project's complexity and the need to immediately think of how to do a fantastic team work. Without even having time to fasten our seat belts, I propose to the plastic surgeon an idea: «Martina, this is a great challenge. I want to be a co-teacher in the first meeting with Roberto Latini on conflict management because there are big risks and I want to be familiar with the environmental situation before beginning my speech. What do you say?» I ask assenting to have the certainty of her yes. Typical *non-verbal communication in form of a sausage* (sausages attract wolves), as my friend Francesco Da Ponte would say. He's the best with children and the worst at parties and in the approaches to the opposite sex. You can imagine it.

«Yes, sure, I think so. Good idea. I speak with Piero (in charge of training), then I ask Roberto (the teacher) if he agrees, I inform the company of your presence and we start next Monday. Of course you have to come at no charge because I cannot pay for this» the Dr. replies precisely and decisively. Wow, the steps' sequence is perfect as the communicative awareness of the economic accounts. This girl is very good, I think to myself.

When it seems everything's in place and each of us is ready to begin the training, the devil steps in and the most classic drawbacks forces to review our programs: at the end, I have to start, then it will be the turn of Roberto and finally Paolo. *Nice failure the casinò.*

On the Friday, before the Monday when I would start the course, I enter *the Marine*'s office to feed me with his experience. In practice, I attack on his breast as if it was that of Monica Bellucci.
«Piero, I need your help. I feel that next Monday in 2MDecori we'll risk a lot. What do you think?» I ask him sitting at his desk from which he controls the open space of his office in Certottica.
«That's true! In your first meeting we risk the success of the course. If you fail, the course fails. If you're successful, we're ok. Slow down, boy, because if you go too fast in bringing people together you can break the mechanism. The pieces don't fit now, the grease between them is still missing. You have to put it. First of all, build harmony and exchange. Then make them a team. At first, do a unique premise, emphasizing the entrepreneur's choice, the courage of the company and their overview. It's a great opportunity for all and I'm glad it's you starting for us. I know you can do it. Think that will be a success, have fun this weekend and Monday morning you will wake up with the solution about what to do. Bye».

Is there a man more direct and effective than Piero Monestier? Improvise, adapt and achieve the goal.

My little ass is very tight with fear, but I trust Piero as he trusts me. I spend a weekend walking, swimming, thinking. The first two things not at the same time.

Sunday evening I try a strategic alliance with Martina, because I am convinced that the reception phase of the participants will be crucial. In front of the mirror I start thinking about how to dress me to put them at ease and to create *harmony*. It's 9 pm and I send this text to Dr. Armellin on her work-phone, trusting that she can telepathically read it before Monday morning in the office.

«Hi Martina .. cute and cuddly tomorrow in 2mdecori, as Madagascar penguins! We're risking our training program's success and I need your help, ok? Objective: to create HARMONY in the "madhouse". Welcome and start will be critical in order to win. If you can, just pick a look to communicate SOFTNESS, that can help to create the right climate among the students. Have a nice evening and thank you for everything :) Ale».

The next day I wake up with a bright, sharp and clear image of what I would do in the afternoon, as Piero expertly anticipated. And while I'm finishing to prepare the slides on my MacBook, Martina calls me: «Hi Ale! I have read the message just this morning in the office, I don't know if I'm soft enough ... I'm dressed casual with a cream suit, canvas beige shoes WITHOUT HEEL, loose hair...».
«You're fantastic! Thank you! See you later!» I reply enthusiastically. In telepathy we have 6 notches.

On Monday, the 28th of may 2012, 1 hour and a half before the start of the course, we are in 2MDecori and we begin to set the meeting room that we already know: we prepare the chairs, the equipment, the training materials, the music. Martina is very soft and reassuring. To be a *team* of *evolved people* means to understand the moments and use the right words to build the desired climate. «Beautiful T-shirt, Ale!» she says to me as we settle the chairs, making me feel even more comfortable. I needed that.

Usually, I change the T-shirt according to the occasions maintaining a constant with dark blue jeans, black karate belt and Prada shoes, in various colors according to the seasons. For the occasion I chose a cotton Nike T-shirt with a white sign "I make it look easy", a gift from one of my footballer client of "F.C. Internazionale Milano" sponsored by Nike. I love wearing positive anchors, they make me feel good. No beard and shaved hair. Those few who remain. No perfume, only a practically odorless deodorant. And above all no barriers between me and the students because communication passes through the stomach, as taught by *the Marine.*

In welcoming, Martina and I are smiling more than Silvio Berlusconi and Mickey Mouse together, we're making our fangs always visible: I have crooked teeth, and she has perfectly white and aligned teeth. You know, a smile that does not show your teeth is not a smile, because it doesn't put people at ease. In the first impact, in fact, human beings instinctively look at the mouth to see if the environment is hostile or friendly: by what they see, they unconsciously perceive danger or absence of danger. In the first case, if they see a closed mouth or a smile where you can't see the white of the teeth, they instinctively search for protection because the environment is perceived as hostile. In the second case, when they see a smile with fangs, as I like to say, they begin to relax and to feel comfortable, ready to a communicative Bunga Bunga. This is the best way to begin any relationship and we know it: AleMarti are always cute and cuddly.

The other things we pay attention to as *a team* of *evolved people* are the movement and the voice's tone. We move slowly and firmly. No visual shock. We receive every person shaking his/her hand with the palm facing upwards. Two words and we warmly accompany people to their place. Then we do three breaths with them and, only after that, we go to welcome another person.

We welcome Adriana, Alberto, Antonio, Damiano, Freddy, Giovanni, Igino, Luca, Nadia, Olivo, Omar, Stefano, Susy, Valerio, Vittorio.

In twenty minutes they're all arrived, except Sabina. She's expected at any moments as Madonna during her concerts. She is very charming and intelligent. With great courage, she slips into the arena at the last moment as Venus in the bed of Mars, reminding everyone who's in charge, including Mars. Let alone Hermes. Everything is communication, so if during the presentation I would not let her in the end, I would have made an unforgivable mistake. But as Mourinho would say: "I'm not idiot." I'm just a guy who likes to have fun and to improvise to keep everyone alert. So *random sequence* and last but not least our Sabi, I think to myself before starting, because we are here thanks to her.

Two words of the plastic surgeon Tutor about some paperworks to be completed and then it's up to me. In my bag I have a crust of Parmesan cheese that my mother had slipped in my work stuff. Do you think it's a normal thing? But this is her way to tell me she loves me and I decide to start right from her bizarre communication, being that a communication course. They are all shocked and I remember Piero's message: «Slow down, boy». Ok, slow down.

What I cautiously called it a "madhouse" turns instead in "a great working family": people are at ease, help and want to build their future together. The credit for this belongs to everyone and in particular to the head of the fish: the ownership, alias Sabina Minute, the general manager Stefano Fontanella and Freddy Rossi, much more than a right arm.

Three great human beings who work in symbiosis:

- Freddy comes from the sports world and he has the culture of "Us" tattooed inside him. If he plays a ski race and at the finish line the interviewer asks him how the first heat went, he's able to answer: «Well, we played a great race, we were good in sliding and very precise on the final wall. We are pleased with our performance. In the second race I feel that we will improve again. Yes we can!». Across the border of knowledge, in another galaxy for me that I live the culture of Us;

- Stefano considers the two companies of which he is general manager as his daughters. And this attitude makes the difference. As Alonso said on his arrival in Maranello: «here the mechanics mount the mirror of the car as if it were their own, that's why Ferrari is a myth!». Stefano talks about his companies with gooseflesh and with the excitement of an everlasting love. If you go with him in production you'll be enchanted by the genesis of their jewelry. That's why things in 2MDecori work;

- Sabina is Sabina.

In a context like this my job is simple: to build a mentality of *exchange* and mutual enrichment developing all their *strengths* and delivering practical communication *tools* to make it even more fluid, effective and fun.

The first day goes great, I feel that we started on the right foot. So on the second day, you never change a winning team. We just have to evolve in the strategy being one step ahead of our audience.

Monday, the 4th June 2012. Martina is always soft and well-mannered, while I wear a Stars Wars blue T-shirt, recalling the color of my first T-shirt. As the guru says, "if you cannot set an anchor and then reactivate it at the right time, better you anchor yourself at the bottom of the sea". Anchored concept, I'd say.

Students welcome us in a wonderful way! They are happy to see us again, there is energy and a strong desire to grow and to participate actively. They have a light in their eyes and a smile on their lips. A good sign.

Sabina's arrival is a good sign too. She takes me aside and tells me that at work you can already see the results of the first meeting with me. How nice! Now I'm much more comfortable. Then, she says with a sweet wink: «nice T-shirt!» because maybe she loves the Star Wars saga, giving me a perfect assist for my next look.

When you put the ball on the line port and the goalkeeper passed out ten meters from you, you just have to put it in, you don't have to be Maradona. You don't have to think about anything, you just have to act. *Said and done*. On Friday the 8th June 2012 I finish my speech wearing a sky-blue T-shirt with the image of the Master Joda of Star Wars on it, dedicated it with my heart and my soul to Sabina and to 2M Decori.

On the last day the teacher's task is also to pave the way for those who will complete the training after him, figuratively building the inclined plane on which to roll the rest of the experience with other teachers. In my case, the infamous different twins, "*Arnold* Roberto Latini *Schwarzenegger*" e "*Danny* Paolo Latini *DeVito*": the first one is tall, hairy, more calm than Valium and the second one is short, bold and shaken like a Churchill (1/6 lemon juice; 1/6 vermouth; 1/6 Cointreau; 1/2 whisky. Shake it vigorously in a shaker and serve it in a tumbler with ice and a grape). Delicious cocktail.

In our third and final meeting there is a great feeling and an extraordinary desire to get involved, including skits, games, presentations, group work and horizontal feedback sessions. Horizontal in the sense that we aren't all lying on the white table in the meeting room to make love in an orgy of passion, but in the sense that everyone says what they perceived. No screen, no barrier, no mask. They're all donating a part of them. And this was the primary goal of my speech, because each feed-back is literally a food back: you have to know how to offer it and appreciate it. You give it going from good to better (what you did well AND what you can improve). You receive it saying THANKS (without any other comment, otherwise it would be like refuse it).

To create the *right environment* for a free and respectful exchange of ideas is the responsibility of everyone, without exception. There aren't free zones in that sense inside a company. If the so-called "totem pole" go to the "steam's and says to him: «Thanks for the cabin you put on. I'm fine here. It's important to me and to my family» and the cabin's head answers with a heartfelt THANK YOU, it is thanks to them both because they have created the right environment to make this exchange happens. And that counts for the compliments as well as the critics. This is to me the only way to grow.

The exchange is the first form of love.
I give something to you and you give something to me. "You give it to me and I'll give it to you", as "Simpletor" would say. As easy as breathing. Sometimes as difficult as climbing eight thousand without a respirator.

Fly
Beyond the walls and the edge of the world
Towards a higher and deeper sky
Of the things that everyone chases
And you does not realize that they are nothing
They are nothing

NEGRAMARO, *Has it ever happened to you*? (Ti è mai successo?)

It happened to me and in the final exchange of feedback the excitement takes over. Now we all give ourselves freely, we can love on the table in the meeting room. The closure is a *Marine's must*, a couple of questions I always dedicate to him: "What will you bring home?" and "What do I bring home of you?". In this way you do the squaring of the circle and you can understand how your path really went.

The answers I receive are moving. Human beings' magic. Among them I remember that of a designer called Alberto, a big, sweet, shy man, father of three children, who answers to the second question as excited as a child, his voice trembling and tears in his eyes: «You bring home... a friend... a friend... a friend» he says, looking me straight in the eye. Incredible.

I answer with his same excitement: « Thank you ... thank you ... thank you, Alberto!» I say in a low voice and with tears in my eyes. I hold on and don't cry. At the end of the lesson we exchange our contacts like two lovers, passing a slip of paper with our phone number behind our back not to be seen by others. Unique moments!

Then when I ask Freddy: «What do you bring home?» He naturally answers « WE bring home...» ha ha ha, what a laughter! When I ask Stefano, he makes a speech that includes all the presents, as a true leader, and then he leaves the last word to Sabina that brings us all in the future, sexy and fearless as only a woman can be. *A lot of stuff.*

In the end I remain with the knowledge that "you have to fight, to swallow bitter pills, to work so hard. Nothing comes for nothing. But we're here and we're fine. We have opened production lines with nothing in hand, only believing. And then the work has come. No one can afford not to try to work with us. Then anything can happen, but we have never lost a customer".

We say goodbye with our hands joined and thanking each other, locked in one embrace, *all together at the same time.* It remains within the spirit of a company "born from a family as a family" with the desire to continue to be.

On the wall I leave the heart, made of post-it notes on which everyone has written in one word what 2MDecori is. Reading them I know that Italy will always make, no matter what happens, because we Italians are special.

On the board I write a mega THANK YOU, I put my puppets (Onion and Penguin) in my bag and, excited, I' ready to go home. I was fine, I enjoyed it, I grew up.

Sabina's waiting for me for the last farewell with a beautiful, full of gratitude *smile with fangs*. The last word should always be left to the boss, let alone when the boss is a woman like her.
«You're cool! You're a Coach! Thank you for everything!» I have the pleasure to listen to.
«Thank you Sabina» I say excitedly.

Is there anything more amazing and wonderful than people?

Not yet satisfied with the emotional well-being in which I'm immersed, I phone Piero to tell him about my feelings and give him my professional feedback about that day. The de-briefing is a decisive stage in the process of building a team, it is the time when emotions are anchored and which will provide improvement areas to work together. And *the Marine* is very aware of that, throwing my feelings on the moon.

«Well. Bravo. I knew it. Congratulations to you. What more could you want from life? But what is success? These emotions are a success! You know what you have to do tomorrow? You have to call that friend of yours, Alberto Bogo (*the Shaman*), who referred you to Piero Monestier. And you have to thank him, because he insisted to get an appointment with me» reminding me that joy has always to be shared.

«Yes, I will do it, thanks Piero! Thank you for everything!» I say in raptures.

«And also thank him for me...» he finishes with his special way of saying Hello.

Has it ever happened to you to wish you were back
to all that you thought you had to run from
and not knowing how to do it
would that there were at least a way, one way to start over again

to think that things weren't so bad after all
that love is when you have nothing to hate anymore
to hang in the balance than fall
it happens to me and now I can stay.

NEGRAMARO, *Has it ever happened to you*? (Ti è mai successo?)

26. SPORT: SIRIO PALLAVOLO PERUGIA

On the way home you will find your children.
Give your children a caress
and say, "this is the caress of the Pope".
PAPA GIOVANNI XXIII

PROLOGUE

In life anything can happen.

You can meet people who will take you on, work with you for months squeezing you like a lemon and then in court, when through the righteousness you ask that they keep the financial obligations they have taken with you *erga omnes*, they pretend they'd never seen you.

Or, you can meet people who are willing to give up everything they have to keep a promise they made to themselves first. These are the *Righteous Men* I told you before: loyal, respectful, and sincere. They express gratitude every day for what they are and for what they have, little or much that is. Staying with them is a joy.

What I have learned, thanks to the experience in Sirio Pallavolo Perugia in the 2008-2009 season, is that it is up to us to choose what to remember and who to keep close, because in life anything can happen. And despite the wrongs, if you think badly of someone you're the first who feels bad. Forgiveness is the only way. Sure, it doesn't give you back what has been lost or that no longer exists, but it returns you the chance to live in a peaceful and happy way.

Nature, you know, doesn't root for anyone. The sky, the sea, the land, do not have it with you or with others. They exist, that's all. Some people say that the world is perfect but incomplete and I think they're right. It's up to you to complete it, like crosswords puzzles. You give a meaning, because there's no sense. Everything is as you see it, it depends on the eyes with which you look at it. In this sense, the reality is something that takes shape from the inside and everything can have a different meaning.

INTRODUCTION

What I'm about to tell you is the story of a sports season in Apollo 13 style: a successful failure. Failure, because we haven't won and none of the staff finished the season. Successful, because in the greatest difficulties we were always together and none of us finished the season. Yes, that's right, it's exactly what happened.

As *the Master* Padoan taught me, that experience was a "paper tiger." If you think tiger remember that it is paper and if you think paper remember that is tiger. According to the Chinese scheme of thought shield/spear, you can think of every experience as a failure or as a success and you can interpret every movement in one way or its opposite. What then makes the difference in time is what do you have inside, what you remember and how you remember it.

That of Perugia is also the story of the inside / outside, i.e. how an experience can be experienced from the inside and how it is told for the consumption of the outside part of the media or of those who had an interest to support a part compared to other. Now I think it's time to present the views of those who lived that incredible human and professional experience from the inside, leaving to the readers the opportunity to draw their own conclusions. In this regard, I think I was the first Mental Coach officially included within a professional team in Italy, I get above myself. Ha ha ha.

For all those who were out, that season is also remembered for the sensational supersonic giant middle finger that Gianni Caprara has done to the fans of Bergamo, at the end of the semifinals of the Champions League defeat against Foppapedretti in the Final Four in Perugia. The image of that missile proudly projected to the sky, resting on the launch base of an outstretched arm parallel to the ground and attached to a body placed in the center of the field to be better noticed, has been around the world and has been the pretext for exemption for good cause of the Sirio Pallavolo Perugia head coach, which was followed by the resignation of the entire staff. That's why none of us have finished the season. To this fact, unique in the history of the Italian volleyball and perhaps also of Italian sport, I mean the resignation of the entire staff (although I'd never seen a finger like that), was given instead very little weight. It was one thing to keep hidden because it has never happened that even the stable professionals, that is assumed by the company regardless of the physiologic alternation of the various Head Coach in the course of time, resigned, risking their professional future in the city in which they live and work.

Let me explain. n the high-level sports world, well-built clubs organize a trusty medical, health, physical and technical staff that doesn't change even if the technical guide does. Generally these professionals are always on the side of the buttons, ie never, ever turn against the company if it decides to change the coach because they do not get the results or for any other reason. So, in fact, there are always two staff in one: one is brought by the head coach, and one is that he finds. Unless something magical and extraordinary happens and changes things. This is the rule in sports.

They're almost all sorry if the head coach is sent away, but no one ever thinks of following him or resigning as a sign of solidarity. Support is expressed only in words, then you have to deal with yourself and hold tight your employment contract by discharging all the responsibilities on the already exonerated Mister. Sorry, but *mors tua vita mea*, it works that way since ever, in sports as in politics, where they don't resign not to lose their seat. In Perugia 2008-2009 we were the exception that proves the rule, so the only thing to point out in Staff Building *all together at the same time*. At least in my opinion.

EXECUTION

At Sirio Pallavolo Perugia, famous and awarded company of the Italian Women Volleyball, Gianni Caprara takes over from the current season. It was in November of 2008. We talk on the phone and he expresses the desire to take me with him in this adventure to work with the staff and with the players. I'm the only person with whom he worked and he trusts me. So, he brings me and finds all others: doctor, physiotherapist, statistics officer, assistant coach, vice-coach, all residents in Perugia. My first task is therefore to align and merge the human resources in the staff, to figure out who you can trust, to explain to them how Gianni Caprara works and build a unique team of evolved people, because to Gianni the team comes first and is the only thing that matters.

On 29th novembre 2008 I leave from Modena, I'm going to Perugia under a snow storm. Even the road that goes down from my hill is blocked by a tree uprooted by the wind. I'm about to give up, but I would have missed one of the most exciting human and professional experiences of my life.

The journey is an odyssey that ends in Ithaca after 7 hours, at Pala Evangelisti, where I would have met the company to define the terms of our collaboration. Perugia's arena isn't a "pigsty" like that of Spezzano, it's huge, and seen from the outside looks like a eye because its coverage is a half moon in laminated beams with glass curtain walls on the sides. It's like taking a cylinder, cut it in two and place one half on the ground.

When I enter the service entrance in the background I hear the sounds of the team that is training and that unmistakable smell of gym, a mixture of sweat, cleaning products for floors, wood floors and balloons. The emotion is very strong, a dream is coming true: returning to work with Gianni after our historic promotion to A1 in 2002 in Spezzano.

In the meantime I became a Coach ceasing to be a professional coach and resisting the lure of Caprara who wanted me as his second in Perugia. «I see my life in Coaching, I thank you but I cannot accept your proposal, now I'm a coach and I want to develop my career in this field» I said on the phone giving up that position. «You're clear and transparent as usual, I'll take you with me as a coach then!» Gianni answered me in that wonderful phone call in early November.

And here I am, with the memory of that moment bouncing in my head like a balloon. Here I am, back in the gym after a life. What will I find? Well, I wonder if Gianni has changed in all that time, I wondered curiously. He won a World Cup, maybe he is completely different from what I remember, I kept wondering while I slowly approached the field in the depths of the locker room, attracted like a magnet by the cries of the players after the point. Finally I see the same scene ever: Gianni at work with his unmistakable style!

Who does not know him well may think he's a conceited or that he wants to make the phenomenon at all costs, because even if you're on the sideline three meters away from him and you're one of his dearest friend he had not seen for years or a family member, he doesn't even greet you. Simply, he is so immersed in what he is doing that he doesn't see you. He only sees the team and gives priority to this. The message is: "when I work, I work and there's nothing more important than the team. And so it is. Then we greet each other, we hug and we do party."

Knowing all this I sit on the sidelines and taste the workout after years in which I did not see my favorite coach in action. The perception that nothing has changed makes me breathe differently and a beatific smile appears on my face. Sometimes I would like to be photographed in these moments, just to see a image of what I'm feeling. In certain situations, you never know if you're an idiot or a prince. I enjoy the workout waiting for the boss.

That's nice to hear the noise of the ball, the screams of the players, the joy for the point, the pulsating life at every exchange! I begin to work with this emotion in my heart, collecting information on the environment, the fans, the players, the staff and the managers. No one knows me and no one knows why I'm there. I am one of those who are watching the team training, sitting on the sidelines along with retirees and I like that, because the information you gather are as fresh as the mountain air in the morning.

When you start a new adventure you must always start from where you can, so I try to identify among staff members and players the people with the biggest group spirit to build everything else around them. Who is the most similar to me? From who do I start? Who I like? These are the guiding questions. Fortunately, who seeks finds.

At the end of the training two eyes sparkling with life and mounted on a beastly body come to greet me: this is Mauro Chiappafreddo, Gianni's vice. Our first meeting is withering. An amazing mutual understanding starts and continues for a whole hour. Mauro is the only man to whom I send messages of love and he does the same with me. We are in love with each other. If one day someone publishes our wiretaps we'll in trouble, it will be impossible to deny the existence of a love story between us.

A moment later, two other bright eyes mounted on a clean face approach me to say hello: this is Guido Marangi, assistant coach and scout-man. Very well, and these are already two, I say to myself, let's drag in all the others, or let's make sure they slip inside themselves, in Sun Tzu style.

Suddenly Gianni arrives and it is a party. We go together to the boss and define the terms of our agreement: I was going to follow the team for at least 8 days per month and continuously available to the technical staff and managers by phone, e-mail, etc... Every month I would have to submit a report on my activities and what was going on in the team. In Perugia I would have slept in Gianni's apartment, being his family still in Russia. Handshake and on.

On 2nd December 2008 I am officially presented to the team in the video room of the arena. At the beginning it is always like walking on eggshells and girls look at me as if I am a UFO, because I'm the only one who doesn't wear the team uniform (this is a detail that makes the difference in sports). I prepared a short and fast speech and I introduce myself, I'm excited and happy to be there. Then we all go to the gym to train for next Saturday competition. Gianni also decided to use me as a sparring. Rust aside, luckily I'm still good I don't cause a lot of damage, taking also some broadsides that are good for the team's morale.

On 19th December 2008, in an official statement on the company website, I am presented to the public and the press: "Sirio Pallavolo Perugia staff is enriched again: the NLP Coach Alessandro Vianello is available to the team since early December. Despar Colussi Perugia is pleased to announce that a new valuable resource is at the service of the players and technical staff".

On the same day we celebrate with the team our first victory together, which took place the previous Saturday in Busto Arsizio. The refreshment is memorable because I don't mind the expense and bring a hangar of sandwiches, cakes, coke and wine (much appreciated by those revelers of the players). As my mother says, "better do things well or not do them at all". In fact she's quite right.

The atmosphere is wonderful and we begin to be *all together at the same time*. In volleyball, and in many team sports, to bring "the pastries" is a beautiful habit. In this way we celebrate birthdays together, new arrivals, great victories and exorcise outrageous mistakes, like hitting the referee directly in cue or beat under the net into the opponent's field. If you have played volleyball you have some crazy stories about these hilarious sports gaffe that are baptized by the word "pastries" and associated with wonderful laughter, even if you're playing the Olympic final.

Among my fondest memories as a player there's that of a friend of mine who jumps and hits the referee in the face with an impressive air missiles, making his glasses jump off his face and making him almost fall from the chair. The match was suspended for ten minutes because nobody would be able to play with laughter. Our coach had to call the two time-outs to let us take a breath, because we could not stop the giggles. Nobody was able to look at the referee without bursting out laughing because he had the balloon's sign imprinted on his cheek and his glasses missed a bar line. Epic. Those "pastries" were unforgettable, we laughed for a whole year.

The "laid tables", as claimed by my friend Giuliano Vantaggi, always help to form great staffs, even when they are set up quickly on the sideline, with cakes, pastries, sandwiches and various drinks in memory of epic moments. Eating, drinking and laughing *all together at the same time* you become a team.

We needed some great moments together in Perugia, because the team was composed of a crazy black American, a shy Chinese who didn't speak a word of Italian, two cheerful Dutch with clogs and typical dresses, an aggressive Caucasian and a mix of experienced players (old chicken makes good soup) and young players debuting in A league, just out of the incubator of youth. The beauty of sport is this: to do with a dozen tubes of different paint a beautiful picture, in which everyone can identify. In this sense, the enemies are the ego, stupidity and lack of time; friends are the common goal, humility, availability, intelligence, skills, fun, time pressure and difficulties.

From a pure technical-tactical point of view, in Perugia things didn't go very well because the company had been wrong at some important evaluation. In particular, the leaders had made a mistake in relation to the purchase of the top player, the Chinese player, because they thought they have hired a great receiver, instead the opposite was true. Unfortunately, when you fail to build the backbone of the team, then the deck is always short. We had a lot of problems during the reception-attack phase and in the league the team couldn't be more balanced because there had to be a number of Italian in the field. The usual Italian-style messes Rules, where the clarity and meritocracy are after demagoguery. So, while in A league championship choices were obliged, in the Champions League we could line up technically a more bilance team, being a European competition where there were no restriction whatsoever on the number of Community players.

To succeed in making that team play well was not an *easy task*.

In any case, in the gym were not joking at all and something was beginning to look good even in the field. In the *staff* everything was all right, there was great understanding with the physiotherapists Mauro Proietti and Laura Rosi, two atomic professionals within the Italian national team. By now we were moving all *at the same pace* and at the presence of the team we were always together and *at the same distance*. This particular field of proxemics may seem silly, but those who work in sports or high-level business knows how important are the perceptions that you give to others.

The more the bar goes up, the more the athletes and the employees look for a way out or a gap to fit in and carry out their own personal interests. When you claim so much and you lead people to overcome their limitations you must be united and be perceived as one, *all together at the same time*. It takes a moment to be penetrated and split in two without lubricant.

In building a team and *a team* of *evolved people*, nothing can be left to chance, so we started to take care of every detail of our verbal and especially non-verbal communication. Even the look makes the difference.

In any pre-game meeting our task was to amplify the head coach's voice in the locker room being silent. They are all able to do so with the voice, the hardest thing is to do it in silence. This can only be done using your body, breath and mind. The delivery that I had established was to look how Caprara wore the uniform and without saying anything to adapt according to what he had chosen. Collar up for him, collar up for us. Collar down for him, collar down for us. Open jacket for him, open jacket for us.

Then, when Gianni emphasized the fundamental tactical themes of the game, we nodded moving our heads up and down *all together at the same time*. The athletes looked at us startled, but they loved having a staff so united in their service. You could read it on their faces what they thought: «What the fuck are doing these morons? Well, come on, but they are cute and cuddly, I like what they do together».

After some time I saw the official team photo and other images of that experience, and I noticed with great pleasure that we were impeccably equal to the head coach. *A lot of stuff.* These are little things that witness a great job, Piccole cose che testimoniano un grande lavoro, a great understanding and a great attention to detail.

The value of a relationship between people can be seen from *how*, not from what. And when the team notes these hidden structures, working together becomes much easier and rewarding. There is respect. «We don't know what they do, but they're doing something, these staff morons!» the athletes thought. The first months were gorgeous, a honeymoon when we were training to become one.

Towards the end of February, while everything is going well, suddenly a bolt from the blue changes the cards on the table. In the middle of the afternoon session, we discover that our company had decided to run for the organization of the Final Four of the Champions League and was succeeded in winning! A manager had in fact thrown into the middle of the field to stop the workout and tell us the great news. Crazy!

Gianni, you know, cannot stand intrusions. In particular, for three reasons: 1. No one can stop the workout; 2. He wants to be consulted before; 3. In this way, the team wouldn't have developed on the field what would serve to excel in the competition, because we would have skipped the two races of the quarter finals, participating in law to the Final Four as a team organizing the event.

The staff wanted to pass the quarter-finals, it would have been a better way to grow through other important races and then we could play on par with the other contenders, maybe away from home and as outsider, because we were surely not the competion's favorites. So, instead of celebrating, we're almost sad thinking about those two inside/outside races that would be needed to build a winning team and that we would not have played.

Our first concern is always the team, not politics or appearances. However, after a moment of natural misgivings, we get to work to better live the month that professionals want to be able to live at least once in their lifetime. From the "problem" we move on to solutions.

The first idea that comes to us is to always train with the yellow and blue Mikasa ball of the Champions League even when we prepare the league games that are played instead with the white, red and green Molten ball. Among the many absurdities and differences in regulations, the balloons one impacted a lot on our performance, because they are made of different materials and take the effects differently. For a beginner there is not much difference, but for a professional it's like going from day to night.

To make the Champions' Mikasa *friendly* we turn it into "Wilson" like Tom Hanks in "Cast Away". Every day we give permissions to a player to take it home, to cuddle it a bit and, if she wants , to sleep with it. They get up to all kind of tricks. The athletes build it a house in the locker room that looks like a sanctuary, they draw a face to it and prepare for it a little suit ad hoc. It soon become our inseparable mascot and a way to have fun together.

The principle is to *familiarize* themselves with the means, like Valentino Rossi when he speaks to his motorcycle locked in the box, alone, on the night before the race. Confidence means trust. For each trip, "Wilson" is with us, dines with the team and takes turns sleeping with anyone who wants it. Personally I've spent about ten nights with it and I felt like when I was child, when I slept hugging my white Spalding before destroying the living room with a spike. Looking back the chandelier is still shaking.

The second major operation we think about is that of inviting a champion for few days with us. In the "Gazzetta dello sport" we read about a great champion of the Italian men's volleyball that at that time was studying as coach and was going to see the training of other technicians around Italy. The idea is to bring home an example, a role model, an inspiration. This myth's name is Andrea Giani.

So, thanks to my friend Roberto Lobietti (who unfortunately no longer exists, we are missing him as much as air) we invite Giangio with us to follow Caprara's workouts. I still remember the excitement at the time of his arrival in Perugia and the surprise in the girls' eyes having him for two days with us, inside our own gym, to participate in our training with our own suit. We wanted him to become, even if only for a few days, one of us.

Said and done. If you want to quickly find out who is a champion go meet Andrea Giani. The thing that has impressed us was his humility and his desire to be at the team's service. When we picked up the balloons he was the first one going. Being huge, never seen such a wide chest like his, and having two shovels instead of hands, for him it was a piece of cake coming back with 12 balloons. Cool!

This is the great lesson we needed to learn in order to prepare the team for the Final Four: the most humble record-man of all with an impressive career, the one with more desire to help others, he's sacrificed for the team more than anyone else. Simply a legend. Collect the balls with him and warm up before playing with him was one of the greatest joys of my life as volleyball player and Coach. Giangio is really *a lot of stuff.*

The third major task was to protect the team from everything and to build our identity. We wanted to give value to our current team, so we asked the company to remove from Pala Evangelisti the old banners of the triumphs of the past who had the face of other teams and other players. The idea was to expose only the banner of the trophy because the coaches and the players pass but the company remains. Or it should have stayed.

In all other world arenas you can see trophies exposed, not winners' faces. Or at least not on the same level, because they can weigh like stones on the shoulders of a young "under construction" team, which still hasn't won. Comparisons are always a bad thing and can generate ghosts with which it is difficult to live peacefully. Let bygones be bygones. «It's useless thinking nostalgically to the times of the great teams of Perugia when you have to do the best with the current team, certainly not up to the crest of the past» we said this to our leaders and they turned a deaf ear.

Unfortunately, the company decided not to decide and to do things by halves, removing the banners of the past but not replacing them with those of won trophies as we asked out loud. This is one of my biggest regret: non having insisted enough, I was not that good at convincing them about the importance of that thing. It cost too much, this was the official reason. Certainly, it cost much less than have everyone against you.

In fact, fans didn't react very well, because it seemed we were about to strip them of their identity or something like that, as if Caprara wanted to remove from the arena Barbolini's face, a great historic coach of Perugia and of the National Italian team, in order to mark his territory. As if to say "this is my home now", take off Massimo Barbolini's icon! As if Caprara suffers from an inferiority complex towards someone... Are you kidding me? Nothing could be more wrong. Nothing of what we did in Perugia was against someone or something, but it was always in favor of our team. Unfortunately we preached in the desert and many of our initiatives were artfully manipulated by those who had an interest in doing so.

The fourth task was to limit the damage that the economic difficulties, combined with poor communication, unfortunately were doing within the team. In addition to the usual technical problems of a badly built sextet, we had to make common cause to the fact that for months we didn't receive our salaries. In practice we had arrived in Perugia in a period of decline, both technical and moral. In volleyball some delay is physiological, but not receiving the salary becomes a drama, especially if the communication given to the team is contradictory and if you notice differences within the same team.

There is nothing worse than being strong with the weak and weak with the strong. This is a surefire way to destroy the mutual respect and sow discord. So, in early March, in order to still keep some friends within the society, I write a letter to the top executives to bring their attention on how it would be appropriate to dealing with the matter in accordance with the results. Of course I take a clear position. Perhaps too much clear.

LETTER TO MANAGEMENT

OBJECT: Strategy

> *Strategy is not a detailed plan or a program of instructions; it is rather a unifying theme that gives coherence and uniqueness of direction to the actions and the decisions of an individual or organization.*
> ROBERT GRANT

Dear Executives,

inspired by my professional situation in Despar Colussi Perugia, as a spectator, as an employee and especially as a Coach interested in the results and the benefit of the team, I would like to bring your attention to some of the strategies and procedures of excellence that aim to improve 'environment, communication, respect among the parties and of course the sports scores.

In my experience:

- in the professional field, esteem is constantly built keeping faith:
to the verbal agreements made with the parties; to written agreements with parties; to the company's achievement of leadership, i.e. to the mission, vision and purpose for which the company exists in the "business world". Unfortunately, it takes just a broken promise to throw to the wind working years. So it is always better not to expose yourself and not to promise if you aren't sure to keep the promises made, regardless of their economic value and their contingent opportunity. In the long run, transparency, consistency and fairness always pay and create value;

- the worst attitude a company may have towards its employees, its suppliers and its customers is to be strong with the weak and weak with the strong, because this behavior results in a loss of style, a loss of esteem at 360 degrees and an internal split that has a direct impact on the results. It will be the strongest to determine the collapse, even though you may think otherwise. This thing doesn't work;

- in sports, you win as a team or you're annulled individually. Holding together a team means decreasing the economic differences through the exploitation of labor and the orientation of resources towards the same goal. All of the behaviors that actually increase or emphasize the contractual differences between players and / or staff members, or certain privileges respect to each other must therefore be avoided because they can de-energize the team and create irreconcilable rifts that inevitably affect the results.

In summary, balance, transparency and honesty create value and produce results.

Therefore, as praxis for payments, for the delivery of awards, bonuses, game uniforms, materials and any other necessary matters for the sporting life, it would be appropriate to start from the smallest up to the largest, reserving the attention and incentives to the smallest economic components, because they will be the real glue and engine of the team.
We pamper the little fishes and stimulate the big ones, not the contrary, because the differences already exist in the contractual terms of opportunities and visibility.

Precisely for a reason of balance, transparency and fairness is important to standardize the payment procedures with a results-oriented communication that can strengthen the team spirit. The regularity and the precision in payments put the company in a strong position with respect to the employees and the outside, and vice versa puts the company in a position of weakness.

If by some reason you cannot respect the agreed deadlines (and it can happen!) it would be absolutely proper, intelligent and respectful warn the employees, in advance and personally, explaining them the reasons for the delay and setting a new date by which those contractual obligations will be fulfilled, always starting from the smallest cost. Never ever it will be the employee having to worry about asking the amount due for his work and how much was freely agreed with the company. In this regard, an effective communication might be the following:

Dear So and So, according to our agreements we would have to pay you what you deserve for your professional services for the month of.. the day.. , but for technical and financial reasons we are here to apologize to you because we cannot meet our obligations within the agreed time. We will do so within the..
Thanks, signed on..

When it will be possible to make the payment, maybe in advance of the date (agreed again), you could use this mode of communication:

Dear So and So, thanking you for patiently waiting, I'm calling to tell you that we have already credited your salary for the month of .. as agreed. Thank you for everything you've done and will do in the interest of the team.
Thanks, signed on ..
As you may have already received, I'm not here to judge, but only to build together an effective and transparent communication, because I love my job and my team.

All the best,
Alessandro

I'm proud of this letter, even if it cost me the rest of my salary... hi hi hi, there is little to laugh about. In any case, I think that in life it is always better to stand up openly and let people know which way you are. Enough hypocrisy! There is a price to pay, but then you will sleep better. I sleep very well and I have a wonderful skin. As the *Czar* taught me, doing something for the team is like making something out of Love. That something always occurs, beyond good and evil, you just have to have faith.

In fact, after countless broken promises, that something occurs also in Perugia, with Gianni's decisive intervention about the payment of the players' salary before the Final Four that would be played on 28 and 29 March 2009. A breath of fresh air! To me it is instead expressed the opposite, i.e. I would not be paid... hi hi hi, there is little to laugh about.

The fifth operation consisted of involving the fans, to put it mildly puzzled by the decision to exclude from the final captain Chiara Arcangeli, from Perugia, who was living it as a disease. On March 22, then six days from the final and unfortunately immediately after a terrible internal beating with Novara, I decide to go meet our "supporters", maintaining a commitment that I had taken during the week with them. My idea was to share with them what we were doing in order to prepare ourselves for the Final Four, seeking support for the team and forgetting any past friction.

Easily said. They were very angry about the result (and who can blame them, wo had made a shameful race) and some of them still did not accept Caprara's choice to substitute the captain of many battles with a Dutch player in her first year in Perugia. But Gianni, if he thinks it's better for the team to play in one way rather than another, is ready to challenge the world. And we are with him. The head coach asks everyone's opinion and then chooses, because that is his job. The staff is responsible to support this choice to the bottom, inside and outside the team. And so it was.

The day after my fantastic speech during the fans meeting, we're slaughtered publicly. In particular, some sporting pacifists types want my and Caprara's death. I'm not kidding, the threats were very heavy and also addressed to our entire family. Perhaps they also discovered that we were the ones to want to remove the banners of the triumphs of the past, but they did not know the other half of the story. I must say that the feeling of being a moving target is challenging, it makes the blood flow faster through your veins. You begin to appreciate the little things in life, a pizza, a cold beer, a night out with your friends saying bullshits. However, if I could go back, I would do it all differently.

In this nice party atmosphere we prepare the Final Four at our best, risking playing away from home while being at home and with almost all the monthly arrears not paid. In this regard, the Chinese player, with a family to support at home and in Italy only to monetize a career in volleyball, is practically on the verge of a nervous breakdown and immediately wants to go back to China.

«Motivator, go and talk to her! You're here for this!» a small executive thunders in a scornful tone. «If you give a check for her, it's easier…» I answers. «Then we're all capable!» he replies more and more unfriendly. In fact, I like winning in an easy way. And I'd like to play the Champions at par, i.e. in the same situation as the others who paid the salaries regularly. However, I do my duty for the team, not for him, and I go. With the precious help of the interpreter, a sweet woman named Po Yin Tam, we sign an Olympic truce until the Champions League final: no more attacks to the executive's Tibetan villages.

There are still a few days to the big event, with the voltage that goes in and out of the team, with the fans who want us dead and with the company that moved to Nepal, totally absorbed in the preparation of the Final Four. The distance with the executives begins to be reaped. But if the difficulties are greater, then the opportunities will be greater.

In this way we start the sixth operation: take care of ourselves among us, partly because the others wanted us dead. Between Tuesday 24 and Wednesday 25 March 2012, we all go to have a great massage and a sunlamp. Introduce yourself to the team in a calm, relaxed and confident way it's the first commitment of a staff during the preparation of decisive games.

To loosen the tension you have to enter firstly into the right mood and then attract the others. Gianni Caprara is absolutely *the No. 1* in this. *The Czar of all the Russias* is just the coach that every player dreams of having at his/her side when the balloons are hot and he/she is playing the most important match of his/her career. Gianni is always lucid and puts you in the right state to express your best. You know you can always trust him, because he will go lucid and determined to the bottom looking danger and opponents right in their faces. And believe me, this thing is the difference that makes the difference.

Now we're settled, so we "fix" the team, organizing a group *sponsorship* on Thursday 26 March after dinner, in Pala Evangelisti's dressing room. The seventh operation cannot be told in detail because certain secrets never go on prescription, they must born and die within the dressing room. I can tell you that everything happened: tears, laughter, screams, silences, hugs. Then we went out and lived for an hour the privilege of being completely alone in the building that would become the theater two days after of the big show of the Final Four. Everything was ready. Each of us had the opportunity to experience that environment alone or with friends, singing or remaining silent, playing or thinking. We were inside the arena in which we will fight to the death.

It happened that we came back to our childhood and we took off our unspeakable cravings of a lifetime. On that magical night everything was possible, even that we could never do in our career, such as smoking a cigarette on the bench or pretending to be the referee to invent the craziest calls or exchanging roles or proclaiming yourself a world champion enjoying the victory in advance. The memory of that *sponsorship* in the locker room and of that night on the field is still very much alive in me and I think also in all others: spaces of pure poetry that only sport can give.

The next day we begin the eighth operation: to give emotional balance to the team (however, this already started a long time ago). So we put in the locker room a great basket of exotic fruits, where each team member was associated with a piece of fruit for a specific reason. In that season we had adopted an explicit procedure for video meetings consisted of letting the girls enter *all together at the same time* with the music and with a different surprise each time. In that mythical staff meeting we were bananas and made an historic fashion show of our underwear. How many laughs, before turning our attention to the video and to the tactics to achieve against Bergamo. When you enjoy the tension is always the right one. In this at least we were perfect.

The semifinal match with Bergamo was a real battle. Gianni chose not to enter in the locker room because we were ready to fight and we knew all about them. In the championship Foppapedretti had always won against us for 3 to 0, but in this race we managed to win a set and we would go to the tie-break if the umpires had not sensationally missed two consecutive decisions at the end of the fourth set: they mistakenly judged a ball out and didn't see a definite touch of the opposing block on the attack of our "crazy American". There is nothing worse than losing in this way, because you have left with an incredible bitter taste.

We felt our possibility to play the tie-break was stolen. Those two unfavorable to us refereeing decisions, which unfortunately ended the match, (defining them questionable is an act of pure sublime romanticism), were a stab to the heart. Bergamo was stronger than us and after it proved that by winning (deservedly) the European Cup, but in a volleyball tie-break everything can happen. We just wanted to play it.

At that very disappointed and painful moment, (yes, there's pain in sports) Gianni was provoked, ridiculed and mocked by someone and unfortunately he reacted badly. Caprara, you know, is not a little lamb and he's not afraid to speak to your face. Some fans and executives of Bergamo, perhaps, had not agreed to forgo a coach who made them win almost everything and that he had decided to bring Russia again on the roof of the world along with his girlfriend Irina Kirillova. In particular, during his first year in Bergamo, he had completed another comeback that has moved to sports history by winning the Scudetto nullifying five match points in Novara. If you are looking for a man who never gives up let me introduce to you Gianni Caprara.

Two things have made it all more mocking:
1. the mistakes' confirmation by the referees themselves, of course microphones and cameras are off. No fraud, just two clamorous oversights;
2. the knowledge that the horoscope of the "Gazzetta dello Sport" is infallible: it had predicted for that day "clamorous refereeing mistakes"for the sign of Scorpio ("crazy American" and Gianni's sign).

But unfortunately the games were done, we were out and they were into the final. Gianni was slammed in the first page in the category "monsters to lock up and then throw away the key" and others were celebrating. Media are like that, they tell only what makes more headlines, take it or leave it.

So in that climate of despair, disappointment and pain, we get to work to prepare the third / fourth place final, where all Gianni's strength and greatness come out. It is never easy to get up after a bad fall, but you have to do it, for yourself and for people around us. In this the Czar reigns supreme, because recharging after a big disappointment requires a great mental energy. You have to quickly pull a line and start over with a smile and the right determination. The show must go on and we are part of it.

So head held high, we win the game for ourselves and nothing else. These are rewards that you understand only with time, because in that moment you just want to bury yourself in a hole. Then you want to throw the medal bronze in the toilet. Only those who have lived totally certain events, giving themselves without sparing a drop of sweat and blood, can understand the sea of emotions they went through in those moments. Those who watch from the comfort of their chair think of a violation of fair play and a lack of sports culture. I think that's quite right, I don't tell this episode to apologize for what I have done and thought, I know.

Gianni, true to himself, after failing to appear at the press conference as a sign of protest, doesn't even take pictures with the team and I choose to do the same, running away at the last moment just before the official shot, only to be with him. People come before the photos and the leader had been through too much to be alone, even though we both know that what we did is not an example to follow. We are human beings and as such we can make mistakes: we have done so, and that's that. He was smoking a cigarette outside the arena and I was there with him in silence. Moments that you remember forever.

Then, overcome by fatigue, I decide to pack my things and go home just like Gianni does. Fortunately for me I counted one's chickens before they're hatched, because another great life lesson was waiting for me in ambush. Before the final competition that would be played at times, I go to Mauro Chiappafreddo, with the backpack on my shoulders and ready to leave Pala Evangelisti forever, and I say to him: «Mauro, I'm exhausted, I'm sick of all this, I take the car and go back to Modena. What about you?». «I stay here! I stay here! Where do you want me to go? I'm here all the way! You left me alone in the picture with the team, thank you! Gianni just left because he cannot watch Irina's matches without helping her.., and now you go away, too. Indeed you come back to Modena! Thanks, how nice of you!» he says, looking at me in a way I will never forget.

So this is a *great man*. Meet Mauro Chiappafreddo, personally and professionally a giant. The chance to work with excellent people is this: they tell you when you're wrong. *Numbers 1* never left you alone in your broth of crap, they will point out what is happening and what may be the consequences of your behavior. They are brave and give themselves, in good times and in bad times. They always take care of you and don't let you banging your head against the wall if you're going in the wrong direction.

So, I swallow, lower my head, connect my 2 remaining neurons and apologize: «You're right Mauro, I'm a jerk, we're going to stay here together till the end and tonight we're going to the Grand Gala to do a world mess. By the way, have you seen Turk's American central … that wild pussy… I like her curly hair and her big high ass… she must also be a "lecher"… » Well, I'm back to "normal" in a second, it takes me a little.

With this desire to say bullshits and laugh together, we sit in our reserved seat behind the field, knowing that we are one: for the world, *we are one*. After a few minutes Gianni arrives. I realize that because he gives me a pat on my head and that caress contained all that he wanted to tell me and that was worth more than a thousand words. Unforgettable. *All together at the same time,* we're soling and rooting for Irina who wins another MVP title, but is unable to bring home her tenth Champions League. That sucker "Old Iri", has not won anything in her career!

At the Gala dinner, we drank a lot and said bullshits as usual. After some Torgiano glasses, I do a wonderful dance among the tables with Veronica Angeloni, arousing the envy of all the present males. True, besides being a great athlete and a great person, she's a galactic pussy. On the field she never gives up, and out of the field you don't want to ever part from her because she's too beautiful and nice. Then, for me not to miss anything as usual, I approach that central American "whore" of Eczecibasi. Embarrassing gaffes, but how many laughs!

In those magical moments the rivalry that animates the teams on the field gives way to respect, to desire to know each other and joking together. We all belong to the same circus. For one night we're all friends, or almost. From the following day you restart to work in order to make those two more points than your opponent. *Life is a circus.*

I don't want to talk about Gianni Caprara's exemption on 13th April 2009. I just tell you that the girls thought it was one of our crazy stagings, but instead it was all true, unfortunately. Reality always goes beyond imagination. In a flash, Gianni takes his things and leaves our former video room. It's over. We all follow him. They all resign, enduring crazy pressures because apart from me, (I obviously resign since Gianni brought me there), others came all from Perugia, lived and worked there for years. Laura Rosi, Mauro Proietti, Guido Marangi, Mauro Chiappafreddo are my heroes. Never seen anything like that! They're great, that's it. They're really *a lot of stuff.*

CONCLUSION

As time passed, you can understand the scope of certain moments and behaviours. Deep gestures, maybe you've seen them done by your loved ones during the course of your life, in different forms, but always with the same meaning.

You know, in each communication there's a *content* part and a *report* part. It is the famous second axiom of communication, where from *how* you understand the relationship that exists. Due to time and to my professional deformation, I'm looking since many years mainly the way in which human beings live their what to uncover the existing connection to read inside people what is called "meta-communication", i.e. the message that goes beyond the message itself. What sometimes becomes the one and only important message, the one you need to "understand" in the original sense of the term.

Lovers find out to be in love when the *how* of their communication changes, when it changes the way they say hello and ask things. They become soft, alluring, sweet, harmonious, seductive. They start to go at the *same pace*, breath in the *same rhythm*, dance together as parakeets during a courtship. It is no coincidence that in some "primitive" populations, the companion of a lifetime is chosen through the ritual of a Dionysian dance.

Guys come to this big party with clear ideas about who they like, or who they think it might be the right person for them. Sometimes intuition is confirmed by a dance, other times it is completely wrong, because what matters is not the head: it is the rhythm, the harmony, the complicity, the naturalness, the dance of bodies dancing together during that magical "feast of love". During this rite the village's Wiseman, or the Shaman if you prefer, decides who is good for someone, giving the official blessing of the tribe based on the feeling that he sees between the two dancers. Those who dance well together are paired for life. Foolproof. Statistically, the best in the world, followed at some distance from arranged marriages in India.

There are houses where you can breathe love.

I slept with Gianni Caprara in many homes because many were our moments together. In all those places where we were under the same roof, before saying goodnight, *the Czar* always went to close the door of his reign with a key. Gianni Caprara is all in that simple, natural and instinctive gesture. The way he protects his family, his friends and his team is what counts and remains in forever. A high, pure, sincere spirit. In that season he transmitted to the whole staff that mentality. His sense of protection towards the team has become our way of being. This is what I carry with me from Perugia, along with another beautiful gesture.

In that mysterious March, before a league game at home, Gianni looks at me and asks: «Ale, do you think we can make it?» referring to the Champions League. «Sure Gianni!» I tell him straight off feeling all his concern and his desire to do well.

As you now know, at that time we were overwhelmed by problems and in constant search for solutions. So, feeling that fear in his eyes that you can only express to a friend, I gather the other staff members in the weight room and, locked in a secret room like a Masonic lodge, I tell them that episode, calling for help, warmth, strength and energy for our boss.

I do not even have time to finish and Gianni enters. He had come to look for us because we were suddenly gone, when we were usually always together. «Well, you're here...» he says surprised when he sees us. «Come on, let's go to the meeting, the girls are waiting for us...» and as he approaches us he spills some tea on his white race sweatshirt, at chest level. A full-blown mess, but as soon as we turn our back to go out, that full-blown mess turns into magic: without the need to say anything, we all get four fingers inside Proietti's tea and we contaminate our white sweatshirts in the same way:

exciting lustful transgression that of getting dirty an immaculate white race uniform for something greater than ourselves.

At that moment I realized that we had become one, a single team of *evolved people*, because we can choose, decide, cut out. The girls' faces in the locker room have done the rest. When they saw us they have sublimated looking at us with that unforgettable feeling of being *all together at the same time*.

I hope you'll experience the same feeling.

27. VOLUNTEERING: RIDERE PER VIVERE

> *The clown is an inventor who discovers something amazing at every step.*
> CLAUDIO MADIA

In a very difficult time of my life my clown friends gave me back the will to live. Staff Building is also dedicated to them, to those cute red nose rascals.

Reading these stories you will understand that I have been saved a lot of times. Ebbene sì. Well, yes. As I told you, I did not miss anything, joys and sorrows *over the top*. Luckily for me I have always had many close friends, when the words "game over" flashed on my display they put a few token for me to continue the game.

At that difficult time of my life I saw all black (sub-visual mode for lovers of GNP) and I had lost confidence in myself and in people. But how is this possible? A Coach who loses confidence in himself? Well yes. Before being a Coach, in fact, I'm a human being, with strengths and weaknesses. I'm proud of this. I do not go around the world to be cool and above myself! And that's why I feel I can help anyone. I always wanted to be "One of us".

Simply, the light went off and I had no water, just as I was all soaped up without towel, with the phone ringing and the coffee on the hob. At that time it was hard to go to work, because the people who choose you need all your energy and all your determination to get where they want. A coach cannot be 99%. There is only 100% or, as some clients of mine say, 110%. All or nothing.

The knowledge of not being 110% was a very complex thing to manage. Being a Coach is a great responsibility and a little voice inside me kept saying over and over: "Ale stop! And settle your car before you get around to arrange someone else's car. Now think about yourself!".

Only a few friends noticed that bad moment, but I suffered like a beast. I felt like a beached dolphin, stranded inside. I gasped for air. For survival instinct, while I breathed as I could, I clung to everything I knew going in search of oxygen, something new that would make me laugh. Laughing to born again, I thought. So when I saw the advertisement of the course for Volunteers of Smile of "Ridere per Vivere", I realized that it was time to make a nice "pit stop clown" to my car.

Said and done. Along with other aspiring little clown, I go for the counterfoil at the council hall of Fiorano Modenese in what would become our new workshop: the *Association Ridere per Vivere Emilia Romagna*. The name is nice: "Ridere per Vivere". And then in Emilia you are fine. Dumpling, pussy, tigelle and lambrusco.

After a chat with the mechanic chief I find out that for the course to begin, all the acceptances had to be confirmed. And then I prayed for it to happen, spreading liberally consensus and enthusiasm: «This is a beautiful course! My cousin in America did it and it changed his life!», the usual things you say to vaguely and cleverly guide people, making an idiot of myself. In ten minutes I had already collected the money ... I'm very good at making an idiot of myself!

Looking at the vehicle registration card I was surprised that mine was the only classic car in a brand-new car park. Good sign. «This is just what I need, a Paris-Dakar, a shot of life, a breath of enthusiasm, a spiritual bunga bunga! Old boot, back to dream!», I said to myself between a smile and another, while I was doing public relations in Mr Bean style. It's amazing how much bullshit I can say in and out of me in the time unit.

But I'm not the only one. In a short time I notice with great pleasure to be in good company in the Association. *If they are not fools, we do not want them*, this was to be their secret base selection criterion, applied with excellent results given the audience of demented present. The clown makes you laugh because it's an idiot too.

Recalling the structure of the self-help groups, that you can see in some American films, we park our vehicle in the garage so as to form a circle, ready to answer these questions: "Who are you? What do you do? How many miles do you have? Why are you here?".

Knowing the style of some of my debuts in society I had prudently placed myself in front of the Clown doctors Giliolo, Tip Tap and Petronilla who did the honors. I would have been in the middle when they would begin to ask questions, then I would have had sufficient time to develop a strategy.

After some innocent (but not virgin) girls, it's my turn finally. I answer in a telegraphic way: «Hello (with a half-paralyzed smile as if I had a botulinum syringe a moment before); Alessandro (raising my left eyebrow as Carlo Ancelotti); 27 years old (looking at the startled reactions of the participants, you can read on their face "but you demonstrate… 200.000 Km…"); I'm here for me (followed by a big smile in Christian De Sica style and a direct glance to those who stood beside me)».

It worked, and apart from the looks of pity for my years, no one wanted to deepen my knowledge. I had made it! I did not want to tell who I was and what I was doing. I was there for me, for Alessandro. Not for the coach. I wanted to remain mysterious as much as possible and return the smile to the child inside of me. Operation that was beginning to work, ih ih ih… actually they had only pity.

After the presentations, it was question time. As I am a professional blunderer in the initial approaches, not to be untrue to myself, I boldly begin to speak and ask Petronilla, a Clown Doctor that is a cross between a teddy bear, Riccardo Cocciante and Lala of the Teletubbies, a curiosity: «to be a clown I need to have your worldwide laugh?». Of course, she answers with her worldwide laugh: «Ha ha ha (44 decibels in line, carried 2 of 3), no, yours is fine too!». Thank goodness.

You must know that when Petronilla laughs, you can hear her three blocks away. She can even cause avalanches in mountain. She's not welcome in alpine resorts. She is the kind of person you dream to meet at the cinema to see a comic film with you: very ignorant and contagious. She starts laughing for some micro-bullshits and never stops. Assured giggles. She can also puts Mortimer in a good mood. She goes directly to ring the bell at your mirror neurons' home and you cannot help but open the door and laugh out loud with her.

Petronilla, in this way I stop disgracing her, is also the inventor of the game "Ninja blanket" and she holds this game's rights on a global scale. It is a registered trademark. The game is simple and incredibly stupid at the same time (it could not be otherwise since she's invented it). I'll briefly explain what it is.

NINJA BLANKET

Essencial pre-requisite: to be totally insane. Location: a bedroom, a dormitory, a campground, an orgy, etc. .. How to play: without a reason, out of nothing, out of the blue, with your brain in neutral and your common sense off, suddenly you have to dive yourself on the blankets of those around you (shouting "Ninja Blanketsssss!!!") to rip them off, with the intention of not giving them back to them. At all costs. Till death do us part. Result: a world war where everything is permitted: pinches, farts, blowjobs, popcorn, pappardelle with deer's balls, etc.. Variants: NINJA PAJAMAS, you can read about that in the last chapter TAM-TAM.

With the same level of idiocy with which I wrote the last lines I start the course and that's exactly what I was looking for, because the whole training develops in search of your clown, the one that lives inside of you, in another dimension. It's impossible to explain the chemistry between us (as a result of the games we play together, of the theatrical improvisations, of the circus acts, of the times when we all laugh *together at the same time*).. Ha ha ha... what a laughter!

The quickest and most effective way to build a team of *evolved people* is just to make them laugh together. The laughter is a human, social and cultural fact. And when you're laughing, joking, kidding, tickling someone, there is a link for sure. This experience among the Clown Doctors has also improved a lot the way I do *team building*, where *fun* and *participation* are at the center of everything.

By now you know, people become a team when they work together to produce something in which they can recognize themselves, when they come into play, when they come out of their comfort zone, when they overcome the difficulties and when they laugh together. This is the recipe for a great Staff Building: *laughing together*.

In this process of evolution of the individuals within a team, the laughter is is decisive, because it involves the whole body being a state of trance that leads to the production of beta endorphins and dopamine. When you laugh the brain lights up like a light bulb involving pre-frontal cortex and the limbic system, logic and emotions, *all together at the same time.*

But we are not here to remove stains from the jaguars ... This book is not a manual, it is a collection of stories. What I'm going to tell you now is the story of a true "Stinky Fool": Leonardo Spina.

On the first day of the course, he shows up with a big smile, a creased, short, white shirt and a sweaty armpit. Since communication is my job, just like his albeit in different fields, it does not pass odorless. I cannot just think that he forgot to wash himself, there must be something else, because he is the founder of Ridere per Vivere and he works with people since a lifetime.

Then, if I think about how I'm paranoid about personal hygiene, something really doesn't square. Before leaving home I have a bidet a hundred times and I brush my teeth with all the brushes that I have (the toilet one included). Once in the classroom, I disinfect tables and chairs, I spray the air with a scent of Sicilian citrus, I smell my armpit and check my breath. I blow some breaths in the air and then I turn around to smell them fast. "I'm so fast that when I turn off the light I'm under the covers before dark", as the legendary Alì used to say. I emit the breaths and then I'm already there to smell them, as I was the sexiest interlocutor eight inches from my face hanging from my soft and warm lips. Sometimes I also pretend to kiss me.

Only when everything is ok and I feel good about myself, i.e. I can do the splits without the risk of embarrassing leaks, I can eat a crunchy chicken livers crouton without breaking my teeth, I can lift my arms without killing with my armpit the people in front of me, only then I let the participants in , so as not to cause involuntary scheme interruptions with my human being smell. "Man has to stink", but away from training classrooms. The basic rules are always the same: be polite, clean, odorless or scented, funny, cute and cuddly. That day Leonardo was certainly polite, nice, cute and cuddly. Let's talk about the rest. This thing really intrigued me, because it could not be an accident.

During his opening speech, perhaps under the influence of axillary gas, Dispettoso, close to Dr. Spinotto, falls asleep on the chair and begins to snore entering forever into legend. Later we discover that Dipettoso is able to fall asleep everywhere, especially during the most inopportune moments, releasing his own clown.

We're all seated in that garage and Leonardo is an authority, the President of our Association... we burst out laughing. Dr. Spinotto, instead of digging a hole and bury himself in shame as I would have done in his place, is instead genuinely happy and lives the incident as a hindrance caused by a crazy divinity: «Coyote God runs the world by contrast and, by the breaking of a serial, recreates reality, giving things a new order through a laughter». Very beautiful, high, pure, sweaty.

From the story of Dr. Spinotto we discover that the clown is a necessary figure, an essential outlet to the life of the whole community, because *the laughter creates a community*. When you laugh with others about yourself, you recover your position, you get up from the fall and come back in the tribe who laughed at you.

The "village idiot" makes a fool of himself for others' good, as the Clown Doctor gives children the opportunity to unburden themselves about something. The violence suffered by children in the hospital, if we cannot understand it, it turns into anger. However and in any case, to be treated children undergo a series of things that remain inside them. That's why the Clown Doctor always asks for permission to enter a room, to return power to the patient, also that of refusing, saying no.

The clown is an adult who is not adult with the child, and for that reason, he gets even beaten. «You have to catch it, you have to catch it!», Leonardo screams movingly. «Make soap bubbles and a sword with a balloon. Then break the bubbles and deliver the sword to the child so that he does the same. And then stay there to catch them if the child wants to beat you, because you give salvation back to him, you return to him the power to control his status and his body, to feel strong and alive. The power to say: I can! I can change my condition, because I'm destined to health, not to disease.»

Emotion.

The "Stinky Fool" has already been through this road: changing the emotions' signs it is a contribution that has to do with your own healing journey. From a laughter, a sparkle of life breaks out. The same sparkle is burst in the life of Leonardo Spina and Sonia Fioravanti and now it's enlightening more lives. Seeing them together was important for all of us, because they are the living witnesses of a rebellion and of a conscious rejection of some unhealthy habits in favor of others. The same rebellion of Norman Cousins, the father of gelotology, who chooses the laughter, from the greek 'gelos' = analgesic.

The result is the *comic therapy*, being the gelotology "the science that studies the relationship between the phenomenon of laughter and health. The result is a new way to help prevent and treat the disease, and in the U.S. finds its maximum expression, but that is rapidly developing in Europe and in the rest of the world. It takes the basics from the most recent studies of Psycho-Neuro-Endocrine-Immunology (PNEI) and tends to seek out and experiment with ways of relating that, involving positively the emotional level of the person, through complex neuroendocrine mechanisms, alter the immune balance from a side and psycho-relational skills on the other". (Alessia Mendini's Thesis - Policlinico Universitario A. Gemelli di Roma - Gelotology: When the laughter becomes science).

Seeing Sonia plaiting Leonardo's hair, while he's telling their story of fear, rebellion and finally healing, it's an image that I'll always carry with me. On that first day together I learned that heart and goodwill alone are not enough. They are the indispensable condition for the rest to work, but then it takes a great motivation and high competence. You can't turn yourself into a Clown Doctor. Those who think that to be a clown in the lane, it means saying four bullshits and welcoming everyone with a smile, make a huge mistake, because the pain you find in the hospital is your own. A pain that can be put under the carpet for a lifetime, but then it turns surely out, when you don't expect it.
The suffering of others are the mirror of yours. The death of others always talk about yours. In some wards it's really hard to enter because you suddenly open those doors that you hoped to have forgotten forever, but they're still there inside you.

The strength of *a team of evolved people*, i.e. a team of people aware of the route and the choice that they did together, lies in knowing that you can always stop and go back and that if you cannot do that there is always someone who can be supportive. The intervention in the hospital is always a staff affair, *all together at the same time* with a red nose. The clown's red nose is the lifeline.

So much in so little.

My finger remains warm all day long after the play of trust with Cleo. I wash it but it remains warm. The emotion of that moment is anchored on the tip of my index. We say goodbye, tired but happy, we're going to meet again tomorrow. It's seven pm. I just have to find out one thing. I go home and, with my son, I go to the dinner organized by some old clown with Leonardo and Sonia in a restaurant in Sassuolo. This was the scene of my last dinner with Gianfranco Milano after his exoneration in December 2011. The tears and the great emotions of that night had kept me away from that place for years. Spontaneously I would never come back, but the desire to sniff Dr. Spinotto gives me the strength to open that door. Officially I'm there to introduce Riccardo to him, but I really wanted to know him better.

I find him stylish, clean and fragrant. "The mystery is revealed thanks to the genius of Sandrino and of us all. Hooray Sandrino!". «Daddy, why do you sing?» Riki asks me on the way home. «Because I learned a new thing».

I find him stylish, clean and fragrant also the next day. So it was not a case of sudden sweaty armpit, but a precise choice of communication. The clown comes from the bottom despite being tall. And here I learn another great lesson: you can do training in another way, what matters is consistency and knowing how to put people at ease, in one way or another. In this Leonardo is a dog.

Let me explain. Ball, my Scottish pastor better known as Lessie, when I come home, (from South Africa or only from buying some bread rolls five minutes), always lies down on his back to say hello and have some cuddles. For ethologists it is a clear sign of submission to the leader of the pack, that is the kind of posture with his genitals exposed which shows the social relationship of the dog within the pack: you're the boss, that's what Ball is saying to me. There may be 20 degrees below zero or 40 above, he always does that. There may be the sun or it can pour, he always does that. To me it is a gesture of great affection, a choice of communication that aims to make you feel better without you doing anything. This is extraordinary.

Let me explain even better. If one of the two goes down, the other perceptually goes up. If the dog goes down you get up. If Dr. Spinotto stinks, of course you feel at ease. You think to yourself: "If he's like that, then here I can also feel free to fart, to fall asleep while he is speaking, to be fully myself. I'm good as I am". Here you feel accepted, even with crooked teeth and smelly feet like those of a clown, (friend of ours). I swear, embarrassing.

This friend of ours could do a whole episode of Real Time "Embarrassing diseases", as long as the smelling-foot is considered a disease. For sure it's embarrassing. If he takes off his shoe in the car, he surely causes a car accident. You put your head out of the window and stop the car in the nearest pitch or you're dead. More lethal than nerve gas. I think that also acts in the part of the brain with which you make yourself those questions that cannot have an answer, like: how can they stink so much? why not to go to a podiatrist? It is inexplicable. There aren't cognitive tools to accept such a thing. And you think about his wife ... children ... relatives ... How did they stand it for all these years?

Oh, and this friend of ours is also famous for eating garlic. Yes, there are those who chew broth (me), who chew tobacco and who chew garlic. Maybe he does it to confuse the smell of aged cheese that comes from his feet, although I think he does that to be sure to destroy your scent particles from above and below, simultaneously. A lethal combined attack. The nice thing is that during the year he let his beard grow to seem Santa Claus. Then he go to some nurseries to bring gifts to children. He is an adorable sixty years old man, (although he's worthy threat). When we found out that, we said in chorus: "Hey, Santa Claus, go to the nurseries, but whatever happens, do not ever take off your shoes otherwise you'll make a killing, ok? And for a few days leave the garlic alone. You do not want to kill all of the reindeer with your breath, do you? Otherwise who will bring your gifts?».

We brought the gifts on the 24th December 2011 during our first intervention in the hospital. Pure emotion. The appointment is at 8 am at the bar, then we change our suit and we are divided into 3 groups led by the old Clown Doctors in order to turn all the wards. We are a dozen. Indeed, "The Dirty Dozen".

On that special day I realized what a child feels wearing Batman's costume. He transforms himself, he really becomes something else. In the room we have reserved, we begin to make ourselves up, joking, caressing and supporting each other in order to contain our excitement. Going from human being to clown is as magic as going from caterpillar to butterfly. From crawling to flying. *A lot of stuff.*

Before leaving for the tour Giliolo tells us what we will find in pediatrics, because for every age group there are things that work and others must be avoided. You have to be prepared to everything, be conscious that you're part of a staff that is moving together. Who does not feel like doing it, can always leave the room or not even enter. «We always ask for permission», Petronilla reminds us. The comic therapy begins from there.

Despite the butterfly wings and the red nose my pulses are sky high. It may be magic, but just as I search for words to explain you my emotion, a poem comes to me.

RED NOSE

So many times I've thought
about your enchanted world ...
I did not know how to do to
get near.
With astonishment and fatigue
you came into my life...
You ravished me and fascinated me
and you brought me in your world...
New friends in my heart
entered with love.
I studied and learned
and I passed the exam.
I went into pediatrics
with you in my pocket it is already magic.
Inside the bathroom by magic
you jump out with a leap ...
You end up on my nose
and I'm ready in my dress.
I pick up the suitcase
I get closer and knock ...
Can I come in? I always ask
and so many people welcome me.
Emotions and feelings
are always overwhelming.
Give everything is my life
I bring endless joy.
I make bubbles for the little ones
and I give balloons to the eldest one.
Thanks for having found me
and accompanied me by the hand ...
You are the most loyal friend
that a clown might have.
I'm a clown, I'm not perfect ...
My name is Peretta

Just an SMS and a 6 notches telepathy, because "the clown is an inventor who discovers something amazing at every step. It is an artist who builds or paints without stopping, making mistakes and restarting, without ever repeating itself, because it has no past and no future, only the present. It does not leave big pieces, but moments that fade away. It never dies: it is more eternal than stone monuments." (CLAUDIO MADIA, *Faccia da clown - manuale per aspiranti pagliacci*.)

In my wonderful journey into the world of clowns... I played with Baraka, Basic, Bianchetto, Bif, Capitozzolo, Cleo, Dipettoso, Gelatina, Giliolo, Yo Yo, Magò, Papuff, Patacicchia, Peretta, Petit, Petronilla, Pianpianino, Piggy, Pimpinella, Pole Pole, Potaci, Scintilla, Sfreevola, Spagnoletta, Tatapì, Timidella, TipTap, Trucciola, Viki and many others.

In my wonderful journey into the world of clowns... I redid the game of the bottle giving a kiss to Peretta. Precisely her. The last time I was on the bus at the secondary school's tour. There was an incredible smell of teenage, we had pimples everywhere and I still didn't call my hair by name.

In my wonderful journey into the world of clowns... once I yelled out loud of a window «Goal». Two young teams were playing football, the ball was in the center of the field. Not happy I went back to the window to yell «Penalty» The ball was in foul side. Not happy I asked for a change «Refereeeeee, I enter through the window!». Denied. Not happy I send him off. I had to give him the red card, you should not behave like that!

In my wonderful journey into the world of clowns... at the "Clown & Clown Festival 2012" I cried with joy as we were overwhelmed by huge red balloons falling on our heads like drops of dew. It was not me to cry with joy, it was the child inside me. I also met Leonardo and he "smelled" as usual. In a world that is constantly changing smelling some certainty is good for the heart. Maybe, *the courage to risk living* lies in going around with your own smell.

In my wonderful journey into the world of clowns... my iPhone's SMS ring tone is Piggy's sweety grunt, a little pig with a red nose.

In my wonderful journey into the world of clowns... trust, contact, listening, expression, Love.

In my wonderful journey into the world of clowns... I am enjoying and spreading the word (TAM-TAM)i.

SECTION V

TAM-TAM

Ale ...
maybe in the future your name shall be truly TAM-TAM,
that read backwards it becomes MAT-MAT (crazy-crazy),
Well, if this will become your name
you'll remember me a little.
Thank you for the excitement and laughter that we made,
I will always remember that.

PERETTA (Perfect without F)

STAFF BUILDING

28. ALL TOGETHER AT THE SAME TIME

> *We can be Heroes, just for one day.*
> DAVID BOWIE, Heroes

All together at the same time we can turn a dream into reality, helping so many people with a small gesture.

What I learned from my personal staff of life is having the courage to share my dreams with others, because only in this way they can become reality.

My goal is to donate a smile.

STAFF BUILDING

29. TRANSPARENCY

> *Tell everything, tell it in advance, tell the truth.*
> JOHN HICKS

A big thing.

As a reward, if you believe, you'll reincarnate to a higher level.

If you're a man you'll have fewer pimples during adolescence, a bigger and better functioning willy (unless you're Rocco Siffredi), a Ferrari that goes with air, the subscription for your team, an annuity as a senator, a mute mother-in-law and last but not least a young, beautiful and "whore" caregiver;

If you are a woman you will not be in the dumps, you'll have the boobs you want, zero cellulite, less assholes men around you and an unlimited supply of high fashion clothing.

30. NINJA PAJAMAS

> *The most completely wasted of all days*
> *is that in which we have not laughed.*
> NICOLAS DE CHAMFORT

PRE-REQUISITE
Congenital and contagious idiocy.

SETTING
Seven star hotel, five-star luxury hotels, five star hotels, four star hotels, three star hotels, two star hotel, a star Hotels, Pensions, Bed & Beakfast, Refuges, Bivouacs, Mountain Cabins, Alpine huts, Hostels, Shared Rooms , Bedrooms, Campsites, Pajama Parties, Orbiting Space Stations and any other place where there is someone wearing a pajamas.

HOW TO PLAY
Pretending indifference, you suddenly pounce like a swooping eagle on some unsuspecting victim's pajamas stripping it off shouting "Ninja Pajamasssss!!".

WHO WINS
Those who survive to their idiocy and manage to wear all the other unsuspecting players' pajamas, in whatever condition they are (players and pajamas).

PULP VERSION
Ninja Pants. Worthy threat clown game... much more libertine, immediate and engaging strip poker. I leave you to imagine what is. The risk of degeneration is lurking in the fray because there is always some woman with a dilated pupil that screams "Ninja Willyyyyy!!!!", triggering the immediate answers of the men with their mouth foaming and screaming "Ninja Pussyyyyy!!!!".

SOUVENIR

Your Staff Building *all together at the same time* "pajamas", along with other gadgets (the proceeds will go for beneficence), is available in the online shop:

http://ale1coach.spreadshirt.it

Enjoy!

31. CONTACTS

Who has a strong enough why, can endure any how.
FRIEDRICH NIETZSCHE

Alessandro Vianello Mental Coach

Site and blog: www.1coach.it

Linkedin: https://it.linkendin.com/in/alessandrovianello1coach

Facebook: http://www.facebook.com/ale1coach

Twitter: https://twitter.com/ale1coach

E-mail: ale1coach@gmail.com

32. MAT-MAT

You will get the best results while having fun and working well on Environment, on Relations and on Performance.
ALESSANDRO VIANELLO

BACKGROUND
Master of architecture.
Degree at the University Institute of Architecture in Venice 108/110 with a thesis in videographic scene of how the environment affects behavior.

RELATIONS
Licensed Nlp Coach.
Master of Global Marketing, Communication & Made in Italy.
Nlp; Coaching; Leadership; Marketing; Systemic thinking; Modeling; Team Building; STAFF BUILDING; Persuasion Engineering; Public Speaking; Networking; Adult-child Communication; Brainstorming.

PERFORMANCE
Licensed Nlp Coach.
PNL; Life, Business, Sport Coaching; Problem Solving; Time Management; Mental Training.

SKILLS
Leadership; Coaching; Mentoring; Strategic Communication; Team Building, Staff Building; Brainstorming (*David's Sling*); NLP; Sports Mental Coach; Football Mental Coach; Golf Mental Coach; Adult-Child Communication; Business Coaching for Managers and Entrepreneurs; Lean Thinking, Lean Solution; Adult-child communication workshops.

PALMARÈS
16 titles in 6 sports: Golf, Football, Tennis, Volleyball, Athletics, Cross-country skiing.

PASSIONS
Sports; Small and Medium Enterprises; adult-child communication; Clown Doctors; Vipassana Metitation; *writing*.

Thanks and see you soon,
Mat-Mat

Dear dad,

thanks for all the pampering you gave me as a child and also for all those you have tried to give me when I grew up. You understand some things only growing.

Thank you for the kindness, softness and sweetness that you've always had with me. You've been a great dad and I miss you so much.

Riccardo is a wonder, would you be mad for him as he would have gone crazy for you. I'm terribly sorry that you have not known each other, but I know you're there.

One day we will play together with Lego that you have kept looking forward. I cherish them like you did.

Every now and then come and see me in a dream,
Alessandro

Dear mom,

thanks cause you worked all your life, grew me, maintained me, cooked, cleaned, ironed, scolded, brought me up. You have not had an easy life, I know. You did the best with what you had.

Thank you for the work culture, the honesty and the education you transmitted to me with your example. These are basic values, the rest comes later, much later.

Also thanks for the quarrels that we have always done and continue to do. Today these quarrels arise only from the fear of losing you.

We are very much alike but yet different.

I love you,
Alessandro

Dear Cri,

Me and you have seen some, lived some, and we have known very well the term "together", while the sun slowly goes down, and you don't want to be that sun.

Thank you for the full time, for the true you, for tight teeth, for faults, for shots in the arm, for aur fantasy. Love matters. Love matters.

These are and will always remain the best years of our lives, and perhaps all that sadness in reality never existed.

Thanks for Riccardo, he is really a lot of stuff.

I love you a mountain,
Ale

Dear Riccardo,

I love you more than heaven and earth together.

Your daddy with the "cabrio-willy",
Alle

STAFF BUILDING

www.ingramcontent.com/pod-product-compliance
Lightning Source LLC
LaVergne TN
LVHW051108080426
835510LV00018B/1957